A perspective
on how our
Society
was Built,
Topics on Power in America

DARREL A NASH

ISBN 978-1-956001-17-4 (paperback)
ISBN 978-1-956001-18-1 (eBook)

Printed in the United States of America

Books by Darrel Nash

Book I: A Perspective on How Our Government Was Built and Some Needed Changes

Book II: A Perspective on How Our Society Was Built, Topics on Power in America

Some History and Reminiscences of The San Luis Valley Colorado, The United States in Microcosm

Contents

Acknowledgements

I wish to acknowledge the ministers I have had over the years who have pushed me to go deeper into my life and examine what should be kept, what should be added, and what should be cast overboard.

A special note of gratitude is given to my friends—persons of color—many of whom are named in Topic III. These people provide me with insights and perspective into the lives of Black and Brown people over the centuries of European and African residence in America.

Opening Salvo

The challenge for all of us is to escape from what we WANT TO BE TRUE and let our hearts and minds discover what IS TRUE.

History should not be about making us feel good or patriotic. History is what happened, recorded or not. If we want to understand what happened or say that we know our country's history, we must see it as it is—all of it—not how we want it to be. If we choose to ignore or can't handle the things we are not proud of, we are saying that we are weak or fragile and can't take the truth—that we can only handle good history. This is contrary to the popular story that we are strong and powerful.

To follow political discussions and actions, a very useful first step is to understand the different kinds of information that we use to understand the world and each other as we go about living today, this week, and really always. Or we can say, "how do we discover the truth?"

One kind of information is statements that perhaps many people agree with, but can never be proven nor disproven no matter how much we study and analyze the statement. A prime example is: "we hold these truths to be self-evident, that all men are created equal; that they are endowed by their Creator with certain unalienable rights; that among these are life, liberty, and the pursuit of happiness." *Thomas Jefferson, Declaration of Independence.*

Here is another: "… the public good, the real welfare of the great body, is the supreme object to be pursued, and that no form of government whatever has any other value than as it may be fitted for the attainment of this objective." *James Madison, Federalist Paper No. 45.*

A second kind of information and this one can be found to be true by experimentation; every time the experiment is done, the result is the same. Water boils at 212 degrees Fahrenheit at sea level, and perhaps a few other conditions such as it has to be pure water, etc. We can always rely on this fact. We use a lot of such information in our daily lives. Even here, however, scientists tell us that when you get to the nano level, things don't behave the way they do in our everyday world.

There is a third kind of information, really a qualification on the one above. It is knowledge gained by scientific research. The example of water boiling at a certain temperature is quite rare. The vast majority of scientific research yields only tentative results. We use these results as the best available, knowing that future research may disclose something else. For example, according to nearly all scientific information, all of the original residents of the Americas came from Asia. We are currently pretty sure this is true, but new scientific discoveries often surprise us.

But even to get to these tentative results requires strict adherence to **rules** of scientific research. First of all, the researcher cannot go into a study with a pre-conceived notion, or more importantly, a preferred outcome. Right away, this invalidates any conclusions from the study. The purpose of the result must be to find truth. **If the purpose is to find confirmation for a belief the researcher already has, the results cannot be reliable and can be truly damaging. As we shall see in the body of this book, many persons in positions of power say that their conclusions come from science. But if the person has violated the requirements of scientific research, it is not science.**

To be dependable, the results of scientific research have to be repeatable by other totally independent researchers. There are other requirements such as how to select the subjects you are studying—a human group or wheat seeds to use two very different examples. There are requirements for sample size depending on the nature of the research. And the sample must be randomly selected from the population.

One further imperative—there is in scientific research the concept called, "other things being equal." This means for example, if you want to find out how different sources of water affect plant growth, you must use the same kind of plant for each experiment. In the real world of research, things are more complicated, but the rule still applies. In the following Topics you will read of "researchers" concluding things about the races in America without taking into account that there are multiple reasons why one group may have different health or academic achievements. The only valid way to make such comparisons is to be sure that all other factors have been accounted for.

This would mean for example, that if you wanted to find out if a disease was more prevalent in one group of people than another, the study must be made on persons in one group having at least the same income, education, housing, kinds of jobs, marital status, the same physical environment, etc. as the other. If this is not done, then conclusions can't be made as to whether the result is due to some characteristic of the group per se, or whether it is due to one of more other factors in the group's environment. Examples are studies finding that persons of African heritage or Indigenous people are more prone to a disease than persons primarily of European heritage. Unless all other conditions are the same, except for heritage, no conclusions can be drawn.

From all this, you may get the idea that it is very challenging to correctly make strong conclusions from scientific studies and therefore, one must be cautious in accepting the findings. And that is true. But as is often the case, we must make decisions based on incomplete and tentative scientific findings.

In modern times "wisdom" often contrasts "faith" with "science." But without faith there can be no accurate science. The scientist seeking to find facts from her/his research must have faith that if the scientific method is used that the research or experiments will lead to the correct result. The scientist without this faith will go into the experiment with pre-conceptions and do things to make sure the result is the one he/she expects or wants.* *I am indebted to Rev. Kathleen Rolenz for this insight.

This description becomes very important for understanding racism—particularly in the US. During slavery, but more aggressively after the Civil War, so-called scientific studies were done with the <u>objective</u> to show the inferiority of African Americans. (Remember, valid research does not start with the goal of getting the answer you want.) Here are some findings from "scientific" research. Skull shapes and sizes were compared with white people to show the intellectual and moral inferiority of African Americans. Feet and hand sizes were compared. The shape of the nose and hair texture were all "found" to show the inferiority of Blacks. The Bible was studied to make conclusions that Blacks were inferior in the sight of God. Or that only white people were created in the Garden of Eden, other "races" come later. Blacks were found to have certain diseases that whites didn't have, including a "running away" disease.* For a much fuller treatment of this issue, see *Stony the Road*, by Henry Louis Gates, Jr.

This categorization of kinds of information is needed to make our way through the mostly political discussions of this book.

The first category does not come from research—it comes from inside us. I call it our internal or moral compass. If we believe Jefferson's words in our heart and soul, then, our actions and advocacy result from this compass. If our internal compass points us in a different direction, then our actions and advocacy will follow where that points. [It is obvious from where our society is now, that many persons in positions of power, and many others in our society, do not believe that all persons are created equal.] Another term for this compass is touchstone or point of reference. If such a statement is your point of reference, you refer back to it when making decisions, both personal and if you are a representative for a group, as the group's point of reference.

In studying for this book, I have discerned other compass points. Here are some.

1. only certain persons have the qualities it takes to make decisions for our government, or more generally for our society. This view is embodied in the text of our Constitution.
2. the purpose of the US is to protect free enterprise where those engaged could amass wealth "get rich" without interference from government, indeed that government exists to enable them to do so. This is not contained in the Constitution, but several founders expressed this, and we know that most were engaged in gaining wealth.
3. government exists to promote **my** religious, moral, and social beliefs. This has a prominent history in the US. Some examples are that 1) many states had laws prohibiting non-Christians from making political decisions; this is prohibited by the Constitution, but the sentiment is often heard today, 2) Sunday blue laws, which enforced adhering to beliefs of some Christian groups, 3) states prohibiting the use of contraceptives, 4) prohibition of marriage between "races," 5) prohibition of same-sex relations and same-sex marriage, 6) prohibition of marriages that are not monogamous, and of course, 7) anti-abortion laws.

These compasses have the same quality as expressed by the "all men are created equal" statement. They are not beliefs that can be proven or disproven by study and analysis. They are the bases for those with these as compass points to advocate for and against issues.

As we shall see, over our 250 or so year history, there are various internal compasses that have been and are used to work toward self-government in the US. I will attempt to identify the points of reference used when the various positions are advocated or acted upon. See if you agree.

In my view, based on the readings and sources for this book and by observing political arguments today, the first compass point, that of "all persons are created equal," has been definitely the minority position for most of our history. The others have dominated our history. Brief periods saw the first one—Reconstruction after the Civil War, and during the 1930s and the part of the 1960s and 1970s when we experienced the civil rights and abortion rights court decisions and federal legislation.

Chief Justice Roberts in his confirmation hearing for the Supreme Court famously said something like, the job of a justice is to call balls and strikes, not to interpret the law. I don't know what the follow-up question was, if any, but a good question could have been, "describe for us your 'strike zone.' Which of these centering positions do you use to establish your 'strike zone?'

So, there are things we can do that will more likely lead us to a measure of truth. **But we are all too familiar with how to obfuscate the truth**. Here are some ways:

One is to so often repeat lies that many people consider them to be true. A lot of social media and TV use this. Sadly, this is now prominent from politicians.

Another is to tell part of the story only. Leave out the rest and so only the part told becomes the whole truth. This is what is done with our popular history.

Match things that don't match in order to convince others of some truth. Another way of saying this is making false analogies. For example, why should I be required to wear a mask when we let illegal immigrants into the US? Or another: Using the National Guard to enforce school integration is another case of Mother Welfare taking away our rights.

Use emotional language to hurt a person or political position. Accusing someone of being a <u>socialist</u> is a time-honored way of shooting down a government program you don't like, for example, funds for Head Start. Here are some others: <u>Tyranny</u> is hurled at those requiring face masks to prevent spreading Covid-19; <u>Destroying the Constitution</u> if you are opposed to prohibiting carrying guns in schools; <u>Destroying our values</u> if a government law or order allows all persons to live in our community; <u>Taking away Christmas</u> if this means showing respect for other religious beliefs; <u>Soft on crime</u> if you believe that a person that has completed prison sentence should have his/her civil rights restored; <u>Murder</u> if this mean allowing pregnant rape victims to choose an abortion; <u>Deep State</u> to describe the competent and dedicated federal bureaucracy; and, <u>Fake News and Lame Stream News</u> to describe national and world renowned newspapers.

There may or may not be reasons why any of these positions should not be supported or that institutions make mistakes—the challenge is to debate the issues with respect and with the intent of reaching conclusions that enhance society.

Finally, beware of arguments using "natural law" as the basis. What is this? It's right up there with "the divine right of kings." These arguments were used during the Renaissance in the battle of ideas. Require the advocate to base what they are saying on evidence.

How Can the Press Best Serve a Democratic Society?

In the nineteen-forties, a panel of scholars struggled over truth in reporting, the marketplace of ideas, and the maintenance of a free and responsible press. Their deliberations are more relevant than ever.

By <u>Michael Luo</u>
July 11, 2020

In 1920, Walter Lippmann, one of the founding editors of The New Republic, and Charles Merz, an editor at the New York World, published an exhaustive examination of the Times' coverage of three years of the Russian revolution. They found that the paper had been overly credulous of the accounts of the State Department, the Russian Embassy, and others, publishing profoundly misleading stories on a subject of vast geopolitical importance. "In the large, the news about Russia is a case of seeing not what was, but what men wished to see," Lippmann and Merz write. **"Human beings are poor witnesses, easily thrown off the scent, easily misled by a personal bias, profoundly influenced by their social environment."**

The solution Lippmann proposed was journalistic objectivity: a reimagination of journalism as a kind of scientific inquiry, subject to the disciplines of testing and verification. In his book "<u>Liberty and the News</u>," Lippman argues that good reporting must be based on the "exercise of the highest scientific virtues"; the best reporters are not "slick persons who scoop the news, but the patient and fearless men of science who have labored to see what the world really is." To Lippmann, who would become the most influential champion of journalistic objectivity, it was a matter of "ascribing no more credibility to a statement than it warrants" and maintaining an "understanding of the quantitative importance of particular facts."

Topic I

In the Beginning

> I am posing the following question right at the beginning for the White reader to think about. Why do we think that someone with a darker skin and different hair than ours is inferior? It is so ingrained in our brains that we just assume it's true. Why?

At the beginning of the Renaissance, a plague began spreading over Europe. No, I'm not talking about the black plague, this one spread among the merchants, explorers, kings, dukes, princes and other royals as well as the Pope and archbishops and bishops and elders in the Protestant churches. It was codified by the Pope in 1451 as a Papal Bull—a proclamation. This said that non-Christians had no rights to personal freedom nor any claim to land or resources. Targeting non-Christians was just a cover for the real intent—to deprive non-Europeans of their basic human rights.

This plague is still with us today. It is called racism. The most prominent effect is the exploitation of Africans and persons of African descent, as well as the Indigenous people of America.* Its cousin, classism, was also imported from Europe and was prominent in the building of our society. **These have deprived untold millions of their opportunities to use and express their talents, brilliance, and dedication.**

And this is why we need to know history. We see this plague in schools failing to teach black and brown children, in prisons with high proportions of black and brown populations compared to their numbers in our society, in appalling housing conditions for those on the lower economic margins, where any black person can be arrested for simply driving or walking down the street. Black and brown people working as guards, drivers, janitors, trash haulers, etc. etc. instead of professional careers where they might have worked had not racism and classism prevented them from doing so. Of course, there are also areas of white poverty.

> *In recent decades, some have considered what name to give the people living in the Americas before the arrival of the Europeans, rather than the name Columbus gave them—indios, (Indians). In considering these names, I have chosen <u>Indigenous people</u> as a way that I think recognizes their being here first and also that they were (are) people whom we recognize as having worth and dignity the same as everyone else. The original residents of the Americas did not have any collective name for themselves— the dominant form of identity was with extended families and language connections. I recognize that whatever name we give to these people it has been first chosen by the dominant white culture.

The mixing of populations

Settlement of what was to become the United States brought together a mix of people from widely separated parts of the world. This is the story of how these populations interacted—and who would come out on top.

The history we are taught in schools and in popular literature includes all these groups, but is woefully lacking in telling the accurate story. We know that the settlers from England and Holland encountered the Indigenous People in the northeast. And we are becoming more aware that Africans were brought here as slaves—captives shipped here to work on farms and other enterprises and received no wages or other compensation. (Owners provided enough food and shelter so that the captives could do the work for which they were purchased.)

In broad outline, there were three cultures—European, African, and the Indigenous people of the Americas. The essential of these three cultures was—and is—this. European culture was one of conquest. Climb the mountain, conquer the enemy, and occupy the land. It also revived the Greek philosophy of learning and research. The Indigenous and the African cultures emphasized living in, rather than conquering, the environment, contemplating the mountain—worshipping certain mountains and physical features of the land, listening to the wind, the animals, and ancestors. Knowledge and values are passed down by story-telling* (unwritten) from generation to generation. I am indebted to Rev. John T. Crestwell for this insight.

*In African cultures, these were called *griots*. Although the understanding of the griot differed by cultures, he or she was generally looked upon as the repository of the group's history and tradition. In some societies, the *griot* was believed to have spiritual powers not possessed by others of the society. [More information can be found on Wikipedia.]

- A **griot** (/ˈɡriːoʊ/; French: [ɡʁi.o]), **jali**, or **jeli** (*djeli* or *djéli* in French spelling) is a West African historian, storyteller, praise singer, poet, or musician. The griot is a repository of oral tradition and is often seen as a leader due to his or her position as an advisor to royal personages. As a result of the former of these two functions, they are sometimes called a bard.

The challenge for us today is to accommodate to these multiple philosophies of life so that we can live together in the American culture.

The European settlers also brought with them the concept that the Indigenous people essentially had no right to their land—their farms, hunting and fishing areas, etc. As noted above, even though most of the settlers were not of the Catholic faith, the justification for depriving Indigenous people of their possessions was based on a Papal Bull—a proclamation—called the Doctrine of Discovery first issued in 1451 by Pope Nicholas V. This proclamation ... specifically sanctioned and promoted the conquest, colonization, and exploitation of non-Christian territories and peoples. Later, the Treaty of Tordesillas (1494), besides dividing the globe equally between Spain and Portugal, clarified that only non-Christian lands fell under the discovery doctrine. This Doctrine has the distinct appearance of the church justifying what the explorers and conquerors were already doing. Here is why this is the likely sequence.

To explore this supposition, look for information on Prince Henry the Navigator of Portugal. A very brief account shows that his first explorations outside of Portugal started around 1415 for the purpose of finding a way to intercept the gold and spice trade from east Africa to what we now call North Africa for the profit of Portugal. In the process of discovery, his ships were blown off course leading to the discovery of Madeira and the Azores. These were then claimed by Portugal (without asking the inhabitants). The development of larger ships enabled the explorers to go farther south along the Atlantic coast of Africa. By 1448, the Portuguese had passed the southern boundary of the Sahara Desert, going around the Muslim land-based trade routes from across the desert. Slaves* and gold began arriving in Portugal. This new trade system cut off and devastated Algiers and Tunis. *Note that already, Europeans viewed the Africans south of the Sahara as a people to enslave.

All European settlers and conquerors found the Doctrine of Discovery a convenient justification—if indeed they believed they needed one—for moving onto lands already occupied by Indigenous people; and for capturing Africans to be shipped to America for slavery. "In 1792, U.S. Secretary of State Thomas Jefferson declared that the Doctrine of Discovery would extend from Europe to the infant US government. The Doctrine and its legacy continue to influence American imperialism and treatment of indigenous peoples." From Wikipedia. To this day the US Government has not revoked the Doctrine of Discovery.

As *Dunbar-Ortiz* teaches us, we must look beyond the common narrative of our country's founding. This narrative is wrong—not so much on the facts and dates but that it gives us the wrong understanding. I might add and by what is left out. From the Indigenous people's perspective, the Europeans from their first arrival were engaged in conquering and destroying the lives and societies of those that were already here. *Dunbar-Ortiz*, p. 2.

There is plenty of evidence that this is true. It is not that we today are prevented from learning this part of our past, it is because we willfully ignore it. Our celebration of Thanksgiving Day is a prime example of this. Our kids are taught that the Indigenous people (Indians) and the Pilgrims had developed a friendship and that the Indigenous people brought food from their farms and from hunting to the Pilgrims for a joint thanksgiving celebration.

This is true as far as it goes. There are plenty of first-hand accounts of the event. The fuller story is that Indigenous groups were already being challenged for their traditional lands by newly arriving Europeans. Alliances were being formed among the Indigenous groups to either ally with or battle the Europeans. Disease brought here by the European fishermen (before arrival of the Pilgrims) had decimated at least one group of Indigenous people, the Patuxent. A member of the Patuxent group, Squanto (or Tisquantum) was a central figure in negotiations with the Pilgrims and among various other Indigenous groups working and fighting to keep what they had. Groups hoping to ally with the Pilgrims brought food from their farms and successes from hunting as a way of cementing this alliance.

> *There are many accounts and historical research sources surrounding how this, "first Thanksgiving" happened. On Wikipedia, by typing in "Squanto," we find over 450 sources for this part of our history. It is only by our own choice that we ignore this history and stick with the story we tell our kids.*

For a much more complete history of the settlement and interactions among the groups brought together here, go to *Howard Zinn, A People's History of the United States.*

Captive Africans

It is obvious that well before the European settlers arrived in North America the only way imagined of treating Africans was to enslave them. The recent celebration of 400 years after the arrival of the first Africans in North America, records that dozens of Africans were captured from a Portuguese slaving ship by British privateers and taken to Hampton Virginia where they were sold into slavery.

In general slavers would try to take the younger people, including children, women and males they would get the most money for. That is a chilling aspect of the slave trade. People are being treated like livestock.

Here is one account: "Angela was taken captive in 1619 during a war in Kongo. She was forced aboard a slave ship, the San Juan Bautista, in Luanda, then a bustling slave-trading port on the cost of West Africa, according to Jamestown Rediscovery. The ship was headed for Vera Cruz, on the coast of Mexico. The ship was overcrowded, "It suffered horrible mortality on the voyage." More than 120 Africans aboard died en route. *Brown, DeNeen L.*

In the middle of the passage, the slave ship was attacked by two English pirate ships—the Treasurer and the White Lion. The pirates climbed aboard the Bautista, hoping to find a bounty of gold. Instead, they found humans—desperate people. The pirates took 60 or so Africans, splitting them between the White Lion and the Treasurer.

The White Lion eventually arrived at Point Comfort, near Hampton, Virginia, where its captain traded the captives for food.

Most of the Africans were bought by wealthy and well-connected English planters including Governor Sir George Yeardley, and the head merchant, Abraham Piersey." According to Jamestown Rediscovery. "The Africans were sold into bondage despite Virginia having no clear-cut laws sanctioning slavery."

How might acknowledgement of this and other parts of US history work to transform society today? That is the central question that this book pursues.

Instead of the actual history, let's imagine an outcome where the captives had not been assumed suitable only as slaves but rather had been considered fellow humans who were in a highly distressed situation. Treating them as fellow humans may have gone like this. The settlers paid a ransom to free them from the privateers and given them temporary food and shelter. Then they said, "Welcome to our town. What would you like to do?" A very good assumption is that the Africans would have said, "we want to go back to our home." The settlers then said, "we don't have any way to send you there. The best we can do is to make you a part of our community. Since you have no possessions, please share what we have. When you have recovered from the ordeal of your capture and long sea voyage, we will help you clear some land so that you can provide for yourselves. You are welcome to join in our town's celebrations and religious ceremonies. Also, feel free to have your own celebrations and religious observances. We are only learning to live in this new land and are learning the ways to grow food and provide shelter. We welcome any knowledge you may have that will make life better for all of us."

17

But by this time, "the well had already been poisoned" so to speak. Europeans had already been fed a steady diet that Africans were non-Christian savages and the Europeans therefore were free to exploit them in ways of the Europeans choosing. The reality was that the captive Africans carried with them diverse religious traditions. About 20 to 30 percent were Muslims. Some had learned of Christianity before capture, but many practiced African spiritual traditions.

The common concept of Africa was and is of an uncivilized area, people living in tribes and subsisting on hunting and primitive agriculture. *Zinn* records that the African culture before and during the time of capture for enslavement was in some ways more advanced and in general more civil than the European society at the time.

African Society at the Time of European Contact

Africa at the time had social hierarchies and a kind of feudalism as did Europe. But in Africa the tribal society was not destroyed as happened in Europe. In Africa, the tribe featured concern for each of its members including less severe punishment for wrong-doing. While it was hierarchical and cruel in some ways compared to England and Holland it was way more civil. In England in 1740, a child could be hanged for stealing. But in the Congo, the idea of private property was a strange one, and thefts were punished with fines or various degrees of servitude. While in England, for example, accused people were beheaded, the heads put on pikes, bodies torn apart on the racks, etc. *Menakem, pp. 59, 60.*

One would be hard-pressed to rate whether European or African cultures were more advanced in the sixteenth century. Africa had large cities, advanced kingdoms including Timbuktu and Mali, used iron instruments in farming, and skills in creating artistic, clothing, and household items.

Far from being thought of as savages, some European traders found African tradesmen easy to deal with. "In 1563, Rasusio, secretary to the rulers on Venice wrote to the Italian merchants: 'Let them go and do business with the King of Timbuktu and Mali and there is no doubt that they will be well received there with their ships and their goods and treated well, and granted the favors that they ask…' " *Zinn p. 26.* Similar reports were received concerning other African settlements including, the Guinea Coast, and Benin.

Degrading Humans

From the beginning, there was a constant message to the African captives that they were less than human. After being marched, sometimes hundreds of miles often by African captors from the inland to the coast, the captives were placed in holding pens, more crowded than what a responsible livestock owner may do. They were then purchased by owners of the slaving ships on the basis of their physical prowess for hard labor, and especially for girls and women, the perceived potential for producing many strong children. Those that had been purchased were then manacled and placed lying down on ships bound for the Americas in areas hardly big enough for each one's body. Many died on these trips called, "the middle passage." By going to *Wikipedia* and typing in "middle passage," you can view diagrams of the slave ships.

"Then they were packed aboard the slave ships, in spaces not much bigger than coffins, chained together in the dark, wet slime of the ship's bottom, choking in the stench of their own excrement. Documents of the time describe the conditions: the height sometimes between decks, was only eighteen inches, so that the unfortunate human beings could not turn around, or even on their sides, the elevation being less than the breadth of their shoulders, and here they are usually chained to the decks by the neck and legs. In such a place the sense of misery and suffocation is so great, that the Negroes are driven to frenzy." *Zinn, p. 28, 29.*

When arriving in the Americas they were auctioned off to slave buyers. There was no regard for group of family connections—each captive was sold individually. It was not uncommon for children to be sold to different slave-masters than their parents, as well as husband and wives being separated. This was no doubt a most lucrative practice for the Europeans. Africans were shipped here by the thousands.

Slave-masters may have been in shock at first to learn that what they had been told about the captive Africans. The message was that these were savages and were waiting to be tamed by the new masters. Instead, they found that these new captives were completely capable of planning and strategizing how to escape and how to show these masters that they could not be easily subdued. Because they were in chains, the owners had more control over them than they did of whites or Indigenous people. The new owners then set about breaking the spirit and self-confidence of the Africans. They were beaten and mutilated, doing whatever it took to let the captives know that they had absolutely no rights. They were taught that their individual needs had no validity—that their only purpose was to serve the master.

The message to them was that just by being African or a descendant of Africans was all that was necessary to be put in this situation. But they were never fully subdued and the lessons had to be repeated on each generation. To emphasize to the Africans that they were at the very bottom of society, they were made chattel slaves. Chattel is an obsolete name for cattle. So as in the case of animals—livestock—the person is owned for life and any offspring of the enslaved person is also owned. By contrast, indentured people* could become "free" by working a number of years, typically seven, for the owner.

> *Indigent Europeans, usually children who could work and young adults were brought to America to work for wealthy families. The terms of indenture were typically that after seven years, the indentured person was free. Sometimes they had learned skilled during their indenture time to enable them to make a living.

It is important to keep in mind that chattel slavery was a created system—not a natural system where some groups are superior to others. Once this is understood, we can get on the path of ridding our nation of these caste systems and class distinctions.

Indigenous People

At the beginning of the 1500s, the population of North America, including Mexico was about forty million, compared to Europe east of the Ural Mountains which was about fifty million. *Dunbar-Ortiz, p. 17.*

The people lived in a relative disease-free environment, because of the combination of surgery, dentistry, herbal medicines and a largely vegetarian diet. Early European settlers noticed that the Indigenous people practiced frequent bathing and wash themselves daily. They made time for many ceremonies and recreational activities.

We like to believe that European settlers arrived on an undeveloped land. We now know that what is now the eastern US was one of seven or eight areas of the world where agriculture arose. The technique of growing corn and probably squash and beans was imported from Mesoamerica.

That this was possible resulted from long established trade routes all across North America. Contrary to the usual belief that North America was an undeveloped continent when the Europeans arrived, all parts of the continent were developed, every part of the continent was connected by trade routes. A major difference was that the Indigenous people mostly adapted to the environment rather than controlling and changing it. *Dunbar-Ortiz,* pp. 15, 16.

The Indigenous people had well-developed governing systems. These varied across the continent. Outside Mesoamerica, these were characterized by governing councils rather than single leaders with discussions and ceremonies to reach consensus on issues.

Tribes, as European Americans understand them, were not the concept the Indigenous people had of their relationships. They organized more as family groups, common language groups, etc. This misunderstanding had devastating effects on Indigenous people when the Europeans asked for "the leader" to negotiate with. The Indigenous people, not willing to name one, sometimes led the European and American governments to appoint a leader and assume that he acted on behalf of a whole group.

Interactions Between Three Groups

Dunbar-Ortiz, describes the system involving the 1) enslaved Africans, 2) the desperate white migrants, and 3) the slave traders and plantation owners whose only goal was profits. To stay in control, the powerful had to turn the poor whites against the Africans and Indigenous people. The message to the poor whites was that they were superior to the other groups and it was only from misfortune that the whites were in a disadvantaged economic and social condition. Most importantly, the poor whites were taught that their interests were the same as the powerful white people, so the poor should not form friendships or coalitions with non-Europeans.

> We often hear in conversations that "that is human nature," often meaning that persons stay in their own groups because we are built this way—that we can't do anything about it. It is true that a part of our brain— the most primitive part (sometimes called the reptilian brain) tells us to be suspicious of strangers, of people that are different than us. It is a protective device that prepares us for "fight or flight" to avoid danger. We share this part of our brain with other animals we consider lower than humans. (This part of the brain also tells our body to work—breathe, heart beat, digestion, etc.) But there are other parts of our brains, much more highly developed in humans, which control our emotions and

our thinking. With these more highly developed parts of brains we cannot argue that we are trapped in the primitive brain, we can <u>decide</u> to be different.

Followers of Jesus learn that there must be a different way. The Good Samaritan story is more than a story of being good to another person. It is about a person who stops along a journey to help an injured person whom he is supposed to hate. Instead, he gives immediate aid, then takes him to someone for further care. His assistance is unconditional. He tells the caregiver that whatever it takes to care for the injured, when I return, I will foot the bill.

And from Judaism: Leviticus Chapter 19, verses 33 and 34 (RSV)

When a stranger sojourns with you in your land, you shall not do him wrong. The stranger who sojourns with you shall be to you as the native among you, [or as one born among you] and you shall love him as yourself; for you were strangers in the land of Egypt; I am the Lord your God.

I believe that a primary reason for religion is for us to use all the resources of our advanced brains to act to the stranger as Jesus and the Hebrew writer would expect us to. In addition to tribalism being "human nature," I say that with our highly developed brains, it is also "human nature" to go beyond our reptilian brains and follow the teachings of great religious leaders who tell us that we are all a part of the human family and that we have responsibilities to each other.

Europeans, starting with Columbus, had no qualms about purchasing or capturing Indigenous people of the Americas to do slave labor. However, forcing Indigenous people to do slave labor did not work out well for the Europeans for various reasons, so they turned mostly to the African slave trade to get captive workers.

Legal Separation of Groups

Direct interactions between the Europeans and Indigenous people were much less common in the northern colonies. Every colony had captive Africans but the South had the largest concentrations. Across the continent, Indigenous people were constantly pushed westward. Wealthier Europeans bought up the more fertile eastern areas, forcing those whites lower on the economic ladder to settle in the west where they were much more in contact and in conflict with Indigenous people. *Zinn, pp. 54, 55.* These displaced persons then were in the unfortunate position of pushing Indigenous people off their land. This, of course, led to direct conflict between these two groups.

Any group, facing loss of their homes and livelihoods, not to mention their culture, would likely do whatever it took to avoid defeat. This desperation of the Indigenous people led to the concept of the Indigenous people as ruthless savages. In turn, the whites were frustrated that governments did not aid them in their battles.

Into this mix of interactions and conflicts came Bacon's Rebellion. Bacon's Rebellion was a significant event in the early settlement of the more southern colonies and set the stage for issues we have still today. The details of who was allied with whom in the Rebellion are complex, so don't spend a lot of time trying to understand all the interactions.

In July 1666, European settlers (without government sanctions) led by Nathaniel Bacon declared war on various groups of Indigenous people who were trying to prevent the settlers from taking land in a section of Virginia across the Potomac River from Maryland. Battles continued and then an armed rebellion that took place in 1676-1677 by Virginia settlers led by Bacon who now had turned his anger against the rule of

Governor William Berkeley. His grievances against the governor were that the Governor would not protect the settlers on Virginia's western frontier. Berkeley, in turn, refused to allow Bacon to take part in fur trading with the Indigenous groups. Bacon believed he was being left out of the political decisions of the Governor.

From this, thousands of Virginians from all classes, including those in indentured servitude and chattel enslavement, rose up in arms against Berkeley, attacking Native Americans, chasing Berkeley from Jamestown, Virginia, and ultimately torching the capital. It seems that frustrations all around coalesced in each group being against the Governor.

What made Bacon's Rebellion especially fearsome for the planters of Virginia was that black slaves and white servants joined forces. The planters responded by working to create in the minds of the indentured servants that they were in a class above the Africans. **This has been a technique throughout American history—convince European Americans on the lower social and economic end that their interests lie more with the ruling class than with other oppressed groups.** In turn, this has led the oppressed whites to commit some of the most violent acts on persons of African descent and on Indigenous people. (Note how often this theme is used in the other Parts of this book.)

Virginia's rulers had a dilemma. They decided it was better to make war on the Indigenous people, gain the support of the white and to divert possible class conflict by turning poor whites against Indigenous people. To show this was a joint revolt by various groups, it is recorded that final surrender was by "four hundred English and Negroes in arms" at one garrison, and three hundred "freemen and African and English bond-servants" in another garrison. The naval commander who subdued the four hundred wrote: "Most of them I persuaded to go to their home, which accordingly they did, except about eighty Negroes and twenty English which would not deliver their arms." *Alexander*, p. 24, *Dunbar-Ortiz*, pp. 61, 62, *Zinn*, pp. 39 – 42.

With the vast numbers of Africans being transported into North America, concerns emerged as to whether the relatively small portion of the population of wealthy Europeans might be in danger of insurrections by the Africans or the Africans in collusion with Indigenous people and the white poor and indentured classes. Bacon's Rebellion was a stark instance where this happened. These groups had found common grounds for rebellion and cooperation.

This fear of too many Africans and their descendants may help explain why Parliament, in 1717, instead of sending those convicted of crimes to jail, instead sent them to their colony in the New World. [meaning that a free passage to America was the punishment] After that, tens of thousands of convicts would be sent to Virginia, Maryland, and other colonies. It also makes understandable why the Virginia Assembly after Bacon's Rebellion gave amnesty to white servants who had rebelled, but not to blacks. Negroes were forbidden to carry any arms, while whites finishing their servitude would get muskets, along with corn and cash. The distinctions of status between white and black servants became more and more clear. *Zinn: pp. 54, 55.*

The Virginia Assembly proclaimed that all white men were superior to black, and went on to offer those they considered "white inferiors" a number of benefits. A law was passed in 1705, to amend a previous law to require that freed white indentured servants were to receive some land, a gun and some corn. Such provisions were to show the whites that it was not in their self-interest to collude with Africans in rebellions. For the whites, there was a promise that at the end of their time of indenture, there was a better future for them. *Zinn, pp. 36, 37, 38.*

"Once the small planter felt less exploited by taxation and began to prosper a little, he became less turbulent, less dangerous, more respectable. He could begin to see his big neighbor not as an extortionist but as a powerful protector of their common interest." *Zinn, pp. 36, 37, 38.*

Again, White people on the lower end of the economic ladder are propagandized into thinking they have more in common with the wealthy classes than with persons of other ethnicities.

The Source of Our Racial and Ethnic Hatred

Our history books tell of early settlers in America coming for religious freedom and the chance to build a new life. What is omitted is the conditions in Europe.

From the time of the crusades and perhaps before, enemies were dealt with by massacres and acts of appalling cruelty.

In the following centuries, this violence carried over into the whole of society. The 1500s and 1600s in England was anything but gentle. People were routinely burned at the stake for heresy, a practice that began in the 12th century and continued until 1612. Torture was an official instrument of the English government until 1640. The famous Tower of London was, in part, a huge torture chamber. One of many torture devices in the Tower, the rack, was used to stretch human bodies and pull them apart. Here is a description of the apparatus at work.

> This caused terrible pain for the victim as well as increasing physical damage as the torture continued. Tendons were ripped, joints separated and bones fractured. The sounds of muscles and tendons tearing apart and snapping provided audible signs of the damage being done. *Menakem, pp, 59, 60.*

During much of the Middle Ages in England, torture wasn't just wildly popular, it was a spectator sport. In his essay *"Violence and Law in Medieval England,"* historian Sean McGlynn puts it this way:

> "Throughout the whole Medieval period there was popular demand for malefactors to receive punishment that was both harsh and purposefully terrifying. This reflected people's enthusiasm and the desire to see justice done. There were even an

executions transfer market: bids were made to stage the executions of condemned men in front of huge crowds ... Mutilations sent a message of warning and deterrence, executions offered the ultimate guarantee against repeat offenders ...with few prisons and no police force, severe punishment was deemed invaluable as a deterrent of crime."

In her book, *A Distant Mirror*, Barbara Tuchman offers this parallel description of everyday life in medieval England.

"The tortures and punishments of civil justice customarily cut off hands and ears, racked, burned, flayed, and pulled apart people's bodies. In everyday life, passers-by saw some criminal flogged with a knotted rope or chained upright in an iron collar. They passed by corpses hanging on the gibbet and decapitated heads and quartered bodies impaled on stakes of city walls."

It is not hard to understand why so many people from England fled to the American colonies. (Fleeing is, of course, a survival response.) Many of the English who colonized America had been traumatized, or had witnessed great brutality first hand. Others were the children and grandchildren of people who had experienced such savagery in England. Foregoing section from: *Menaken*, pp. 59, 60.

Menaken's thesis in the book is that violence infects our bodies and is inherited by the offspring—both the oppressed **and the perpetrator**. It is carried until it is faced and dealt with. If Menaken is right, the descendants of these perpetrators (probably most white people) still carry the violence in our DNA.

To me, this helps explain the abhorrent actions of the slave traders who loaded African captives onto ships that were cruel beyond imagining, the beatings, mutilations, rapes, lynchings done by the captors—the plantation owners, later depicting Africans as animals, as well as, the Salem witchcraft episode, beating and rape of women by owners, the sweatshops of early America, the mistreatment of many of the indentures servants, and in general treating those without power as not worthy of an adequate income, safe working conditions, access to health, access to adequate education to name some.

I suspect that many of the slavers, the plantation owners, were descendants of the oppressed. I also suspect that even today those that carry out mass murders with military-style rifles, inner city shootings, etc. are all carrying in their bodies the generations-old damage inflicted on their ancestors. It helps me understand the sadistic behavior of some police officers, prison guards, as well as the US Government torture of Iraqi and Afghan prisons and keeping immigrant children in cages, all in the twenty-first century.

Thus, American society has always been violent by design. The European settlers, primarily English and Dutch in the northeast, brought with them a caste system in which a few wealthy individuals owned property and were able to acquire workers* to enable the few to become wealthier. How did they do this? Basically, it was to sell their products for as much as possible and to cut production costs all they could. The wider the margin between the selling price and cost of production, the more the wealthy acquired so that they could become wealthier. *If necessary, they could use violence or the threat of violence to get and hold these workers because they had the political power to do so.

There is, of course, nothing inherently wrong with a business working to maximize income and minimize costs. What is wrong, morally, is to use **power** to obtain the resources at less than cost and to use **power** to force buyers to pay more than would be the case without this power.

The history of this period, without always being specific, is that European settlement of North America relied on two resources—land and labor. Land was obtained not by purchase, but by removing Indigenous people from their traditional lands by force and trickery. The other was to obtain slave labor by either buying white indentured servants or by buying African captives. The advantage of buying an indentured servant or an African captive is that these people could be kept without the need to pay them wages sufficient for them to remain in the owners' service. The most valuable asset of some of our nation's founders was their enslaved people.

Indentured servants, were mostly younger persons, men and women who were brought from Europe to work for the wealthy who usually footed the bill for their passage from Europe and room and board during the indentured period. Even though some of the indentured servants were brought here voluntarily—or by an arrangement with parents, many were children just gathered up by the hundreds on streets of England and shipped to Virginia. What happened to the majority of these children is not known. *Zinn,* pp. 43, 44.

The general concept for indentured servants was that after seven or so years, they were free from their indenturer and to go and seek his or her own means of making a living. Few of these indentured servants ever got beyond a subsistence or at least a modestly adequate income.

During the time they were indentured, they had no legal rights, indeed, laws were passed to assure this. Serving on juries was not even considered. It was common to beat and whip the servants, women were raped without any legal recourse. Governor Berkeley of Virginia reported that four out of five indentured servants died of disease after arrival in America. Maryland court records show many suicides.

Even less known than the status of indentured servants were the conditions of free persons, who had no property and had to make a living squatting on less fertile land away from the eastern seaboard, by becoming an employee, or attempt to live off the profit of a small business. In general, these people were little better off than enslaved people. The following cases are from *Zinn*.

In the 1660s, Carolina, which included most of the land between what is now Virginia and Florida, set up Fundamental Constitutions written by John Locke (an Englishman, often called the father of liberalism). These set up feudal-type systems which resulted in eight barons owning 40 percent of the colony's land. After a rebellion against this arrangement, rich speculators took an additional half million acres of good farmland leaving the poor people to squat on small parcels of poorer land and who were then in constant battle with landlords to collect rent.

In Boston, the wealthy, working with the clergy and by careful marriage arrangements, controlled trade and commerce to assure most of the profits went to themselves. The foundations were thus laid for the controlling class in seventeenth century Boston. This is a case, as noted above, where sellers used their power to charge more for their goods than they could have without this power.

New York in the colonial period was like a feudal kingdom. The Dutch controlled the Hudson River Valley, with enormous landed estates. There was a farmers' revolt in 1689 and the leader hanged. Under Governor Fletcher, three-fourths of the land in New York was granted to about thirty people. He gave a friend a half million acres for a token annual payment. In the early 1700s, a group of speculators received a grant of 2 million acres.

In Maine in 1636, an employer of workmen and fishermen complained that his employees "fell into a mutiny" because he had withheld their wages. A few years later, workers in shipyards engaged in worker slowdown because of food shortages among them.

In Boston, men rioted because they were forced to serve in the navy. Also, Boston officials reported a great number of families who could barely survive, due to lack of food. *Zinn*, pp. 48, 49, 50.

All the major cities built poorhouses in the 1730s, which took in old people, widows, disabled, orphans, war veterans, and new immigrants.

As noted above, in European society there were social classes and what we today call ethnic hierarchies. The British, Dutch, and French vied for possession of the northeast, with the British winning out. However, the Dutch residents were able to maintain some of the top economic, social, and political positions, especially in New York.

America's First Targeted Ethnic Group—The Ulster Irish

For most of the colonies those of English descent were in top position. But *Dunbar-Ortiz* introduces one group in particular from the British Isles—the Ulster Irish. In the power hierarchy, the Ulster Irish group, also known as Scots-Irish, Scotch-Irish, Protestant Irish and maybe other names, was below the English. The group migrated from the counties of northern Ireland.

Britain, at that time, controlled, or sought to control, all of the British Isles. It colonized northern Ireland by moving groups from other parts of the British Isles to northern Ireland. (UIster usually means the six counties of the Irish island that are a part of the United Kingdom.) What eventually became known in America as the Ulster Irish, was mostly transplants from Scotland. *Dunbar-Ortiz* reports that there were also, Welch, English, and even French Huguenots. But they all became identified as Ulster Irish. [Because there were several groups, I choose to use the more inclusive name, "Ulster Irish."] The one thing the group had in common is that they migrated from northern Ireland. Most adhered to the Presbyterian including Covenanter, or more generally, the Calvinist faith tradition.

The Ulster Irish brought to America a long history of battles for survival in northern Ireland. Any summary does not do justice to this history, but here is an attempt. The Ulster Irish had moved into territory belonging to the native Irish, most of whom were Catholic. There were complex and violent interactions among the Ulster Irish, the native Irish, and the British royalty. Britain wished to tame the Irish and establish the Church of England. The transplants and refugees were seeking a combination of freedom from the Church of England, and an escape from poverty in the Scottish Lowlands. Decades-long battles between the Irish and Ulster Irish were brutal. *Dolan* pp. 3 – 8. The Ulster Irish brought these methods of engaging in war to America.

By 1630 the new settlers in Ulster—21,000 Britons, including some Welsh and 150,000 Lowland Scots—were more numerous than British settlers in all of North America. Antagonism between the Irish and the Ulster-Irish was a constant of life. Conditions were desperate in northern Ireland, so that there was a mass migration of Ulster Irish to British North America.

"In one of history's great migrations, nearly a quarter million Scotch-Irish left Ulster for British North America between 1717 and 1775. Although a number left for religious reasons, the majority lost out due to British-Irish policies, which brought economic ruin to Ireland's wool and linens industries. Hard times were magnified by prolonged drought, and so the settlers moved across the Atlantic.

"The majority of Ulster Irish settlers were cash-poor and had to indenture themselves to pay for their passage to North America. Once settled, they came to predominate as soldiers-settlers." Most initially landed in Pennsylvania, and large numbers eventually migrated to the southern colonies and back country by way of moving down the Appalachian Mountains. They moved onto Indigenous land* (either by negotiating with Indigenous people or more commonly simply by squatting) in the British backcountry. Although the majority remained landless and poor, some became merchants and owners of plantations which were worked by slaves, as well as politically powerful. For the British and later the Americans, they made up the officers' corps and were soldiers of the regular army, as well as the frontier-ranging militias that cleared areas for settlement on lands Indigenous people considered their own. *Dunbar-Ortiz, pp. 52, 53.*

*Even though the Ulster Irish occupied a lower rung on the European social ladder, they, as did the other Europeans, in practice subscribed to the Doctrine of Discovery which held that non-Christians had no rights to land.

Throughout the mid-1650s and into the 1760s, in the American colonies, these Ulster Irish moved west and south. At one point, Indigenous war parties closed the road south from Pennsylvania. Some of the toughest Ulster Irish fighters battled the Indigenous groups. Several of the church leaders saw the incursion of their people into Indigenous people's land as not in keeping with the church's religious holdings. (Church leaders were also distraught that many of the immigrants were falling away from the church.)

Regardless of the qualms of many of the leaders, beginning in the late 1740s, settlers were pouring into regions of Indigenous peoples' territory. This, along with other factors led to open warfare on the frontier. As one official put it in 1750, "Numbers of the worst sort of Irish had been to mark places and were determined to have gone over the Hills this summer or in the fall." These migrations angered the Indigenous people, who once again were being pushed from their lands, which lends to "Quarrels between Indians and the Trespassers." Traders and diseases followed the settlers. In 1751, a county court indicted John McAlister for carrying "Quantities of Rum and other strong Liquors above the Quantity of one gallon amongst the Indians at their Towns and beyond Christian inhabitants." Two years later, the same court brought charges against eleven such settlers. The proprietors and their agents saw no way to keep the frontier quiet except "to get the Indians to burn the Log houses" of squatters. *Griffin, p. 166.*

These Ulster Irish seem to have been the first European ethnic group that the British Americans considered "undesirable." It was a kind of class consciousness—a class fear. *Zinn, pp. 36, 37, 38.* This may seem surprising to today's descendants of the Ulster Irish, many of whom have important and comfortable positions in our society. But also, some of these descendants are at the bottom of the income ladder, especially in Appalachia.

Around 1700, the Virginia House of Burgesses declared:

The Christian servants in this country for the most part consists of the worser sort of the people of Europe. And since ... such members of Irish* and other nations have been brought in of which a great many have been soldiers in the late wars [in Ireland] that according to our present circumstances we can hardly govern them and if they were fitted with arms and had the opportunity of meeting together by musters, we have just reason to fears they may rise against us.

> *The Burgesses were referring to the Ulster Irish (Scotch-Irish, Scots-Irish, Protestant Irish). For several decades, in the 1700s the Ulster Irish were simply referred to as Irish by the power structure in North America. The Ulster Irish were okay with being called Irish. By the 1830s, settlers in America who were Irish Catholic started to outnumber the Protestant Irish, the Catholic Irish were now commonly called Irish. As a result, Scotch-Irish became the customary term to describe Protestant immigrants from Ireland. The Irish Protestants in America were happy to be identified as separate from Catholics.

The reason for describing this group, in addition to their large numbers, is that the largely English entrepreneurs and plantation owners found the Ulster Irish a useful source especially as the land owners pushed into new lands farther west from the Atlantic shore. As noted above, the Ulster Irish were on the front lines of pushing out Indigenous people so that plantation owners could occupy the newly acquired land. While records of Bacon's Rebellion, described above, do not identify ethnicities of the White participants in the rebellion, it is highly likely that both with the status of the poor whites, and the location—Western Virginia—that many of the participants were Ulster Irish.

At the time of the American Revolution, few if any of these people were a part of the top rung of power. But they were on the side of the colonies, indeed, relished the chance to battle the British. "They were among the most vocal agitators for independence from Great Britain and volunteered in large numbers as soldiers in the revolutionary armies." *Wikipedia* October 2020. As one Captain Heinrichs of the Hessian Jager Corp, writing a letter during the War wrote, "Call this war, my dearest friends, by whatever name you may, only call it not the American Rebellion, it is nothing less than an Irish-Scottish Presbyterian Rebellion." *Nash,* p. 29.

In the summer and fall of 1780, Britain turned its attention to the south—Virginia and the Carolinas. The British had captured Charleston and no doubt thought the entire state was in their hands. But a militia group from South Carolina's backcountry took up a guerilla war with the invading British. The guerrillas were ferocious and paid little attention to formal rules of war. Many of the fighters were Ulster Irish, who already hated the British but were further inflamed by British treatment of them during the Revolutionary War. The guerillas without at first help from regular troops fought a battle on King's Mountain, South Carolina. The British lost more than one thousand men, roughly 20 percent of Cornwallis's entire army. *Ferling,* p. 96. The Battle of Kings Mountain was proclaimed as "the turning point of the American Revolution" by Thomas Jefferson. Wikipedia, October 2020.

After the Revolution, some Ulster Irish entered the top rung of society by way of military leadership; the most famous is Andrew Jackson. Since then, many descendants of the group have made important contributions to our society in politics, education, the military, and religion. Twenty US presidents have lineages going back to these Ulster Irish. They have been influential as presidents, businessmen and educators. ... Many settled in Appalachia where throughout our history they have maintained the stories and music of the immigrant Ulster Irish. As noted above, this area is also where there has been a condition of poverty that so far has not been resolved. We will re-visit this group in later Topics as their challenges and contribution to the nation's history is identified.

Turning European Ethnic Groups into Whites

The Ulster Irish were just one of a number of immigrant groups from western European countries. As most of these groups came to America in significant numbers, many were first shunned. As time went on, those in power found that they could gain allies by downplaying these groups' ethnicities and encouraging them to rather just think of themselves as <u>White</u>. This is called "assimilation," in this case, encouraging people to think of themselves first as Whites and then using this to advance the notion that they are superior to oppressed people. With the concept of being White, the power structures could more easily ally them against <u>Black</u> people and Indigenous people. As *Diangelo* and others teach us, White and Black are social constructs—not biological differences.

"All of your polkas, or pubs, or pizzas and more got tossed into the crucible of race, where ethnicities got pulverized into whiteness. That whiteness is slapdash, pieced together from the European identities at hand." *Dyson*, p. 45. "So much has been invested in whiteness that it is hard to let it go. It is often defensive, resentful, full of denial and amnesia. The only way to save our nation and, yes, to save yourselves, is to let go of whiteness and the vision for America history it supports." *Dyson*, p. 49.

References for Topic I

Alexander, Michelle, The New Jim Crow, Mass Incarceration in the Age of Colorblindness, The New Press, 38 Greene Street, New York 10013, 2012.

Brown, DeNeen L., The Dawn of American Slavery, Washington Post, May 1, 2019.

Diangelo, Robin, What Does it Mean to be White?, Developing White Racial Literacy, Peter Lang, New York, ISBN 978-1-4331-3110-3, 2016.

Diangelo, Robin, White Fragility, Why It's so Hard for White People to Talk About Racism, Beacon Press, Boston, ISBN 9780807047415, 2018.

Dolan, Jay P., The Irish Americans, Bloomsbury Press, 175 Fifth Avenue, New York 10010, ISBN-13: 978-1-59691-419-3, 2008.

Dunbar-Ortiz, Roxanne, An Indigenous Peoples History of the United States, Beacon Press, Boston, ISBN978-0-8070-5783-4, 2014.

Dyson, Michael Eric, Tears We Cannot Stop, A Sermon to White America, St. Martin's Press, 175 Fifth Avenue, New York 10010, ISBN 9781250135995, 2017.

Griffin, Patrick, The People with No Name, Ireland's Ulster Scots, American's Scots Irish, and the Creation of a British Atlantic World, 1689 – 1764, Princeton University Press, Princeton University Press, 41 William Street, Princeton NJ 08540, 2001.

Menakem, Resmas, My Grandmother's Hands, Racialized Trauma and the Pathway to Mending Our Hearts and Bodies, Central Recovery Press, 3321 N. Buffalo Drive, Las Vegas, NV 89129, ISBN: 9781942094470, 2017.

Nash, Ralph G., et. al., Martin, A Martin Family Genealogy, Scotland, Ireland, North America, Library of Congress catalogue No. 80-82674, (undated, about 1980).

Zinn, Howard, A People's History of the United States, Harper Perennial Modern Classics, New York, ISBN 978-0-06-196558-6, 2003.

Topic II

The War is On—Now What?

This Part covers issues from the time of the Declaration through the launching of the federal government under the U.S. Constitution. The society we have today was largely built during this period. In turn, that was built on the political and social structures of the colonial period, as outlined in Topic I.

Introduction

Self Image of the Colonies

Animosity toward the British united the thirteen colonies and so, as is well-known, colonial representatives met in Philadelphia and on July 4, 1776 issued the Declaration of Independence from Great Britain. It said by the authority of the colonies they are now free and independent states. The Congress had already commissioned George Washington and other former British officers to lead an insurrection against the British troops.

But there was little else that these proclaimed states held in common. Two important points of agreement were, as when they were colonies, each was an independent state, (sovereign is the term they used) with no responsibility to each other.* The other, closely following the first was that paying taxes was to be avoided. A well-known reason for seeking independence was "taxation without representation." Less well recognized was the aversion to paying taxes at all. This aversion among other things caused misery among Washington's fighting men, the most famous is the winter of 1777-1778 at Valley Forge. This aversion to taxes by the Americans will be evident as the story continues here and in later Topics. **Mutual support was pledged, however, as we shall see, even during the most dire part of the War, sovereignty was treated more importantly than mutual support.**

Declaration of Independence

The Declaration of Independence was much like a sixteen-year-old telling his parents he's moving out. Where will you live, what will you do for money, his parents might ask. Don't bother me, I'll do it my way, might be the response. Well, my way results in pounding the streets, looking for a place to live, your shoes wearing out (think Valley Forge), begging for food and clothing and giving out pieces of paper promising to pay back loans from good-natured people. The equivalent to the new government is that it was impoverished and had no way of raising money except to petition the states for funds. So, it issued paper money—little more than unsecured promissory notes—with no assurance that this paper would have any value to buy things. These promises to pay were not only given to other countries, but to the soldiers of the new country—the very ones on whom victory was dependent.

Like the sixteen-year-old, the Revolution was focused only on independence. No consideration was given as to what kind of society the new country hoped for. But in either case, the sixteen-year-old or the new country, some big decisions had to be made. *Chernow*, p. 243.

Articles of Confederation

Following the Declaration, the states prepared the Articles of Confederation. These expressed supreme optimism that the states could function with very few restrictions. Each was independent of the other and expressed little regard for the welfare of the others; more importantly, the common belief was that the new government created by Congress required very little support from the states.

Constitutional Convention

By the middle of the 1780s, the fallacies of this loose confederation of states were obvious to several of the leaders, among whom were Washington, Alexander Hamilton, Robert Morris of New Jersey, and James Madison. This led eventually to the calling of a Constitutional Convention. Delegates from each of the thirteen states eventually attended.

Strong disagreements existed among the Convention delegates as to what the Constitution should be. Some wanted the substantial sovereignty that the states had under the Articles, small states were worried about being overwhelmed by larger states, the south would not give up on the right to enslave Africans and their descendants. And except especially for Hamilton, most pushed for the states to retain considerable power. The outcome of the Convention was the draft of a constitution that was submitted to the states for ratification.

Ratifying Convention

When the voting public read what the Convention proposed, most were appalled. They were expecting some modifications to the Articles. What was proposed was a whole new government.

Most likely a surprise to people today, ratification was a hard-fought battle. Many states had reasons for keeping the Confederation. Few agreed for the need for a strong central government. Some southern states would have walked away if restrictions on enslaving Africans and their descendants were included. In order to get to the nine-state approval before the Constitution went into effect, some changes were made, most importantly, the adding of the Bill of Rights—the first ten amendments that we have today.

Articles of Confederation—Summary.

Now for a more in-depth look at these documents. First, the Articles of Confederation. This codified how the states would relate to each other and with foreign governments. *The summary is at the end of this Topic.*
Here are the important provisions.

> Asserts the sovereignty of each state, except for the specific powers delegated to the confederation government: "Each state retains its sovereignty, freedom, and independence, and every power, jurisdiction, and right, which is not by this Confederation expressly delegated."

Note that the reference and concept was *Confederation*. No thought was given to establishing a *nation*. As will be recognized, the provision of sovereignty of states has been with us since the beginning. Right away, this affected the pursuit of the War. States claimed this sovereignty when money and manpower were required to engage the British. States asserted their rights to decide whether to fulfill the requests.

> Declares the purpose of the confederation: "The said States hereby severally enter into a firm league of

> friendship with each other, for their common defense, the security of their liberties, and their mutual and general welfare, binding themselves to assist each other, against all force offered to, or attacks made upon them, or any of them, on account of religion, sovereignty, trade, or any other pretense whatever."

The wording is important here. Again, not thinking of this new political organization as a *nation*, they entered into a *"league of friendship."* This may be the preference of many people even today—it is certainly idealistic. This would have been great were it not for important factors facing them. One was the power of Great Britain and other European powers against a rag-tag army. The other was that there were crushing social needs among the population of the States as reviewed in Topic I. These also threatened the success of this new entity. And even though this Article pledges mutual support—an attack on one is an attack on all, unfortunately most states took the previous Article, State sovereignty, more seriously than they did mutual support.

> Allocates one vote in the Congress of the Confederation (the "United States in Congress Assembled") to each state, which is entitled to a delegation of between two and seven members. Members of Congress are to be appointed by state legislatures. No congressman may serve more than three out of any six years.

Again, note the wording. The *Congress of the Confederation*. The main point here is that each state got one vote in Congress. States could send a delegation, but the delegates of a state had to decide how to caste the vote of the state. And note the term limitations of congressmen. The underlying tone here is that no one should gain power by way of gaining experience and wisdom on governing. Omitted from this provision, but most important is that each State had strict provisions on who among the population could vote on as a congressional delegate. Voters had to be free white property-owning men. And several states had religious restrictions.

> Only the central government may declare war, or conduct foreign political or commercial relations. No states may form any sub-national groups. No state may tax or interfere with treaty stipulations already proposed. No state or official may accept foreign gifts or titles, and granting any title of nobility is forbidden to all. No state may wage war without permission of Congress, unless invaded or under imminent attack on the frontier; no state may maintain a peacetime standing army or navy, unless infested by pirates, but every State is required to keep ready, a well-trained, disciplined, and equipped militia.

This article largely carried over into the Constitution. This provides that only the central government may declare war. The exception seems to be that if attacked by Indigenous parties, mostly on the western frontier, the state may wage war.

It is so unfortunate that the last phrase, **"but every State is required to keep ready, a well-trained, disciplined, and equipped militia"** was not made the wording of our Second Amendment, rather than what we have. The wording in the Articles is unambiguous, but more importantly makes way more sense.

> Expenditures by the United States of America will be paid with funds raised by state legislatures, and apportioned to the states in proportion to the real property values of each. Also, Congress may request

requisitions (demands for payments or supplies)
from the states in proportion with their population,
or take credit.

These provisions caused almost fatal problems. In keeping with
each state being a sovereignty, Congress could ask, but the states may or
may not respond. And most freely ignored the provision that the state
pay "in proportion to the real property values of each." Several states just
sent revenue in the amount they felt appropriate.

> … to establish <u>courts for appeals in all cases of</u>
> <u>captures</u>, but no member of Congress may be
> appointed a judge; to set weights and measures
> (including coins), and for Congress to serve as a final
> court for disputes between states.

The court system was way less developed than under the
Constitution. This is all the Articles of Confederation says on the subject.

> The United States in Congress assembled may
> appoint a president who shall not serve longer than
> one year per three-year term of the Congress.

The power of the president has changed beyond all recognition
since then. Note that Congress **may** appoint a president. So, this also
means it may not. There were 10 US presidents during the period of the
Articles of Confederation. Most served just a few months and there were
gaps when there was no president. See *Wikipedia*, Articles of Confederation.

The desire of each of the new states to be separate from other states
was expressed as each being a "sovereign." For clarity, the meaning of
sovereignty according to Collins Dictionary of Law, 2006, "sovereignty

is the union and exercise of all human power possessed in a state; it is a combination of all power, it is the power to do everything in a state without accountability; to make laws, to execute and to apply them; to impose and collect taxes, and levy, contributions, to make war or peace; to form treaties of alliance or of commerce with foreign nations, and the like."

This extreme definition was not wholly adopted by the new government. Some concessions were made to the national government; however, this was given in the most grudging way. The one power given to the national government which is of consequence today, was that only it could wage war.

In summary: All these restrictions of the power of government seems to be reaction against the British monarchy and Parliament, rather than conceiving how a functioning government could be created. It was like throwing out the baby with the bath water.

Articles of Confederation—Main Provisions

A Weak Federal Government

From the beginning the founders* wanted a weak and limited government—so Congress was only a kind of committee and their sole activity was to empower General Washington and a few others. The only governmental organization was the Congress and that consisted of one vote from each of the newly created "states." Most of the residents who expressed positions considered themselves citizens of their states—not of a nation. The concept of being a US citizen had not taken hold. It was most common for people to identify their states as their "countries" and most outside the military had never traveled far from their homes. *Maier points out that there were large numbers that were involved in the process of creating our government. This is no doubt true, but there seems to have been a relative few that were able to get their viewpoints adopted, even though compromise was usually necessary.

Alexander Hamilton, among others, always looking beyond the present situation, became greatly concerned about the weaknesses of the United States. Anyone in a position of power, he said, who took the effort to view the dire circumstances of Washington's army, could have easily concluded that something had to be done if these new "free and independent states" were to survive.

Hamilton rose from an outsider in America to be appointed Washington's *aid-de-camp*. *Chernow*, p. 85. (What we might think of as chief of staff). We read in our history books that the Revolution was fought by battles here and there, but with long periods where there were no battles. During these off-times, Hamilton immersed himself in readings on government and thinking about what was needed to have a strong government for America. All this led him to the conclusion that a much stronger central government was needed, and therefore, that the Articles of Confederation were severely deficient. Not only was this Confederation not strong enough to win the War, a strong central government was needed to provide for the needs of the fledgling nation. He thought the Confederation was no more than, "a fragile alliance of miniature countries." As noted above, Hamilton thought Congress had optimistically chosen the path of a Confederation without considering what it would take to build and survive as an independent entity. *Chernow*, p. 157. Many in the power structure held different views. There was sentiment for even weakening any central authority further by disbanding Congress when the War was over. "The constant session of Congress cannot be necessary in times of peace," said Thomas Jefferson, who wanted to replace it with a committee. *Chernow*, p. 183.

Hamilton argued that the Declaration had declared the United States to be a sovereign nation, but the national government lacked the power to actually be sovereign. The US had almost lost the war and since then it has been in constant danger of breaking up. He said the nation can't continue and when it does, it will break into waring states that can easily be captured or controlled by European nations. *Ferling*, pp. 4, 5.

Hamilton wanted a stronger connection to a government for all of the Confederation. There must be a concern for this stronger government that looked beyond the thirteen sovereign states. There must be an American spirit. The Congress created by the Articles was too weak, either to prosecute the war, or to govern once peace was achieved. What was needed was a government strong enough to require respect, both domestically and from the European powers. Chief among his concerns was who would lend this ragtag government money? The Articles dealt with a central government having too much power, but overlooked the likelihood that a government with too little power leads to anarchy.

This strong central government was essential, according to Hamilton, otherwise the states would continuously take more power to themselves and further weaken the central government. There was little in the Articles which would hold the Confederation together, thus there was the danger of each state going its own way. He could see the larger states taking advantage of the smaller states in disputes such as boundaries and commercial competition. Since tariffs were a main source of revenue for the states. There could be resort to violence—even war—over which state had the authority to collect tariffs.

Hamilton was concerned that the weaknesses of the Articles were so severe that the nation would not survive. His strongest concerns were that there was no federal judiciary, no strong executive, no authority of the Confederation over individuals, and **no taxing power.** *Chernow*, p. 157, 158.

Severely Restrict Taxing Power of the Federal Government

Most of those in power believed that if the Confederation needed money, it should come from somewhere else. Tariffs on imports were a favorite. Using tariffs makes it seem like the importer (the seller) pays the tariffs. The reality is that the consumers pay a lot of—maybe all of—the tariff charges because now the selling price is higher. Another favorite was to sell land owned by the government (which was taken from Indigenous people). Finally, tax those without political power. One of the early conflicts after the adoption of the Constitution was the Whiskey Rebellion. Congress decided to tax whiskey, which was mostly produced on the frontier—western Pennsylvania, etc., thus relieving those in power—all living close to the Atlantic seaboard—from taxation. The whiskey producers rebelled and were put down by the fledgling federal government.

The mostly Scotch-Irish frontiersmen of western Pennsylvania, who regarded liquor as a beloved refreshment, had the highest per capita concentration of homemade stills in America. In places, whiskey was so ubiquitous that it doubled as money. The rough-hewn backwoods farmers grew abundant wheat that they couldn't transport over the Allegheny Mountains, which crossed only by narrow horse paths. They solved the problem by distilling the grain into whiskey, pouring it into kegs and toting them on horseback cross the mountains to eastern markets. Some whiskey was also shipped down the Mississippi. Local farmers believed they unfairly bore the economic brunt of Hamilton's excise tax and also reasoned any interference with their recreational consumption of homemade brew. Chernow, Hamilton pp. 469, 470.

It is hard to fathom today, for all except the most tax-hating people, how much opposition to paying taxes existed in the beginning years. When reviewing debates on taxes, I have a viewpoint on judging the arguments. The viewpoint is that if you want something, the right thing to do is pay for it. Whether it's having a public library, petitioning the mayor to pave your street, or having an educated population, someone or some entity has to provide it; those who benefit from the good or service need to pay for it. So those that argue against paying taxes either want something free, or it is a way of saying they don't want the good or service (a public library, a paved street, or an educated population).

I am particularly in favor of a strong public education system. This is necessary so that the people can responsibly participate in democracy (people rule). John Stuart Mill, an English philosopher in the 1800s wrote, "The first question in respect to any political institutions is how far they tend to foster in the members of the community the various desirable qualities, ... moral, intellectual, and active." Mill, p. 337. So, if we want a democracy, we have to pay for it.

A reminder; here is the wording from the Articles.

Expenditures by the United States of America will be paid with funds raised by state legislatures, and apportioned to the states in proportion to the real property values of each. Also, Congress may request requisitions (demands for payments or supplies) from the states in proportion with their population, or take credit.

As already noted, the states took the provision in the Articles that each was sovereign more seriously than any obligation to financially support Congress. Hamilton was convinced that the failure to grant this authority would weaken—even destroy this new nation. The lack of funding for Congressional expenditures did not mean that expenditures were unnecessary. Quite the contrary.

In these desperate times of war with Great Britain, Congress resorted to borrowing and printing money. This in turn resulted in the money becoming less valuable and to no one's surprise, a loss of credit. This was the time that Hamilton first got to thinking about a national bank. In his conception it would be capitalized by both foreign loans and promises of private lenders. Chernow, p. 124.

Not only was the War effort way under-funded, but with individual states deciding how they would financially support Congress, Hamilton rightfully feared that the states would fight with each other, accusing one another of not paying their fair amount, then threatening to pull back on their own payments to Congress, etc. So rather than the Articles pulling the states together, it was creating conflicts and disunity. Chernow, p. 170.

No Provision for Financial Responsibility

The concept of the Confederation of States with a voluntary association with a federal government was leading to disaster. For the first part of the War, funding for Washington's army went fairly smoothly with states, regional conventions, local committees, town meetings, etc. providing funds. This looks more like today's GoFundMe, rather than a serious way to run a government.

By 1778, Congress was insolvent. France had started making loans, but was not as generous as expected and the states were still reluctant. Congress had requested ninety-five million dollars from the states but only got half that amount. That's when Washington went to meet with them for a month in January 1779. What he found was a totally weak Congress that had no power or willingness to make the states pay what was requested. This convinced him that Congress needed authority to directly collect taxes. But since there was no such authority, what it did was to print paper money. This money was indeed, just paper. If it was considered a promise to repay at some future date, the face value of the money was to a large extent imaginary. Not only this, individual states were also printing paper money. *Ferling*, p. 82.

Almost by himself among the leaders of the Revolution, Hamilton during down time as Washington's aide-du-camp, read and studied vociferously *writings* by European authors on how successful governments worked. He wanted to know how the United States could become economically independent. Among the authors he concentrated on were, Hume, Wyndam Beawes, Richard Price, and Malachy Postlethwayt. He was most impressed with Postlethwayt's Universal Dictionary of Trade and Commerce which concentrated on how a government and a nation could be strong financially. Hamilton was especially interested in the discussion on "production" "manufactures" and "exportation." *Ferling,* p. 84.

Malachy **Postlethwayt** (1707? – 1767) was a British commercial expert famous for his publication of the commercial dictionary titled The Universal Dictionary *of Trade and Commerce* in 1757. The dictionary was a translation and adaptation of the *Dictionnaire universel du commerce* of the French Inspector General of the Manufactures for the King, <u>Jacques Savary des Brûlons</u>.[1]

Postlethwayt wrote several works on the benefits to the British economy from the African slave trade to the colonies in North America. *Wikipedia*

One of the few people that had the same concerns as Hamilton about the inability of Congress to obtain funding necessary for survival of the Confederation was Robert Morris, a Philadelphia businessman. Soon after surrender of the British at Yorktown, Congress appointed Morris as its finance officer. (To be clear, there was no such thing as a separate executive branch with the Confederation.) Morris, then appointed a collector of taxes for each state and knowing of Hamilton's knowledge chose Hamilton as collector of taxes for New York.

In this position, Hamilton not only had direct experience with the lack of funding for the War, but had to combat the notion that somehow after the War, the Confederation could survive without taxes altogether. He wrote that such delusions should be unmasked. *Chernow,* p. 171. Recall the analogy of the sixteen-year-old above.

The position of New York tax collector confirmed and amplified the worries that Hamilton already had about states' responsiveness to requests for taxes to fund the Confederation. In one instance, New York was requested to send eight million dollars, but sent only four hundred thousand. He therefore was more convinced than ever that Congress needed to directly levy taxes. His idea was to tax imports, land, poll taxes (meaning each person would be taxed) as well as some commodities. *Ferling,* p. 136.

Constitutional Convention—Arguments Over a Strong Federal Government

Within eighteen months of the end of the war, a consensus was building that Congress must have more power. New York and Massachusetts were among the early states that pushed for a strengthening of the national government. From what we know, the first action on the road for more federal power was a conference at Mount Vernon where delegates from Maryland and Virginia met to resolve a dispute over navigation on the Potomac River. This led, after twists and turns, to the calling of the Constitutional Convention. The Virginia delegates at Mount Vernon wanted this process to be used to resolve other disputes between states and so called for a more general conference in Annapolis which was held early in 1786 to solve trade issues.

Later in 1786, the Virginia Assembly proposed a Continental Convention to consider "such regulations as may be judged necessary" to resolve disputes between the states. The original proposal was confined to this issue. Madison and William Grayson, a Virginia congressman, who saw the need as strongly as Hamilton, viewed the Convention, which would meet in Annapolis, as the beginning of a process to "fix the other defects" in the Articles of Confederation. They thought it would be better to handle all the problems at the same time. Those favoring a stronger national government became known as Nationalists or Consolidationists. *Ferling*, p. 182.

The New York legislature named six commissioners to the Annapolis conference; in the end, only Hamilton and one other attended. If Hamilton had not gone to Annapolis, he may have not gone to the Philadelphia Constitutional Convention or ended up writing a good number of the *Federalist Papers* urging adoption of the Constitution. *Chernow*, p. 2.

The Annapolis attendees soon agreed that the commercial disputes among the states were symptomatic of underlying flaws in the political framework, and they arrived at a breathtaking conclusion, "they would urge the states to send delegates to a convention in Philadelphia in May 1787 with all states sending representatives" to amend the Articles of Confederation.

They proposed the Convention have "enlarged powers" and to take up "other matters" as the situation warranted, in order to have a Federal Government needed for a nation. New York elected Hamilton to go to the Philadelphia convention, along with John Lansing, Jr. and Robert Yates. Both Madison and Hamilton realizing that Washington was the one person that could bring the states together, so they worked to get Washington to attend; he had since retired to his plantation and wanted to stay there. *Chernow*, p. 223, *Feruling*, p. 183.

Most went to Philadelphia with the understanding that their mandate was to revise the Articles of Confederation. But very soon after they got down to business, way more radical proposals were presented. Edmund Randolph of Virginia presented a plan, which became known, as the Virginia Plan. This was mostly the brainchild of James Madison who wanted to get rid of the Articles altogether and instead create a strong national government—which was the basic design of what was later adopted and created the government we have now.

Hamilton expressed agreement with Randolph and presented a motion that the Convention proceed to adopt this approach. Delegates agreed overwhelmingly that "a national government ought to be established consisting of a supreme legislature, executive and judiciary." Yates at once exposed the irreparable split in the New York delegation by voting against Hamilton's motion. *Chernow*, p. 230.

Other plans, notably the New Jersey Plan were offered which contained many of the provisions of the existing Articles. *Chernow*, p. 231. Most of the other proposals were some variation on making changes or modifying the Articles including some New York delegates, and Virginia delegates, as well as the delegates from Massachusetts, South Carolina, New Hampshire delegation. *Maier*, pp. 122, 123, 362, p. 366, p. 454.

These alternative proposals largely centered around the idea that the new nation was still just a confederation of states, so that if the federal government wanted to require something of its citizens, it had to go through the states. Also, there was a general concept that the federal budget, was something like a personal bank account. For an individual not looking to the future, the concept would be, as long as there is money in the account—why work, we have money? The equivalent concept for the federal budget was that only when the budget was running low, because of war or other special circumstances, was there a need to raise funds. This then led to great debates over how individual states would react when the feds asked them for money. Most of the debaters saw all kinds of problems with the US imposing requirements on the states.

Among other presentations, Hamilton took the opportunity to shoot down any idea that the United States could concentrate on domestic affairs and ignore what other powerful nations were doing. We cannot have tranquility in this country unless we are strong enough to be respected abroad—isolation was not an option. *Chernow*, p. 235.

While these debates were going on, there was a rebellion in western Massachusetts, led by a Revolutionary War veteran, named Daniel Shay. Many in that area were in dire straits economically. The rebellion was against economic and civil rights injustices. But the state needed to collect more taxes and so was trying to collect from these insurgents. Things came to a head when the rebels tried to seize a federal armory in western Massachusetts. The federal government could not defend its property, so had to rely on Massachusetts and a privately funded militia. *Wikipedia, September 2020.*

Shay's Rebellion, was a wake-up call. Those working to strengthen the central government had not given attention to the fact that important segments of the population, as well as state and US government had serious indebtedness. Hamilton saw this as an opportunity to show his knowledge and push the states into creating a central government that could raise revenue through taxes and one that was a <u>reliable barrower</u>

that could pay off debts when due. In a speech to the New York Assembly, he argued that if the central government didn't take control, powerful oligarchs would seize control looking out for their own interests—not the welfare the nation.

[It is frightening that this has a modern equivalent as will be covered in Topic IV.] Hamilton argued that the nation would be back in the situation it was in during the War when it could not eve buy essential military equipment. He told the body that, as leaders, it must guard against the short-sighted viewpoints of the general population. He was concerned that most people would favor state power over federal because they are more likely to deal with concerns the people can see on a daily basis. I suspect by "most people" he considered this to be those in a position of power.

To make his point, he reported that since the end of the War, as a continuation of irresponsibility during the War, five states have paid nothing to the federal government, and payments from the other eight keep going down each year. We are headed for a breakup of the union— we will be subject to the whims of the states and the powerful nations of Europe. Is this what you want? Do not let the United States perish from fears over the "imaginary danger for the specter of power of Congress."

At this time, Hamilton's fears and proposals were taken as too extreme by most of the delegates. He would have liked to do away with state governments, but admitted this wouldn't happen. His idea of a federal government was to draw on the British model—"the best the world had ever produced. Its drawback was that it discouraged change," but admitted that such a step would "shock public opinion too much." *Ferling*, p. 183, 184, 185.

But many delegates were aware of the precarious condition of the fledgling nation if it could not raise revenues without first going through the states. One would think that after the experience of Washington's army at Valley Forge, it would be obvious that a there must be an assured means for the central government to raise revenue. Indeed, there were strong advocates for such a provision. Edmund Randolph and Madison of Virginia argued that Congress had to have "full scope, and complete command over the resources of the nation." Then it would be able to "borrow with ease." "If its capacity to command the resources of the nation were compromised—lenders would have no confidence in its ability to repay loans." Randolph argued, as had several others, that ideas that states would pay voluntarily would lead to bickering among the states, even leading to civil war and weaken us when dealing with foreign nations. He and Madison advocated, contrary to the argument that nations could always raise funds to pay off debt, they could only do that if it had full authority "over the resources of the nation." They argued, Congress had to have "full scope, and complete command over the resources of the nation." Without this, the existence of the nation was in doubt. *Maier* p.272, 273. Likewise, New York's, Robert Livingston argued, "experience has shown that requisitions were nothing but, 'pompous petitions for public charity.'" Further, "what hope have we for barrowing unless we have something to pledge for repayment?" *Maier* p. 364.

Even Jefferson, a strong proponent of state sovereignty, saw the danger of uncertain sources of revenue for the central government. Possibly using his lawyerly skills, said the Constitution provided the means to tax individuals directly. His basis was that the House of Representatives provides for being "chosen by the people directly," therefore within the fundamental principle that people could be taxed by their representatives or by their own consent. If the people don't like what their representatives do, they can vote them out of office. *Maier* p. 444. Ultimately, the amendments that were adopted left Congress's power in place. *Maier* p. 463.

In all this debate, in spite of strong feelings of support or opposition, it appears that no one had a clear definition of "direct taxes." James Madison is said to have had trouble explaining what and what was not a direct tax. It took an amendment to the Constitution, Amendment XVI ratified in 1913 to specifically allow for taxes on personal income at the federal level.

Ratification

"The drama formally began on September 17, 1787, when the Constitutional Convention (or as contemporaries called it the federal Convention) adjourned and released to the public the Constitution. The convention met in secret and there are no minutes of the proceedings. At that point, the Constitution was nothing more than a proposal. In fact, it was a proposal from a body of men who had acted without authority since the delegates had been appointed to propose changes to the Articles of Confederation, not to design a new government. The federal Convention specified how the Constitution should be ratified. The proposed Constitution was to be approved by a special "ratifying convention, conventions elected by "We the People" in each of the states." The Convention also specified that once nine states ratified the Constitution, it would go into effect for all those that had ratified it. Once nine states had done so, there was tremendous pressure on the others to ratify. But this opened the way for strong opponents to the proposed Constitution to argue that they could go it alone. We know, of course, that those arguing for this lost. *Maier,* p. ix.

Talk about a coup. These men, although they were mostly the same people who created the first United States government, now had worked outside the government and proposed sending Congress packing and setting up a totally new government.

Considerable drama took place in the ratification process. The threats, subterfuge, bargaining, strategizing are interesting, but largely outside the scope of this Topic. Some states vied to become first to ratify, for others, including New York and Virginia there was strong sentiment for not ratifying and considering leaving the union. States such as New York saw their advantages restricted, small states were concerned with being overwhelmed by larger states, southern states wished to preserve the institution of slavery at all costs. The result was a Grand Compromise. This is in contrast to the usual modern concept that the Constitution was the work of geniuses and that it is a finely-tuned almost perfect document for outlining a strong governmental system.

As the ratification debates wore on for months, a few delegates, primarily Hamilton, Madison, and John Jay became alarmed that ratification was doomed. From discussions, they developed the idea of writing opinion pieces (with made up authors like "Publius," to hide the real author) and getting them published in major newspapers, primarily in New York where ratification was critical—but also was strongly contested. There were eventually 85 such pieces published. These have since been collected and publicized as *The Federalist Papers*. These pieces presented strong arguments for ratifying the Constitution. Contrary to some modern champions of the *Federalist Papers*, these were not an objective interpretation of the proposed Constitution rather, they were straightforward advocacy. As often happens with strong advocacy, the purpose of the papers was to win the argument—consistency, respect, and logic often took a back seat. *

> Even so, there are elements in the *Papers* that explain the thinking of at least the author. One in particular, is helpful to me, *Federalist Paper No. 68*, where the author, most likely Alexander Hamilton, provides the reason for establishing the Electoral College. This *Paper* shows that the Electoral College was not established, as some present-day writers have insisted, to protect small states from the domination of large states. The Electoral College was established so that "the sense of the people should operate in the choice of the person to whom so important a trust was to be confided. ... Nothing was more to be desired that

that every practicable obstacle should be opposed to cabal, intrigue, and corruption. These most deadly adversaries of republican government might naturally have been expected to make their approaches from more than one quarter, but chiefly from **the desire of foreign powers to gain an improper ascendant in our councils.**" *It's true that the Electoral College gives lower population states a greater say in the election of president, but that was not the reason it was created. Making states' rights a central part of the Constitution was done for other reasons.

Opposition to a standing army

The issue of whether to have a standing army are farthest from our debates today. It was primary at the beginning of the republic. Recall this provision from the Articles.

> Expenditures by the United States of America will be paid with funds raised by state legislatures, and apportioned to the states in proportion to the real property values of each. Also, Congress may request requisitions (demands for payments or supplies) from the states in proportion with their population, or take credit.

We do not think about how fragile the government was during the War and in creating the government which forms a lot of what we have today. Nor do we consider how far the primary concerns of those days differ from our major issues today. There was no assurance that the thirteen states that signed onto the Articles of Confederation would eventually become a nation. As covered above, the states were as much or more concerned about keeping their sovereignty than they were about winning the War. Among the actions taken were opposing long-term enlistments in the Continental army because of the fear that soldiers would start to have more allegiance to the federal system than to their home states. Those who are reading this for the first time must be astounded by the almost **universal opposition to the US having a standing army**. By contrast, today, a majority of Americans consider our nation's military, "the arsenal of democracy."

Many of the states had the same few objections to the Constitution. Those that opposed the Constitution in its form before amendments wanted, first, that federal powers would be confined only to those expressly granted, second, a fuller representation in Congress, third, restrictions on Congress's "unlimited powers of taxation," fourth, **that there should be restrictions on its power to create a standing army**, and finally, to restrain its ability to overrule state provisions for congressional elections. *Maier,* p. 339.

Here are arguments on a standing army from prominent figures of the day.

Richard Henry Lee of Virginia stated the Constitution should say "standing armies in times of peace are dangerous to liberty." *Maier* p. 56.

Dissident Pennsylvania assemblymen raised an impressive number of arguments including … Congress's right to maintain an army... *Maier* p. 65.

At the Pennsylvania convention, Robert Whitehall said, the Constitution gives Congress all the powers of raising and maintaining armies … *Maier* p. 109, and Whitehall declared that, "standing armies in times of peace are a danger to liberty" and "ought not to be kept up … *Maier* p. 119.

Eldridge Gerry of Massachusetts criticized … Congress's power to raise a standing army … *Maier* p. 45.

Virginia's George Mason's criticisms became something of a platform for critics of the Constitution because it allowed for, "the danger of a standing army in peace." *Maier* p. 46.

Virginia's Patrick Henry proposed amendments including requiring a two-thirds vote by Congress to raise a standing army. *Maier*, p. 296.

Although coming later in the process—when debating the first amendments to the Constitution, Richard Henry Lee of Virginia was opposed to the amendments for among other reasons, "Standing Armies in peace" was still in place. *Maier*, p. 454.

In the House of Representatives, amendments were proposed and rejected. [Including] one that would require a two-thirds vote in the both houses to "raise and maintain a standing army of regular troops in times of peace." *Maier* p. 453.

Richard Henry Lee of Virginia was outraged by the weakening of the amendments by the Senate and House which themselves fell short of what the Virginia convention had recommended, among which was "Standing armies in Peace." *Maier* p. 454.

Jefferson's bill of rights included, "clearly and without the aid of sophistry" ... "protection against standing armies." *Maier* p. 444.

In Maryland, there was a debate, after ratifying the Constitution because some members voted to ratify with the understanding the amendments would be forthcoming, including, "imposed limits on Congress's power to an army except in time of war, 'and then only during the war.' " *Maier* p. 245,

New Hampshire added three amendments, including, "require the consent of three-fourth of the members of both houses of Congress to raise a "standing Army in peacetime." *Maier* p. 316.

The New York majority delegates "would require a two-thirds vote of both houses to raise a standing army in times of peace, restrict the federal government's use of state militias without a state's consent ..." *Maier* pp. 370. 371.

James Madison agreed "that a standing army is one of the greatest mischiefs that can happen." The best way to avoid it was "to render it unnecessary" by giving the general government authority to call up the militia instead. *Maier* p. 282.

As the following show, supporters, though few in number, argued in favor of a standing army.

James Wilson, a Pennsylvania delegate, argued that worries about a standing army were unfounded. All governments, including the US Confederation had to "maintain the appearance of strength even in times of tranquility ... *Maier* p. 79.

Federalist speakers in the Virginia convention answering Patrick Henry's scattershot attacks on the Constitution, said "a standing army" was essential for defense and preferable to depending on the militia ... *Maier* p. 272.

George Nicholas of Virginia stated that making Congress's use of the militia subject to the "caprice" of state legislatures would undermine its power to provide for the general defense and, ironically, force it to turn from the militia to a regular army, which the opposition wanted to avoid. *Maier* pp. 282, 283.

Chattel Slavery not Open for Compromise

Now on to an issue that haunts us still today.

The issue of slavery was not a part of the Articles of Confederation. However, one of the few significant actions by Congress during the Confederation era, was the passage of the Northwest Ordinance of 1787. This Act organized the Northwest Territory and laid the groundwork for the eventual creation of new states. The Act provided that the land north of the Ohio River and west of the (present) western border of Pennsylvania and east of the Mississippi River where states were eventually admitted to the union would never be slave states. *Wikipedia, October 2020.*

Enslavement was always an issue each step of the way toward creating a union. As early as when working out the peace treaty to end the War, enslavement became a major issue. Initially there was a provision to place a ban on the British "carrying away any Negroes or other property" after the war. What this meant to the American holders of the captive Africans was that the British should return enslaved people who had defected to the British lines or else pay compensation.

The British, however, claimed that the former enslaved people had been freed once they joined the British. Hamilton supported the British position. He said that the runaways had been promised freedom; this provision "tends to bring back to servitude men once made free." We cannot now return them back to the Americans, which would be an "odious and immoral a thing as can be conceived. Hamilton, the fierce defender of private property—for whom contracts were sacred—expressly denied the legitimacy of any agreement that stripped people of their freedom. *Chernow*, p. 213.

The north never relied on enslavement as much as the south, where it was used to build the tobacco and cotton plantations. When Thomas Jefferson drafted the Declaration of Independence, enslaved people were 49 percent of the population of Virginia. Enslaved people in South Carolina outnumbered whites. Southern delegates severely criticized Hamilton.

Northern financial and mercantile interests usually were aligned with Hamilton but were opposed because he was pushing for a strong federal system. What they did not admit to was their own aristocratic lives were enabled by the of enslavement of captive Africans and their descendants. **The national consensus that the enslavement issue should be tabled to preserve the union meant that the southern plantation economy was effectively ruled off-limits to political discussion, while Hamilton's proposed financial system was extensively debated** (see below). *Chernow*, p, 211.

During the ratification debates, the proponents of enslavement would not compromise. The only concession was that after 1808 importing of Africans for the purpose of enslavement was prohibited (Constitution, Article I, Section 9, paragraph 1). Maier, pp. 42, 43. George Mason called this "a fatal" provision. He passionately condemned not only the importing of captured Africans trade, but enslavement itself as an institution that retarded industry, discredited labor, and fostered tyrannical habits in owners. (He nevertheless held people in enslavement his entire life.) Enslavement was a moral evil, and "providence punishes national sins" he predicted, "by national calamities." *Maier*, pp. 283, 284.

The issue of slavery always hovered over the Constitutional Convention. Madison observed that "the states were divided into different interests not by their difference in size, but principally from their having or not having slaves. … the conflict did not lie between the large and small states. It lay between the northern and southern." The southern states supported the Virginia Plan in exchange for protecting the institution of slavery. Charles Pinckey of South Carolina stated baldly, **"South Carolina and Georgia cannot do without slaves." The issue was so explosive that the word slavery did not appear in the Constitution; it was replaced by people "held to service or labor."** *Chernow*, p. 238.

George Mason was ready to leave those states out of the Union unless they agreed to discontinue "this disgraceful trade," but Madison disagreed. "Great as the evil is," he said, "a dismemberment of the Union would be worse." *Maier*, pp. 283, 284. Since the Constitution allowed Congress to end the trade after twenty years, which it could not do under the Articles of Confederation, it was a step forward. Slaveholders got a concession providing for the return of fugitive enslaved persons (Article IV, Section 2, paragraph 3).

Madison's views on enslavement were similar to Jefferson's. He was a relatively humane master for the nearly 120 enslaved people that he inherited once instructing an overseer to "treat the negroes with all the humanity and kindness consistent with their necessary subordination and work,"—meaning I guess, don't beat them unless you have to, to keep them subjugated. In the mid-1780s, he supported a bill in the Virginia Assembly to abolish enslavement slowly but then began to duck the issue because it was a severe political liability.

Madison never tried to defend the morality of enslavement—at the Constitutional Convention, he called it "the most oppressive dominion ever exercised by man over man"—but neither did he distinguish himself in trying to eliminate it. As a part of the planter class, he was as dependent on the enslaved people as any of the others. In his final years, he belonged to the American Colonization Society, which favored emancipation and resettlement of the former enslaved people in Africa. Over his career, Madison's political survival in Virginia and national politics required endless prevarication on the enslavement issue. *Chernow,* p. 213.

Southern states had to argue with everything they could think of to hold the others with them because they could not defend their position without help from other states. Virginia was vulnerable because of its "immense proportion" of enslaved people; by Randolph's calculations, 236,000 enslaved people to 352,000 whites. This alarms "gentlemen who have been long accustomed to the contemplation of this subject." The other states combined had over 330,000 men capable of bearing arms; the Virginia militia consisted of 50,000 men, "too few to mount an effective defense against attacks by foreign enemies, Indians, or **insurgent slaves**." *Maier,* p. 274.

Though a passionate critic of enslavement, Hamilton knew that this inflammatory issue could wreck the union. Publicly, he couldn't be both the supporter of a strong national government and a radical abolitionist. He certainly couldn't push through program for a strong national currency and financial responsibility (see below) if he stirred up the enslavement question, which was probably a futile battle anyway. So, he was silent on the enslavement issue. But in a newspaper piece in February 1791, it was most likely Hamilton using the pen name "Civis" wrote about Madison and Jefferson: "**As to the negroes, you must be tender upon that subject ... Who talk most about liberty and quality ...? Is it not those who hold the bill of rights in one hand and a whip for affrighted slaves in the other?**" If Hamilton wrote this, he was updating a gibe by the English radical Thomas Day, who had written in 1776, "**If there be an object truly ridiculous in nature, it is an American patriot, signing resolutions of independence with the one hand and with the other brandishing a whip over his affrighted slaves.**" *Chernow,* p. 307.

Was this Democracy?

Throughout the debates on ratification, there was an overall presumption that when issues were being discussed, the basic concern was for the benefit of "the people." Topic I of this book sets the groundwork for challenging this assumption. It is more fully developed in *Nash*, where it is estimated that less than 20 percent of the people living in the United States had a voice in any aspect of government. *Nash, pp.16, 17.* At the time the Constitution was being framed and debated, voting was restricted to white male property owners. Excluded were: women, men not owning property, Africans and descendants of Africans held in captivity, indentured servants, and in some cases non-Christians or even Catholics. In addition, Indigenous people were totally ignored and restricted from voting. Thus, when viewing the process of ratifying the Constitution, keep in mind that the debaters did not come from the excluded classes. Even if some argued for the welfare of the excluded classes, it was from the standpoint of the debaters—not the excluded people themselves.

This exclusion from the process was especially pernicious when arguments were made the states were closer to the people than the federal government and therefore, the primacy—even the sovereignty of the states—should be maintained. Especially in the decades and centuries following the ratification of the Constitution, it has been the states that maintained and even made worse the oppression of marginalized groups while it has most often been the federal government that has brought the rights of oppressed groups closer to those of others. Lincoln's decision to go to war against secession, Roosevelt's New Deal, and Civil Rights legislation and Supreme Court rulings in the 1960s all were actions of the federal government. (Quite obviously, the federal government has not always been on the side of removing oppressions.)

George Mason observed that the delegates to the Philadelphia Convention were the top rung of society. The vast majority had served in

Congress, many had served in state governments when these governments were organized, others were officers in the Continental army. Also, many were wealthy businessmen owning vast properties including treating enslaved persons as property. As we shall see, many held the paper money issued when there was no backing for it and they had a big interest in getting this changed into something of value. *Ferling*, p. 184, 185.

And a reminder—neither women, non-landing owning whites, indigenous people, non-Christian, nor Africans and their descendants were represented. *Zinn* makes this observation—the essence of the behavior of the power class identified in this and the following Topics. "When economic interest is seen behind the political classes of the Constitution, then the document becomes not simply the work of wise men trying to establish a decent and orderly society, but the work of certain groups trying to maintain their privileges, while giving just enough rights and liberties to enough people to ensure popular support." *Zinn*, p. 97.

Hamilton was unabashed about who should hold power. The natural state of affairs is that there will always be a division between the few who were wealthy and the many who were not. Those who had were not inclined to change very much. Thus, they should be the governing class because they were more likely to judge what is right and "check the imprudence of democracy." He expressed the views of many of the powerful class that fought the Revolution to rid themselves of Britain so they could pursue their own nation where property owners, financiers, and international traders ruled. There was no interest in democracy—people rule—in fact, this was to be avoided. *Ferling*, pp. 185, 186, 187.

This was the environment in which our Constitution came into being. When interpretations of the Constitution are done today by justices and others, it is important to keep in mind that they are doing so from this basic position of "the founders." Today, many conservatives agree with the ideas of having only the rich in power, so agree with Hamilton. Their strategy for accomplishing this is to keep the federal government weak, a goal that Jefferson sought. They like to cite Madison's statement in *Federalist Paper No. 45*, (see below) where he states that the federal government's powers would be few and defined, the state government's powers would be many and un-enumerated. The Constitution does not go this far. Proponents of a limited Federal Government prefer the more expansive language in *Federalist Paper Number 45*, rather than The Tenth Amendment. "The powers delegated by the proposed Constitution to the federal government are few and defined. Those which remain with the State governments are numerous and indefinite." The Tenth Amendment says, "The powers not delegated to the United States by the Constitution nor prohibited by it to the States, are reserved to the States respectively or to the people."

Launching of the US Government.

This review of launching the government goes through the presidency of John Adams. Up until that time, there were multiple reasons why the United States would not survive. By time of the Jefferson presidency, the nation was on a more stable footing of financial responsibility as well as the desire to govern responsibly. The section is drawn largely from *Chernow* and *Ferling*.

Weaknesses of the federal government was especially galling to western frontiersmen who were barely eking out a living. Even though the British had agreed to surrender the Ohio Valley, they did not do so and the US had no power to enforce the terms of the surrender. The frontiersmen viewed the British as preventing them from moving onto fertile land. And Spain was preventing US shipments on the Mississippi River. The frontiersmen felt abandoned and were increasingly hostile to those in the east.

Then the federal government poured salt in the wounds by imposing a whiskey tax, a product almost totally produced in the west. The frontiersmen refused to pay, resulting in what is called the Whiskey

Rebellion organized in western Pennsylvania. Washington and Hamilton were directly involved in the military campaign to defeat the rebels.

Although not specifically identified, it is highly likely that many participants in the Whiskey Rebellion were descendants of the Ulster Irish who were considered undesirable by the British colonial governments in pre-Revolutionary decades. Western Pennsylvania was a prime destination for the settlers from Ulster in Ireland.

To get started, Washington and others had to create a government based on the limited guidance in the Constitution. The Constitution did not even suggest a cabinet, so Washington had to invent one. He named four officers to run departments: Hamilton as secretary of the treasury, Jefferson as secretary of state, Henry Knox as secretary of war, and Edmund Randolph of Virginia as attorney general.

From the beginning, Hamilton and Jefferson were at loggerheads. Jefferson was in Paris during the creation and ratification of the Constitution. His view was that the Constitution creators had gone way off course. He retained the dream expressed in the Articles of Confederation for state sovereignty. We know from above in this Topic that Washington and Hamilton, the two officials that had military experience in the War, saw the dangers of a weak central government which almost resulted in defeat of the new nation.

When Washington named Hamilton as secretary of the treasury, Hamilton must have been overjoyed. Why else had he consumed every word of dry economic texts during the war or the three-volume memoir of Jacques Necker, the French finance minister. Since his military days, he had been studying and developing in his mind how a financial system for the US might work. The treasury position allowed him to put these ideas into practice. **Hamilton was now in charge of the national economy.**

Friends warned him of the dangers in taking the Treasury Department job, because many in power thought it was just like British rule, which they had fought a war to get rid of. This was indeed the case, everything that Hamilton planned to create to transform America into a powerful, modern nation-state—a central bank, a funded debt, a mint, a customs service, manufacturing subsidies, and so on—had a good deal in common with the British system. Earlier, it was observed that the colonists didn't have a clear idea of why they were fighting the British, aside from not liking to pay taxes. They had not thought out what they were **for**.

When Robert Morris, who had been Superintendent of Finance for the Congress in 1781, told him he would be in for a very rough time, Hamilton replied that "it is the situation in which I can do most good." In debating the Constitution, Hamilton knew that the issue of federal taxation and tax collectors had provoked the biggest brouhaha. As chief tax collector, he would be blamed for everything the opponents didn't like. *Chernow, pp.* 319, 320.

Hamilton started the treasury job by taking on the handling of the federal and states' debts. A related decision of Hamilton's was to create a national bank in order to create confidence in America's debt repayment. These were hard no-win projects, causing Jefferson to further distance himself from the positions of Hamilton. Jefferson strongly opposed a national bank as did many other leaders. Their view was such a bank would take from the poor and give to the rich.

Hamilton faced two issues. One was to convince those involved with creating the government that strong finances were an essential to the survival of the government. The other issue was who was to pay and how to collect the required funds. The almost universal answer to the second issue was "someone else."

Hamilton's views on financing government were revolutionary—not only for the new United States—but for the powerful European nations. Hamilton believed that the federal budget should be available for the public to see. This was the view of Jacques Necker who had the audacity of letting the public see the national budget of France. Before that, the royalty could spend the crown's treasure any way they wanted—no doubt a lot going to themselves and those they favored. Neither how the funds were obtained nor how they were spent was accompanied by any analysis. *Chernow, p.* 287.

Jacques Necker was Finance Minister of France from 1777 to 1781. He was controversial in France for a number of reasons internal to France, but also, he opposed France's financing of America's Revolutionary War. *Wikipedia*, Sept. 2020.

In Hamilton's view, the overriding necessity of the new nation was for its government to have enough resources (wealth) to show its power to other nations and to meet its obligations to its citizens. His main approach, therefore, was to show creditors that the US would pay obligations when due. To do this, he had to acquire revenue for the government—therefore his drive to create a national currency and pay off the debts of the various states.

Hamilton had to make several no-win decisions on the way to creating a currency that would be accepted both nationally and among the European powers. One such decisions related to retiring War debts to Americans. During the Revolution, many affluent people in the US had invested in bonds, and many war veterans had been paid with paper money that had no backing. With the lack of revenue due to operating under the Confederation (states refusing to pay assessments to Congress), this paper money lost much of its face value. Many of the veterans, those on the front lines of winning the War, now needed cash or had given up on ever having their paper money redeemed, therefore sold the it to speculators for as little as fifteen cents for a one dollar bill. Hamilton mistakenly expected that with his program to create a sound federal currency that these obligations would regain their face value.

By the time Jefferson, the future secretary of state arrived in New York from Europe, Hamilton was full-steam ahead with his funding scheme. Jefferson was appalled by Hamilton's plans. Jefferson had no doubt that the original holders of government paper had been cheated of rightful gains by speculators who were "fraudulent purchasers of this paper ... Immense sums were thus filched from the poor and ignorant and fortunes accumulated by those who had themselves been poor enough before."

Jefferson was still of the mind-set that liberty was best assured by small government; and even if a central government was necessary, it should have a weak executive. When he observed Hamilton creating a strong central government with a strong executive, which took sovereignty from the states, it was everything Jefferson was against.

Hamilton then had to decide, if he should redeem the paper money from the speculators at full face value or should the money be paid to the original holders? After much pondering, he wrote that "after the most mature reflection" about whether to reward original holders and punish current speculators, he had decided against this approach as "ruinous to public credit." The problem was partly that such "discrimination" in favor of former debt holders was unworkable. The government would have to find the original owners and how much they sold their paper for. This would be impossible to do.

He finally came to this reasoning; neither side was a noble seller nor a noble buyer. The sellers had willingly sold their paper and did not trust that the US would ever redeem it. His reasoning was that the first holders were not simply noble victims, nor were the current buyers simply predatory speculators. The original investors had gotten cash when they wanted it and had shown little faith in the country's future. Speculators, had taken a risk when buying the paper—they had no assurance that the government would ever redeem it. By this argument, Hamilton had established a rule that has governed securities trading to this day—that securities are freely transferrable and that the buyers assume all the risk of the security falling in value. Of course, they receive the benefit if the price increases. That the government would not interfere with a prior sale and purchase, Hamilton thought, was so important that it outweighed the controversy that his act created. This led to the future world strength of US currency—and political controversy for Hamilton.

Then there was the matter of debts held by the States, many of which had no system for how these would ever be repaid. Hamilton took the plunge and consolidated all federal and state debt into a federal debt. He wrote, "The Secretary, after mature reflection on this point, entertains a full conviction that an assumption of the debts of the particular states by the union and a like provision for them as for those debts of the particular states by the union and a like provision for them as for those of the union will be a measure of sound policy and substantial justice." The mechanism for assuming these debts was to issue federal bonds to the debt-holders.

This profoundly increased the power of the federal government. Hamilton concluded that the bondholders would now have a stake in a strong federal government and would pull their loyalty more to the federal government and away from their state. He was not so much interested in enriching creditors or the privileged class as he was to ensure that the federal government could survive and operate as a nation among nations. *Chernow,* pp. 297, 298, 299.

Hamilton's creation of the US financial system greatly concerned James Madison. The two had put their life and reputations on the line to bring the Constitution to existence. Madison, of course, fervently believed in the need for a stronger federal government, but thought Hamilton was going way too far. Now Madison's views were migrating closer to Jefferson's (his long-term friend) regarding the powers of the federal government.

By the end of Washington's presidency, the nation's politicians had divided into two groups—the **federalists**, most prominently Washington and Hamilton, but also John Adams; and the **republicans**, headed by Jefferson, Madison, Monroe and others.

Even though Jefferson was vice president in John Adam's presidency, he and Adams fought fiercely and Jefferson took no part in Adam's administration. Moreover, Jefferson had believed rumors he was hearing that Hamilton—not a part of the Adams administration—was out of the government was planning to create an army that would be used to put down the nationalists. The nationalists were increasingly vocal that there should not be a strong federal government—a position at odds that many, including particularly Madison, had at the time of Ratification.

Madison and Jefferson were now arguing that each state must decide on its own whether powers granted in the Constitution had been exceeded and if so, the state should declare these null and void. This was the opposite of Madison's position at the time of drafting the Constitution. The idea that states could "opt out" has been an albatross on our nation over the centuries. This idea of state nullification has been with us ever since. It is the same idea that led to state secession—that state participation in the federal government was optional.

> For today's readers, the names of various factions may be confusing. At the time of ratifying the Constitution and organized the new government, Federalists were those that pushed for a strong central government. Today federalists are those that strongly favor a limited federal government. Thus, the *Federalist Society*, organized in the 1990s, pushes very hard to interpret the Constitution as it was, in their view, <u>originally intended</u>, so they argue that the power of the federal government should be severely limited. (see Topic V)

Whose Nation is it?

This issue was farthest from the minds of the authors of the Articles. However, it was agreed by all of the thirteen now "states" that only white male property owners were eligible to vote. Most had religious restrictions prohibiting non-Christians from voting or holding public office. Thus, the nation was built on the interests of those eligible voters. Most of the "founders" believed that the nation should be governed by the elite, that is to say, men like themselves.

There was no mention of concepts such as democracy, republic, nation, citizens' rights, rights for Indigenous people, nor what should happen to enslaved people. But the idea of citizen participation could not be kept from many that had been lower on the social and economic ladder. Others besides the elite read the Declaration and thought maybe they also were included in the phrase, "all men are created equal." Some property-owners found they could vote and took seriously the words in the preamble to the Constitution, "we the people of the United States."

Some of these new voters with less education and considered "less refined" than the top rung were elected to state and national offices. But what the original leaders were concerned about was that they would start demanding economic policies that they could benefit from, but may cost the wealthy in some way. *Ferling*, p. 3.

Patrick Henry of Virginia and Melancton Smith of New York were among the few proponents of a political representation of people in lower social and economic classes. Smith made the point that political representation should be a mirror of the whole population. This was how governing bodies would find out what the whole population needed and wanted. He feared that if this did not happen, the government will be run by a "natural aristocracy," or worse, "a government of oppression." Without making some changes, Smith said, the elite already have an advantage in governing and they were experienced in directing the decisions to their viewpoints. *Maier*, pp. 295, 354, 355.

These ideas ran counter to both the beliefs of Madison and Hamilton. In *Federalist Paper No. 10.** Madison saw the threat of "majoritarian tyranny" if the various community interests were represented directly. He wanted only the ruling class to be elected and thought that this would happen if there were large electoral districts so that men of superior talents whose wisdom may discern the true interests of the country, rather than yield to "temporary or partial considerations of the people. Note above that Smith said this class already had the advantage. *It is easy to skip over what Madison is saying in Federalist Paper No. 10. He seems to be arguing for large districts from which to choose congressional representatives so that you get a moderating of extreme positions. Within the phrases he warns against fractious types. Looked at this way, Madison's argument sounds ultimately reasonable.

In answering Smith, Hamilton said that not all of a community's interests should be represented in the legislature. "No idea is more erroneous than this," he said. "Only such interests are proper to be represented, as are involved in the powers of the General Government," such as commerce, taxation, and the like.* In some cases, it is necessary to ignore the opinions of the majority, but in any case, they are still dependent on the majority to get elected so must listen to them. (This assumes "the majority" were allowed to vote.) Finally, he argued that if the elite men were elected, they should be allowed to serve. With this he ignores Smith who thought that a mix of the community should be its representative. *Maier*, p. 354, 355, 356.

*The argument may be true for the issues that Hamilton says the government will be involved in. Today, the government is involved in much more—so by extension, we need representation in all the things the government is involved in.

So, I guess the "founders" needed the whole population to be a part of the nation, but did not want to let them be a part of the governing. <u>If we give these people a voice in governing, they will want all kinds of fluff, like safe working conditions, a decent wage for everyone, protection of women against oppression and abuse, freeing captives who were forced to work for those that had enslaved them, and giving Indigenous people a voice in who occupies the land</u>. The powerful class needed people to manufacture goods, transport to markets, build roads and bridges, houses and buildings, grow and harvest crops, man the ships, work on the docks, manufacture military hardware, move to the frontier, etc. Who among the elite were willing to do any of these tasks? Yet, the position of the powerful class was that the workers should have no say in their government.

SUMMARY OF ARTICLES OF CONFEDERATION

1. Establishes the name of the confederation with these words: The stile of this confederacy shall be *The United States of America.*

2. Asserts the sovereignty of each state, except for the specific powers delegated to the confederation government: "Each state retains its sovereignty, freedom, and independence, and every power, jurisdiction, and right, which is not by this Confederation expressly delegated."

3. Declares the purpose of the confederation: "The said States hereby severally enter into a firm league of friendship with each other, for their common defense, the security of their liberties, and their mutual and general welfare, binding themselves to assist each other, against all force offered to, or attacks made upon them, or any of them, on account of religion, sovereignty, trade, or any other pretense whatever."

4. Elaborates upon the intent "to secure and perpetuate mutual friendship and intercourse among the people of the different States in this union," and to establish equal treatment and freedom of movement for the free inhabitants of each state to pass unhindered between the states, excluding "paupers, vagabonds, and fugitives from justice." All these people are entitled to equal rights established by the state into which they travel. If a crime is committed in one state and the perpetrator flees to another state, he will be extradited to and tried in the state in which the crime was committed.

5. Allocates one vote in the Congress of the Confederation (the "United States in Congress Assembled") to each state, which

is entitled to a delegation of between two and seven members. Members of Congress are to be appointed by state legislatures. No congressman may serve more than three out of any six years.

6. Only the central government may declare war, or conduct foreign political or commercial relations. No state or official may accept foreign gifts or titles, and granting any title of nobility is forbidden to all. No states may form any sub-national groups. No state may tax or interfere with treaty stipulations <u>already proposed</u>. No state may wage war without permission of Congress, unless invaded or under imminent attack on the frontier; no state may maintain a peacetime standing army or navy, unless infested by pirates, but every State is required to keep ready, a well-trained, disciplined, and equipped militia.

7. Whenever an army is raised for common defense, the state legislatures shall assign military ranks of colonel and below.

8. Expenditures by the United States of America will be paid with funds raised by state legislatures, and apportioned to the states in proportion to the real property values of each.

9. Powers and functions of the United States in Congress Assembled.

    o   Grants to the United States in Congress assembled the sole and exclusive right and power to determine peace and war; to exchange ambassadors; to enter into treaties and alliances, with some provisos; to establish rules for deciding all cases of captures or prizes on land or water; to grant <u>letters of marque and reprisal</u> (documents authorizing <u>privateers</u>) in times of peace; to appoint courts for the trial of pirates and crimes committed on the high seas; to establish <u>courts for appeals in all cases of captures</u>, but no member of Congress may be appointed a judge; to set weights and measures (including coins), and for Congress to serve as a final court for disputes between states.

o The court will be composed of jointly appointed commissioners or Congress shall appoint them. Each commissioner is bound by oath to be impartial. The court's decision is final.

o Congress shall regulate the post offices; appoint officers in the military; and regulate the armed forces.

o The United States in Congress assembled may appoint a president who shall not serve longer than one year per three-year term of the Congress.

o Congress may request requisitions (demands for payments or supplies) from the states in proportion with their population, or take credit.

o Congress may not declare war, enter into treaties and alliances, appropriate money, or appoint a commander in chief without nine states assented. Congress shall keep a journal of proceedings and adjourn for periods not to exceed six months.

10. When Congress is in recess, any of the powers of Congress may be executed by "The committee of the states, or any nine of them", except for those powers of Congress which require nine states *in* Congress to execute.

11. If Canada (referring to the British Province of Quebec) accedes to this confederation, it will be admitted.[16] No other colony could be admitted without the consent of nine states.

12. Reaffirms that the Confederation accepts war debt incurred by Congress before the existence of the Articles.

13. Declares that the Articles shall be perpetual, and may be altered only with the approval of Congress and the ratification of all the state legislatures.

References for Topic II

Chernow, Ron, Alexander Hamilton, Penguin Group (USAS) Inc. 375 Hudson Street, New York 10014, ISBN 0 14 30-3475 8, 2005.

Ferling, John, Jefferson and Hamilton, The Rivalry That Forged A Nation, Bloomsbury Press, 1385 Broadway, New York, 10018, ISBN 978-1-60819-528-2, 2013.

Maier, Pauline, Ratification, The People Debate the Constitution, 1787 – 1788, Simon and Schuster, Inc. 1230 Avenue of the Americas, New York, 10020, ISBN 978-0-684-86855-4, 2010.

Mill, John Stuart, Representative Government, Great Books of the Western World, Volume 43, The University of Chicago, 1952.

Nash, Darrel A, A Perspective on How Our Government Was Built, And Some Needed Changes, Rose Dog Books, 585 Alpha Drive, Suite 103, Pittsburg PA 15238, ISBN 978-1-4809-7915-4, 2018.

Topic III

Racism in America

Several years ago, I thought, no wonder the US is such a rich
country. We took the land from the Indigenous people and
took the labor from captive Africans and their descendants.
This wealth is far from being shared by all citizens,
especially those from which we took wealth.

The Plague Crosses the Atlantic

Parts I and II introduce the enslavement of Africans and their descendants
in North America. Recall the moral plague that had already been carried
by the earliest American settlers which caused them to believe that
captured Africans were only to be enslaved—not fellow humans that
needed rescuing and respite from their long ordeal of being captured and
shipped across the Atlantic in conditions worse than the way animals
were treated.

> "The term *negro* didn't come into use until the
> 1450s when Portuguese traders came to what is
> now Senegal and called the area, *terra dos negroes,*
> (land of the blacks). At that time, it was an ethnic

designation—not a racial term that would come into use much later. Europeans criticized some of the behavior of Africans, but this was largely from ignorance, thinking their cultural practices included devil worship. At that time, it was not different from looking down on Europeans from other parts of the continent." *Mann*, pp. 514, 515.

During the whole colonial period, in the entire area of what would become the United States, white persons held Africans and their descendants in slavery without any apparent concern that this was morally wrong. White New Englanders, especially benefitted from the slave trade—this area having developed into a thriving shipping economy throughout the Atlantic and Caribbean.

But the Southern whites had the most to gain by enslavement. This is where the captives were put to work, first in tobacco fields, then cotton, etc. Without the requirement to pay wages to these workers, the owners could get rich, buy more land, buy more captives, and build mansions for themselves. Enslavement was so lucrative for the white captors that by the time of the Revolution, these Africans and their descendants made up significant portions of the population of the South.

Dutch, Portuguese, and English purchasers of the captive Africans had little knowledge of those they held in captivity. Only a few captors in what was to become the United States seem to have known that thousands of captives were trained in military tactics in their home regions. When the African captives organized military campaigns, it took many captors by surprise and led to great fear that these campaigns could be repeated. Mann, pp. 432, 433. From Topic II we see this was a strong factor for some southern states to ratify the constitution—to get the backing of the central government when slave rebellions happened.

By the time of the Revolution, the American captors had long realized the errors of what they had been told that the African captives were of low intelligence and therefore would have to submit to the demands of the captors. Experiencing the multiple ways of resistance by the captives, the political structures in these colonies/states were in constant fear of rebellions and therefore needed overwhelming military capabilities to protect themselves.

To try to break the resistance of the captives, the owners took to severe beatings, amputations, rape, etc. (Recall from Topic I that settlers from Britain were accustomed to using and seeing such atrocities.) And the final aggression, Africans and their descendants alone from all others held in various forms of forced labor*, were proclaimed by most of the colonies to be owned for life as well as the lives of their descendants. It became known as chattel** slavery. Others held in bondage, the indentured servants, were held for a fixed number of years—often seven—and then they were set free. *Article IV Section 2 of the US Constitution, calls this "held to service or labor." The Thirteenth Amendment calls it "involuntary servitude." **This is the ownership practice for livestock in western civilization.

The Lie Goes Mainstream

A story, still being told in some schools, museums, and visitor centers, especially in the South, is that the enslaved African descendants were better off in America than they could have been in Africa, so the US had done them a favor by bringing them here. **This could have some credibility if instead of those who were brought here in chains and forced into labor without pay, would have been recruited and willingly migrated to America.** The Recruiters would have had to convince potential migrants that they could have a good life in America, would by paid today's equivalent of perhaps $20 or 25 an hour, (maybe even more to work in cotton fields*) provide for their families, and allowed to retain all of their celebrations, religious practices, and family connections—in short, their culture—that they had in Africa. And then, of course, that the promises largely had been realized. Instead, the captives were deprived of nearly everything that makes someone a person. *I only recently learned of how working in the cotton fields was so painful and damaging to the hands and feet.

Much of the popular history of the US is told as a political story—which presidents did what, dates and issues of the wars, etc. but to get a more complete and accurate history of the US, we must expand our search to power groups outside political history.* Especially after the Civil War, the principal actors were powerful private interest groups. As will be discussed in more detail below, great influences in our society were promulgated yes, by the political process but also more aggressively by wealthy landowners, newspapers, college professors, "scientists," physicians, religious leaders, and others of influence. The goal of these people in positions of power, still existing in too many circles, was to re-create the conditions for African descendants that were in place before the Civil War, that is, to hold African descendants in subjugation to white people.

*The lives of all Americans, white, Black, Indigenous people, the many immigrant groups, and those working in mills and shops in the northeast under extremely dangerous conditions and with few rights, are of course, important to understand our past. This Topic concentrates on the treatment of persons of African descent—the most vexing and long-term blot on our society. **I put *scientists* in quotes because as one trained in the scientific method, I am appalled to see how persons wearing the cloak of scientist, misused their position to produce or proclaim results they wanted, rather than conducting research to find the truth.

Popular History

The turmoil leading up to the Civil War is a part of most history books. What I remember from studying history in elementary and secondary school is that there was a disagreement between the northern states and the southern states about how the enslaved people were treated. The issue of whether enslavement was immoral never came up. According to that narration, the north claimed those enslaved were forced to work in the cotton fields, the south claimed that the enslaved people were happy and enjoyed celebrating. <u>The problem with stopping here is that</u> <u>one of these claims is a lie.</u>

Then after the War, carpet baggers came from the north going to the south and, as I recall learning, that the carpet baggers were trying to harm the freed slaves. Then the "radical Republicans" decided they would impeach President Andrew Johnson. I don't remember why they were called radical, but it wasn't a good thing.

All of this is a gross distortion. More for what it didn't say than what it did.

America Goes for the Bottom

Topic II covers how the US Constitution would not have been ratified had not enslavement been codified into it. The Southern states, especially would not have joined. The one concession for the US Constitution made by the enslavers was to agree to discontinue importation of African captives after 20 years. Otherwise, things could go on as before. Even though enslaved people were not even recognized as people by most in power, they were considered three-fifths of a person when it came time to enumerate the population of each state to determine how many representatives the state would get for the US Congress. For further discussion see, *Nash*.

After the Revolution, there was talk and sentiment among some of the white residents for freeing people from enslavement. The discussion at the time introduced the word "manumission." The dictionary definition is "the act of freeing slaves." It is obvious from the context what the proponents meant was "sending them back to Africa." Luminaries from Thomas Jefferson to Abraham Lincoln expressed the belief that descendants of Africans were of a lower moral and intellectual order. These men expressed their opinion that the enslaved lacked the imagination and energy to compete and live in America as free persons and therefore, the most humane action was to send them back to Africa. By this time, of course, many of the captives had several generations between themselves and their African ancestors. (Liberia was established as a nation and many freed persons of African descent migrated there to begin a new life.)

Agitation for ending chattel slavery grew stronger as the nation achieved some international power after the War of 1812. Great Britain ended slavery in 1833 adding justification to the argument of ending it in the US. It became a national issue as new lands were taken from the Indigenous people and territories achieved the status of applying for statehood. (Territories could apply for statehood when "the count of settlers outnumbered the indigenous population, which in most cases required forced removal of the indigenous inhabitants." *Dunbar-Ortiz, Roxanne, pp. 3, 124*.)

The Northwest Ordinance in 1785; among other provisions stated that the area north of the Ohio River and east of the Mississippi River were declared off-limits to slaveholding. The area west of the Mississippi River was not included, so there was great competition to grant or deny slave-holding in these areas when they were admitted to statehood. Missouri and Kansas were at the center of this controversy and the battles there was one of the major initiating events of the Civil War.

Reconstruction

Civil War amendments to the Constitution abolished slavery and required seceding states to rewrite their constitutions before being readmitted to the Union where their Constitutions prohibited voting by persons of African descent and other ethnic or religious groups that may have previously been prevented from voting.

After the southern states re-did their Constitutions so that they could re-join the Union, voters elected significant numbers of Black men to their constitutional conventions and to their legislatures.

Here is a brief accounting of Blacks in public office—mirroring the attitude of the White power structure toward Blacks. The first Black senator and representatives were: Sen. Hiram Revels, of Mississippi, Reps. Benjamin S. Turner of Alabama, Robert DeLarge, Joseph Rainey, and Robert Elliot of South Carolina, Josiah Walls, of Florida, and Jefferson

Long of Georgia. All of these men were Republicans—the party of Lincoln. In Mississippi and South Carolina, Blacks were a majority of the population. Together with pro-Union whites, Republicans took control of these legislatures. Across the south, several congressional districts were made up of a majority of Black voters.

It didn't take long for the Democrats, the party of planters, enslavement, and secession and the power pushing back on Reconstruction, came up with the idea of voter suppression. This most likely was the first instance of violence to suppress votes. Before that prohibition from voting was done by legal means. Very early after the War, the Ku Klux Klan emerged as a secret vigilante group, terrorizing freedmen and their White allies. Starting in 1868, especially in Louisiana, Mississippi, North Carolina and South Carolina, paramilitary organizations such as the White League and Red Shirts began working openly to intimidate Blacks so that they wouldn't vote.

In 1866, Congress passed the Civil Rights Act which dissolved nearly all the governments of the states that had seceded. It divided the South into five military districts where through the Freedmen's Bureau, it worked to protect the voting rights of Blacks as provided for under the newly revised constitutions of these states.

But this was short-lived. It happened due to the election of 1866. The results were disputed between Rutherford B. Hayes, the Democrat, and Samuel Tilden, the Republican. The House of Representatives settled the issue by naming Hayes the winner. To get the Democrats—especially Southern Democrats—to acquiesce in Hayes's victory, Hayes and the Republicans agreed to withdraw all U.S. federal troops from the Southern U.S. and thus brought Reconstruction to come to an end.

This began the 80-year reign of the solid South, where Democratic candidates who opposed the civil rights of Black people won nearly all elective offices. Their tolerance and involvement with the KKK and other organizations brought the reign of terror in the South that is not totally gone today. *Wikipedia, October 2020.*

At the beginning of the twentieth century, Black people had been almost totally eliminated from political power. The KKK and the reign of terror were in full force. By 1900, Louisiana had fewer than 6,000 registered Black voters, down from a high of 130,000 and Alabama had 3,000 down from 181,000, figures typical for most southern states. *Gates*, pp. 186, 187.

There were African Americans ready and able to argue against the propaganda of Black inferiority being published in popular magazines and journals. In 1884, George Washington Williams argued that the nation should look to history, not to science.* He reminds readers of the history of the treatment of the descendants of Africans in America from the tortures and deaths of the middle passage, of women forced into slavery, the breaking up of families and much more. Instead of the common themes of the US being built by the knowledge and dedication of white Americans, he argues that the progress made in this country was made by accumulating wealth on the backs of the enslaved people, that without this, there would be no American power. *Science had apparently been so misused in those decades, that persons seeking to truly understand the social conditions in society rejected science as a way of gaining knowledge.

Frederick Douglass also gave a forceful rebuttal to Black inferiority in 1894. "It is a formula of Southern origin, and has a strong bias against the negro. It handicaps his cause with all the prejudice known to exist against him. It has been accepted by the good people of the North, as I think, without investigation. It is a crafty invention. ..."

"The device is not new. It as an old trick. It has been oft repeated, and with similar purpose and effect. For truth, it gives us falsehood. For innocence, it gives us guilt. [Note that this strategy was not invented in the present time.] It removes the burden of proof from the old master class, and imposes it upon the negro. It puts upon a race a work which belongs to the nation. It belongs to the craftiness often displayed by disputants, who aim to make the worse appear the better reason. It gives bad names to good things, and good names to bad things. ..." "I repeat, and my contention is, that this negro problem formula lays the fault at the door of the negro, and removes it from the door of the White man, shields the guilty, and blames the innocent. Makes the negro responsible and not the nation." *Gates*, pp.89, 90.

One would think that anyone reading the works of Williams, Douglass, and others that their writings would persuade white people to re-think the propaganda that they were being fed. But there was little in the way of changing the attitudes of the power structure toward the descendants of Africans for decades. Those of African descent who pushed back were lonely voices, with very little visible support from whites.

Educated white persons had the training and the resources to push back against the vitriol of painting the descendants of Africa as a separate species or as humans incapable of managing their own lives, or what was feared most by whites, having political power to help shape the nation's law to create a more just society. But, "good" white people fell silent. Consider a possibly reason for this silence. By acknowledging Black people as fully capable to be personally responsible and able to perform in any capacity in our society, that whites were/are afraid that we may have to give up the power we have over Blacks and other oppressed people.

> Here we have the thousands of years-old question. "Then the Lord said to Cain, where is Abel, your brother? He said, I do not know; am I my brother's keeper?" *Genesis 4, v. 9, 10, RSV.*

Redemption

Our history books call the period in US history after the Civil War, Reconstruction. This was supposedly a time when the nation was to be bound back together. It also was the period when the descendants of Africans gained political power. They were elected to Congress and to state legislatures. They started businesses and organized churches. A great surprise to the white power structure is that former slaves, who had purposely been held illiterate were able, ready, and prepared to perform in these responsible positions. No doubt, some were elected to positions for which they were not qualified—as happens today among all ethnic groups.

Reconstruction was not at all what Southern white power groups wanted. They therefore set out to reclaim the power structure existing before the War, meaning that the African descendants had to be subjugated but without the structure of slavery. This was given the term <u>Redemption</u>. The term Redemption caused me confusion until I read Gates' definition. A better term to describe the period after Reconstruction would be <u>Destruction</u>. We have only partly recovered from the Destruction.

While our history books tell us about Reconstruction, the period of Redemption is new to most of us. According to *Henry Louis Gates, Jr.,* the period known as Redemption immediately followed Reconstruction (1865 – 1877) "**when the gains of Reconstruction were systematically erased** and the country witnessed the rise of a white supremacist ideology that, we might say, went rogue." This ideology is still with us. "I define the Redemption era as starting in 1877, when the last of the former Confederate states were reclaimed by Southern Democrats, and reaching its zenith in horror—the highest point of the lowest low—with the screening by President Woodrow Wilson at the White House in 1915 of D. W. Griffith's *The Birth of a Nation.*" *Gates, Henry Louis Jr.*, pp. 152, 153.

It is well to keep in mind that for many decades, the Republican Party, the party of Lincoln, was known as the one that freed the enslaved people. The Democratic Party was made up largely of those that opposed to freeing the enslaved. In the 1877 presidential election, the Democrats gave in to the Republicans in return for getting federal troops removed. It was not until Franklin Roosevelt's administration that the Democratic Party firmly took on the mantle of being on the side of giving Black persons more power and even then, as will be recorded below, his administration had a mixed performance. And it was the administration of Nixon that put the Republican Party firmly on the side of restricting rights and powers of Black persons with his "southern strategy."

In the 1940s, 1950s and later, leaders in the US and many citizens were obsessed with propaganda and infiltration of ideas from Soviet communism and its allies. From the Korean War, we got this fear of *brain-washing*, that US prisoners would be brain-washed and come home and foist their new beliefs onto gullible Americans.

But all this is nothing compared to the **vile, vitriolic, lies** promulgated with most force against persons with African ancestry in the era of Redemption and drilled into the minds of most white Americans. As a nation, we must know about and understand the effects of Redemption that we are burdened with today. It is a plague that we have not rid ourselves of. All readers who are white are urged to take the test below. Where do you stand?

This brain washing was done at every level of government and by many powerful organizations, including newspapers and magazines, major universities, especially in the North, and religion (meaning Christian churches and Christian religious leaders). It started mainly in the South, but worked its way outward to encompass the whole nation.

I was born into and grew up in this environment.

Here is a sample of statements and posters that *Gates* provides readers from the period of Redemption. If the following seem incredible to you, read *Gates* book for yourself.

Books and articles: God created white people, Adam and Eve. Others were not in the Garden of Eden, but rather were a part of the animal kingdom. The Negro is not a part of the Abrahamic family. Charles Carroll a minister from Missouri

*God did two creations, one of white people, the other of African. There is scientific proof of this. Charles Carroll

*Noah took Africans onto the ark, but as a part of allowing one pair of each animal species. Charles Carroll

*God created speaking apes so that humans could put these animals to their service. Charles Carroll

Posters and post cards: orangutans, gorillas, chimpanzees, and Africans are shown in one picture giving the message that these are all sub-human species.

*Comparing an "idealized" white person—large forehead, moderate sized nose, distinct chin beside an African with sloping forehead, large nose, and receding chin, presumably showing White intelligence.

*Scientists Say Negro Still in Ape Stage, Races Positively Not Equal

*Mongrelization—End of Civilization The white Blood Will be Lost Forever

Let's take a test. What do you believe?

	Strongly agree	It makes some sense	Strongly disagree
Black people are subhuman like gorillas, chimpanzees, and orangutans			
Head size and facial features are indicators of intelligence			
Black people are slothful, lazy			
Black people are genetically disease-prone			
Black people are happy to have others tell them what to do			

Black people don't and won't take directions			
Black men are weak, don't take initiatives			
Black men are rapists			
Young Black men are angry and dangerous			
Since Black people are less healthy and less intelligent, it is wasteful to spend money on providing equal access to education, etc.			
Adam and Eve were white, so they could not have been the parents of Black children			
Offspring of different races are mongrels and therefore interracial mating should be illegal			

All of the above were widely believed among the white population of the US in the Redemption era. How many of these beliefs are still with us?

How many checks did you put in each column?

None of the statements have any basis from studies conducted to get to the truth.

In social science research where I am trained, there is always the recognition that there are multiple factors (or reasons) for a certain result. This area of science doesn't have the option of doing experiments in labs to reach conclusions, rather, it must study the world as it is and try to expand our knowledge. Unless all or many of the major factors in this complex world are taken into account, the final conclusions of research are weak—even erroneous.

An example from real life is that some studies show Black Americans to be more disease-prone than white people. What is left out are multiple reasons why this may be the case—access to health care, living near waste dumps, chemical and petroleum processing plants, substantially lower income which reduces choices in diet, living conditions, etc., more are employed in dangerous occupations like animal slaughter, trash collection, etc. Finally, an important finding is that the lives of every Black person is more stressful the for others simply by the generations-long and daily insults that they are exposed to—referred to below as microaggressions. Unless these factors are taken into account, it is not possible to conclude anything about the tendency to diseases of Black people compared to White.

Of course, racism didn't start with Reconstruction. Think of the recent "celebration" of the first Africans arriving in what would be the US at Hampton Virginia covered in Topic II. Pirates had raided a Portuguese ship thinking it was carrying gold. Instead, they found African captives. The pirates then headed to Hampton and sold the captives to the White settlers as slaves.

One could immediately raise the question, why did the settlers buy them? Couldn't they have instead paid a ransom for the captives and set them free? It is obvious, they had already been brain-washed into believing that the captives were "less than" and that slavery was the only option for treating them.

Our understanding of the origin of humans and human groups has advanced greatly in the past hundred years, most definitively by DNA analysis. This tells us all *homo sapiens* are descendants of Africans. The differences in what we look like make up one one-thousandths of our DNA. The other 999 parts are common to all of us. We also know that the concept of race is a cruel myth. But the essential truths were realized a century ago by W. E. B. Du Bois and others.

Du Bois writing in the early 1900s that "scientists" had been trying to find ways to definitely say that Blacks were of a different race than whites. They tried skin color, hair texture, cranial measurements and language. None of these worked because individuals varied so much within their own ancestry that separate races could not be identified. He said that "science" had identified two or three great families of humans. He cited Darwin who concluded that even though there are differences, the likenesses are much greater and this confirms the brotherhood of all humans. Cited in *Gates*, pp. 71.

> What Du Bois didn't say is that "scientists" might make conclusions. But that doesn't automatically say that these scientists used proper scientific methods to reach their conclusions or whether they were just using their status as a basis for making pronouncements.

Here are some of the falsehoods created by "experts." *The Surgical Peculiarities of the American Negro* (1896) was written by Rudolph Matas, a professor of surgery at Tulane University. From other "experts" Mattas reviewed the supposed weakness of those of African ancestry. He claimed to find that, first the centuries of slavery had created social weakness by itself on top of the inherent inferiorities of the former slaves had made them incapable of being anything but "indigent, dependent, and defective classes in the Southern States." This is a permanent condition and so cannot rise to anything else. He says that if you are "thinking men" you have to accept the findings of experts. Hmmm. *Gates*, pp. 71, 72.

Matas concludes with a number of "findings." "The North American Negro, as he is known at present in the United States, is anthropologically, physiologically, and pathologically different from his original African ancestors and from his uncivilized brothers in the West Coast of Africa of the present generation," due to being under the influence of the white man and adapting to the climate. *Gates*, pp. 71, 72. **Matas even admits to the practice of white owners raping women of African ancestry as a factor in making the American Negro different from his African ancestors.** But he calls it miscegenation.

Matas also reported that illness and early death was less than that of whites under slavery. But since freedom has been attained, "its morbidity and mortality have enormously increased." *Gates*, pp. 71, 72. (I do not know if this was true, but it doesn't sound true. Keep in mind the requirements of sound social science research noted above.)

Readers may wish to explore this further. For now, from *Wikipedia* we learn that a historian U. B. Phillips found several enslaved people got "a quart of cornmeal and a half pound of salt pork per day for the adult and proportioned down for children. This was supplemented by sweet potatoes, field peas, syrup, rice, fruit, and 'garden sass' (vegetables). Kenneth F. Kiple writing in 1981 records, "the poor quality of food led to slaves that were either 'physically impaired or chronically ill.'"

Diet, of course, is only one factor in health. Other major factors had to be the psychological damage of forced and brutal labor, family separations, deprivation of culture, beatings, rape and on and on lasting for as much as 10 generations.

Matas reported that as a physician, he could say that from a purely surgical standpoint, "the white and the negro are practically alike." But from a statistical viewpoint, (what was his source) the health problems of the negro were due to the unfavorable environment. (One solution not proposed would have been to enable or provide income and access to health care more in line with what white citizens had.) But he also attributed the lower health and living data to moral deficiency, bad heredity, vice, and dependency among an "ethnologically inferior and passive race struggling against a superior, aggressive, and dominant culture." *Gates*, pp. 71, 72.

In contrast to these "findings" here is what a modern researcher shows. The "persistent sense of otherness" experienced by persons of color take a psychological and physiological toil. Social science research has demonstrated that the cumulative effect of micro-aggressions* "assail the self-esteem of recipients, produce anger and frustration, deplete psychic energy, lower feelings of well-being and worthiness, produce physical health problems, shorten life expectancy, and deny minority populations equal access and opportunity in education, employment and health care. *Tatum* p. 53. *Micro-aggressions are the <u>supposedly</u> small insults and injuries receive just because you are Black or any other oppressed group. Being followed in stores by a clerk, someone being surprised that you speak "proper English," expecting you to be good at basketball or singing, and on and on.

The white "analysts" were recognizing what DuBois wrote, that physical appearances did not explain differences in the races; they therefore searched for other explanations. At Columbia University in New York City, a professor, William Dunning, continued the vile propaganda noted above. Dunning summarizes the case for doing away with Reconstruction. His argument was that slavery was a natural system for the two groups to live together, so after freeing the slaves, a system had to be developed to keep the oppressor/oppressed system. His ideas were so widespread that he and his students became known as the Dunning School. *Gates, p. 73.*

Charles Carroll, a minister from Missouri, went farther than Dunning. Instead of two races, Carroll argued that religion and science now agreed that Negroes are not human, but animals—talking apes—

so that white people could more easily treat them as the animals that they were. Carroll's *The Negro, a Beast: or, "In the image of God"* (1900). Carroll tells us: Noah took Negroes along with other animals onto the ark and then his descendants took the Negroes along with domesticated plants, animals, and instruments wherever they went. This was God's plan to develop the superb white civilizations that we have today. *Gates, p. 73, 74, 75.*

These "findings" were widely distributed and widely believed among the white population. They poison our beliefs today—perhaps not the most repulsive statements—but the common belief of the inferiority of persons of color. But how far away from this are we? We see students placing nooses around school campuses, white students calling students of color the "n" word, and all sorts of physical violence, like dragging a Black man to death tied behind a pickup truck. We see white people doing all kinds of things to avoid having persons of color living in "their" neighborhood and working to keep their kids in all white or mostly all white schools. You don't think this is widespread? Look at the results of your test. As white persons, we must ask what this oppression does to Black persons' physical, economic, psychological, and emotional well-being. And what does it do to us?

There are many more "studies" and "treatises" cited by *Gates*. What the "researchers" and interpreters didn't know or didn't care, is what this did to the daily lives of people at the margins of society. For example, in 1927, the Supreme Court voting eight to one upheld a Virginia sterilization law in which Oliver Wendell Holmes, Jr., wrote: "It is better for all the world if, instead of waiting to execute degenerate off-spring for crime to let them starve for their imbecility, society can prevent those who are manifestly unfit from continuing their kind … Three generations of imbeciles are enough." Statements of this kind are covered more fully below.

Let's pause here. How much of these "scientific" findings do you believe? Remember the test above I urged you to take? Also keep in mind the basic requirements of valid scientific research—1) research must be done to seek the truth, not to set out to prove what you want to believe, and 2) especially in social science research, there are multiple factors that affect the way things are in the real world, unless the several important factors are taken into account in the research, the findings are not valid. To take a prime example from above, there were and are many reasons why persons with darkest skin might not do well on intelligence exams, among the reasons is that it is well-known that persons with darker skin are more oppressed in multiple ways than persons with lighter skin. Even within Black society, darker-skinned persons are sometimes looked down on or worse by lighter-skinned persons, no doubt a holdover from the days of enslavement. See, Tatum, p. 123.

Remember in the Topics I and II, that the political leaders and others with political clout considered themselves to be a wise group that must manage the affairs of the colonies/nation. You got into this group mostly by family connections. This mentality continued into the Redemption period when white southerners worked to restore the oppressor/oppressed conditions during slavery. Who are these leaders in this period? Notice how this plague of white superiority had infected the entire nation that we are living in today.

I will insert here that these writers did not invent the vitriol of Black inferiority. Here are the words of John C. Calhoun, a towering political figure from South Carolina primarily in the decades after the passing of the founding fathers.

Calhoun was increasingly disturbed by the newly developing abolition movement. He argued that if this happened, it would "raise them to a political and social equality with their former owner, by giving them the right of voting and holding public offices under the Federal Government." Northern politicians and their black allies would then complete a social revolution not for a moral reason, but to gain political patronage from them. They could then further the economic exploitation by the northern states of the South.

He said if this happens, the South will be reduced to poverty in an all-black region, if the northern spoilsmen, exploiters, and fanatics are not stopped. *Niven, pp. 324, 325.* Calhoun increasingly argued for "nullification" which was an argument introduced by Madison of all persons. This concept was that states had the right to nullify any action of the Federal government, if in the state's opinion violated the Constitutional separation of state and federal power. This thinking helped the South justify seceding from the Union.

The *Atlantic Monthly*, founded in 1857, still published today and valued by liberals, by the time of Redemption, was publishing articles on why the Negroes could not survive in "our" country. "In February 1882, the magazine ran an article called 'Negro Types, written by Jonathan Baxter Harrison in his *Studies in the South* series. He continued the false narrative " 'the uncouth, strangely shaped animal-looking Negro or mulatto, who seems mentally, even more than by his physical characteristics, to belong to a race entirely distinct from that of the white race around them. He is not so much hostile or antagonistic as alien, unimpressible, inaccessible. He cannot be influenced or guided to any extent. He must have his way. He will only do so much work, and will labor only under conditions natural and desirable to him.'" *Gates*, pp. 81, 82.

In 1884, *Atlantic Monthly* published writings in a forum which included a piece by a Harvard paleontologist. In it he wrote that the negroes were unfit to even manage their own civilization. Even though they have been enslaved and thus had the benefit of learning from the whites, in each generation they will go back to the ways before being brought to America. He seemed to be saying that since Black people are incapable of living in the American society, that it was a mistake to have enslaved them in the first place—not what plantation owners would want to hear. *Gates*, pp. 81, 82.

According to Joel Chandler Harris, a writer for the *Atlanta Constitution*, the Georgia Constitutional Convention to rewrite its constitution, went like this. The election went on for three days to give negroes a chance to vote in as many precincts as possible. The ballot boxes were not protected. [Sound like a familiar charge?] The worst fears of the whites actually happened. The negroes, now with their new power, supported by Congress and the War Department "and filled with the conceit produced by the flattery and cajolery of the carpet-bag sycophants, were beginning to assume an attitude which would have been threatening and offensive even if their skins had been white as snow." [I don't know how much of this can now be verified or refuted. It certainly supported those working to restore White dominance.] *Gates*, pp. 102, 103.

Fear of Black persons and supporters would take over state legislators in the South resulting from the requirement that states rewrite their constitutions was published was by Joel Chandler Harris claiming that all these carpet baggers from the north and others "were intent on stirring up a new revolution in the hope that the negroes might be prevailed upon to sack cities and towns, and destroy the white population." *Gates*, p. 95. Popular magazines, such as *Harpers Weekly* carried forth the messages of Black inferiority with articles and cartoons.

In this period there were more pamphlets, signs, cartoons, etc. of what legislatures looked like with descendants of Africans as legislators. One published in *Harpers Weekly* in 1974, shows Black legislators in near fisticuffs with each other, while the white chairman is ducking for cover.

As time went on, the advocates of Blacks as inferior in all the ways mentioned above, were winning the propaganda war throughout the country. Recall what I referred to as brain-washing. The nation was in the throes of brain-washing. Have we recovered? Does this have any familiar rings in our society today? The extent of this plague (see Topic II for my definition) went throughout the country, and was intensified during Reconstruction. Northerners flocked to these propaganda barrages. One was James Shepard Pike, a former Radical Republican, who made a vicious assault on the "Negro Government" of South Carolina. Barbarism has overtaken civilization and the former slaves have overtaken the master according to Pike. *Gates*, pp. 152, 153.

James Nast also was brain-washed. He was an early advocate of ending slavery, but by 1874, his cartoons in *Harpers Weekly* showed Black legislators in South Caroline in the most uncivil and uncivilized manner, calling each other every name that could be imagined. White legislators are pictures trying to avoid violence. *Gates*, pp. 152, 153.

Here's more. The following writings are by Ralph Waldo Emerson, a towering Euro-American intellectual in the middle 1800s, member of the Unitarian Church in Concord, Massachusetts, former minister who opposed slavery, Indian removal, and Mexican Annexation, nevertheless bought into the reigning supposedly "scientifically-grounded" public assumptions about race and the inevitability of colonial expansion.

"I believe that nobody now regards the maxim that all men are born equal as anything more than a convenient hypothesis or an extravagant declamation. For the reverse is true—that all men are born unequal in personal powers and in those essential circumstances, of time, parentage, country, and fortune. The least knowledge or natural history of man adds another important particular to these; namely, what class of men he belongs to—European, Moor, Tartar, African? Because, Nature has plainly assigned different degrees of intellect to these different races, and the barriers between are insurmountable. This inequality is an indication that some should lead, and some should serve.

"If we speak in general of the two classes Man and Beast, we say that they are separated by the distinction of reason and want of it.

"I saw ten, twenty, a hundred large lipped, low browed black men in the streets who, except in the mere matter of language, did not exceed the sagacity of the elephant. Now is it true that these were created superior to this wise animal, and designed to control it? And in comparison with the highest orders of men, the Africans will stand so low as to make the difference which subsists between themselves and the sagacious beast inconsiderable. It follows from this, that this is a distinction which cannot be much insisted on." *Porte, Joel*, ed., *Emerson in His Journals*, pp. 19-21.

"Strange history this of abolition. The Negro must be very old and belongs, one would say, to the fossil formations. What right has he to be intruding into the late and civil daylight of this dynasty of the Caucasians and Saxons? It is plain that so inferior a race must perish shortly like the poor Indians. There is always a place for the superior." *Porte, Joel,* ed., *Emerson in His Journals,* p. 245.

"It is very certain that the strong British race, which has now overrun so much of this continent, must also overrun that tract (Texas), and Mexico and Oregon also, and it will in the course of ages be of small importance by what particular occasions and methods it was done. It is a secular question." *Gilman, William H., ed., Selected Writings of Ralph Waldo Emerson* p. 119,

[The] "imperial Saxon race, which nature cannot bear to lose, and, after cooping it up for a thousand years in yonder England, gives a hundred Englands, a hundred Mexicos. All the bloods it shall absorb and domineer: and more than Mexicos—the secrets of water and steam, the spasms of electricity, the ductility of metals, the chariot of air, the ruddered balloon ..." from Emerson's essay "Fate" *Gilman, William H., ed., Selected Writings of Ralph Waldo Emerson* pp. 384-385.

"I think it cannot be maintained by any candid person that the African race have ever occupied or do promise to occupy any very high place in the human family. Their present condition is the strongest proof that they cannot. The Irish cannot, the American Indian cannot, the Chinese cannot. Before the energy of the Caucasian race all other races have quailed and done obedience." *Allard, Linda, ed., The Journals and Miscellaneous Notebooks of Ralph Waldo Emerson,* p. 152.

What strikes me in these Emerson writings is how contagious the brain-washing of the Redemption period was. The plague was alive. We often optimistically believe that more education and learning leads to higher thoughts and viewpoints—recognizing the worth and dignity of all persons. We also assume that those with the most brain power is able to discern truth from falsehoods. Yet, Emerson was led downward from his earlier moral stands by the brain-washing done by Harvard professors and others.

Gates shows a sample of the images of the descendants of Africans all in an unfavorable light and all the while depicting white supremacy. It was a real live effort at brain washing. It was done by the private power structure—not so much by government. But of course, governments supported and reinforced the propaganda machine.

> Words don't begin to communicate the images of Blacks as animals, slothful, dangerous, ignorant, creating dangerous half-bloods, etc. I encourage the reader to view these in *Gates* and other archives. They show the depths to which "good" people can fall.

This fear of the descendants of Africa, led to real terror among the Blacks as the KKK got power and created the **reign of terror** in the south and into northern states. When you were finished with your day's work and ready to turn in for the night, each night was a time to fear that a ruckus would start outside your home. You could see hooded men and burning crosses. A crowd would demand that your husband come out. He might be whipped, mutilated, and then hung and afterwards his body set on fire. Or one of your neighbors would come running and shout that our church had been set on fire. Lynching of Black people was a public spectacle. White parents took their kids to watch. Treating horrific torture and murder as a spectator sport seems to be a carryover from European ancestry.

> How far away from that mentality are we? What would it take for us as a society to go back to those times— mostly ending in the 1960s? When Michael Brown was killed in Ferguson Missouri after an altercation with the police, his body was left lying in the street

for several hours, "because it is a crime scene." His body was left for all to gawk at all this time. And people standing around watching the Minneapolis policeman holding his knee on George Floyd's neck until he suffocated. Is this much different than when lynching Black people was a public spectacle?

Reviewing all the vitriol put out by the white power structure (academic, publishing, political) Gates asks, "What possible rationale demanded this many debased representations of the recently freed Black people be produced in the final third of the nineteenth century? How many ways can one call a woman or a man a 'nigger' or a 'coon?' ... Why in the world was it necessary to produce tens of thousands, perhaps hundreds of thousands, of these separate and distinct racist images to demean the status of the newly freed slaves ...?" *Gates* p. 129.

Within the last decade or two, the answer to Gates' question is becoming clear. Analyses find that the behavior of white people is due to White Fragility. See *DiAngelo* and the following.

> "White fragility comes from the delusion that Black bodies are incredibly strong and frightening and impervious to pain. They can handle anything short of total destruction. But white bodies are extremely weak and vulnerable, especially to Black bodies. So, it's the job of Black bodies to care for white bodies, sooth them, and protect them—especially from other Black bodies." ... "Because white bodies are so vulnerable to Black ones, when a Black body is not subservient to a white one, it must be brutalized or destroyed. There can be no mercy, no second thoughts, and no halfway measures. Because Black bodies are nearly invulnerable, this brutality and

destruction must be swift, and it must be ruthless."
Mechakem, p. 98.

You don't agree? Think about the guy that shot Trayvon Martin and multiple police killing of African Americans.

Publication of cartoons, pamphlets, and "scientific" studies was not enough. Thomas Dixon, a lawyer, legislator, and traveling minister wrote a book, *The Clansmen: An Historical Romance of the Ku Klux Klan.* A movie based on this book by the name of *The Birth of a Nation* came out in 1915. These productions embodied every negative attribute to Black people that could be imagined. They pushed the message that white people, especially white women, should fear Black people. Black people, according to this message were about to take revenge on white people and take control of the country.

At this time, the KKK was at the peak of its power, having gained legislative representation in Indiana and other states along that geographic tier. Here is an account by my mother, who grew up eastern Kansas, recalling an event from the early 1920s.

> "Evidently, the Ku Klux Klan also came to Eskridge [Kansas]. They had a special movie once. Glenn [her husband, my dad] and I were invited. We saw or entered a very, very dark tent (near my father's hardware store). Could not even see who was sitting next to us. It was showing the negroes in the south as very wrong people who preyed on white. My father had a questioning look when we came out. I was dazed and ignorant. Then shortly, I noticed stores had a sign saying 100 percent American. That sounded good. Then suddenly one or two merchants had to leave town on a few hours' notice on charges of rape, etc. [She doesn't say, I presume these were Black

people or supporters of Black people.] A cross was burned on the hill West of town. I was approached to ask if I wanted to join a secret club. I declined. Everyone seemed suspicious."

"I believe Glenn and Carl [a friend], decided to go and see what it was all about. Glenn and Carl, I knew sometimes, went to meetings in Eskridge or even Harveyville. Everything was so kept secret from their wives and since most were heads of parties, we just wondered and waited."

My mother concludes by saying that "the Ku Klux Klan is a very large organization and seems to be contrived by the Devil and his suitors, always trying to belittle anything good and how it can entice more and more people to join." From a manuscript hand written in the 1980s, pp. 48, 49.

There is no doubt that the movie my parents experienced was *The Birth of a Nation*. And as you can read, she didn't buy in to the message that white women were in danger from Black men.

Although not recorded anywhere, tidbits of conversations among my siblings lead us to wondering if my father and his friend, Carl, had initially supported and secretly joined but then torpedoed the KKK by putting sugar in car gas tanks at a meeting. Anyway, the KKK were not much of a force in that area for very long.

According to historian, David Blight, productions such as *The Birth of a Nation* explains; "The lasting significance of this epic film is that by using its vile, worse than false message, cast a long-lasting image that Reconstruction was a failure, "directed by deranged radicals and sex-crazed Blacks, especially those mulattos given unwarranted political power." Some concluded, however, that these attacks led to Blacks organizing to counter the image and was important in the NAACP gaining some public support. Gates, pp. 156, 157.

But, of course, the KKK was far from defeated and still isn't. Theodore Bilbo, an admitted Klansman was elected to the US Senate, where in 1938, he led one of the longest filibusters to thwart a bill making lynching a federal crime.

At one point, he rose to speak on behalf of his constituents—not the entire state of Mississippi but the white voters there—and in opposition to the interest of half the state. He spoke in defense of the right to kill Black citizens as white southerners saw fit.

"If you succeed in the passage of this bill," Bilbo told his Senate colleagues, "you will open the floodgates of hell in the South. Raping, mobbing, lynching, race riots, and crime will be increased a thousand-fold, and upon your garments and the garments of those who are responsible for the passage of the measure will be the blood of the raped and outraged daughters of Dixie, as well as the blood of the perpetrators of these crimes that the red-blooded Anglo-Saxon White Southern men will not tolerate." *Wilkerson*, Page 303.

As you will read below, the creators of these hateful, hurtful images of persons of African ancestry knew exactly what they were doing. These stereotypes are with us today. In the book, *Why are All the Black Kids Sitting Together in the Cafeteria?*, author *Beverly Daniel Tatum, PhD*, a clinical psychologist, writes that the stereotyping of groups begins at an early age. When preschoolers were asked to draw pictures of Indians, all pictured them with feathers. Most included a tomahawk or knife and pictured the person in violent or aggressive terms. *Tatum* p. 84. Now we see why the hateful campaign against persons of African ancestry was so successful.

My definition of stereotyping people is the assumption that you know everything about another person based on one or two things that you observe, like looks or accent.

Eugenics

As the decades after the Civil War moved on, the proponents of Black inferiority—that Black is a group to be feared—took to new arguments to support the old positions. One was the emerging "science" of eugenics. The term was introduced by a British biologist, Francis Galton in 1883. One Daniel J. Kevles paints the picture of the industrial revolution as "man's mastery over inanimate nature." What this meant for the proponents of eugenics was that man was now in control of his destiny. Eugenics, in this view, would find those persons who had the desirable genetics and then through selective breeding, create a superior race and illuminate "undesirable people." Can you believe it??

> For those not familiar with eugenics, it is most easily understood as the human equivalent of animal breeding—livestock, dogs, race horses, etc. The goal is to select for breeding a superior female and superior male of a breed so that the offspring are superior—give the most milk, have the biggest hams, win top prize in the dog show, etc. Animal breeders rid their herds of those with "undesirable" traits by neutering, sending these to the slaughterhouse, etc. Eugenics would apply this strategy to humans. If you don't believe this, read on.

In 1904, Galton argued that eugenics must be "introduced into the national consciousness, like a new religion." ... Oliver Wendell Holmes, Sr. a physician and writer, expressed the thought, "If genius and talent are inherited, as Mr. Galton **has so conclusively shown**, why should not deep-rooted moral defects … those themselves … in the descendants of moral monster?"(bold added) *Gates*, 75, 76, 77.

There are lots of problems with the use of selective breeding for humans—not the least is which a moral one. If a newborn doesn't come out as having the supposedly acceptable traits, do you kill them or sterilize them as is often done in animal breeding? But the bigger problem of "breeding for superior characteristics" is that there are so many dimensions to being a human that it is impossible to define what a superior or even an acceptable person would be genetically. And who should have the power to say? As a society, were we about to start killing people that we didn't want? If you think "no," read on.

Though farmers had known for millennia the benefits of cross breeding and selective breeding of animals and plants to create certain desirable traits, Gregor Johann Mendel's pea plant experiments conducted between 1856 and 1863 established many of the rules of heredity, now referred to as the laws of Mendelian inheritance. Among human populations just like other livings things, it was long and widely understood that people have strong resemblances to their parents, grandparents, etc.

In this case, science was properly understood—where Galton and his followers went wrong was in the moral realm. He placed himself and his followers in the position that they were the arbiters of the "desirable traits." Who among us would be willing to have "scientists" doctors, college professors, etc. decide if we or our children, grandchildren, etc. have the "desirable traits?" Are we too short, too tall, nose too flat, mother failed in school, father couldn't hold a job, on and on?

If you are a person of color living at this time, and your ancestors having gone through enslavement, and then you are experiencing the Redemption, imagine how you think you will survive in this new era where selective breeding for humans is being pushed. Most likely, you don't have optimistic views of your survival.

A wide spectrum of "educated" people seized on this new "science" of eugenics. Charles Davenport, PhD, Harvard, thought that mental capacity could be attained through properly controlled reproduction—selective breeding in a word. He went from there to advocating sterilization arguing that "poor people, minorities, and criminals were unfit to reproduce." He argued that "the most progressive revolution in history" could occur if "human matings" could be placed on the same high plane as that of horse breeding."

Indiana passed a law in 1907 to outlaw interracial marriage* and mandating sterilization "to prevent procreation of confirmed criminals, idiots, imbeciles, and rapists." Charles Eliot, president of Harvard joined in, praising Indiana for blazing the trail for all states to protect against "moral degeneracy." What Eliot missed was **his own moral failings.** Other states followed Indiana's lead in establishing laws banning interracial marriages often citing scientific findings for their actions. *Gates,* 75, 76, 77.

> These experts overlooked the millennia-old knowledge that cross breeding is one way of **improving** animals and plants. In a crass sense, interracial marriage is the human form or cross breeding. The difference, of course, is that marriage is done for love—not as a program to create a superior population. Barack Obama, of mixed parentage, as defined by the eugenicists, is arguably one of the most intelligent persons to have served as president of the US.

For many years, the entire Harvard organization was the center of the eugenics movement. Stanford, Yale, and the University of Virginia also provided much support. You will not find mention of this status in today's advertisements for these august institutions.

Ibram X. Kendi writes of the popularity of eugenics: "**The eugenics movement created believers, not evidence.** White Americans wanted to believe that the racial, ethnic, class, and gender hierarchies in the US were natural and normal."

As if what we have been deluged with so far was not enough, great concern developed over the results of an intelligence test given to soldiers during WWI, the creation of Harvard psychologist professor Robert Yerkes and summarized by Stephen Jay Gould in *The Measurement of Man*. He concluded that the US was a nation of morons. This was fuel for the fire of eugenicists who leaped to the conclusion that the country was being overrun 'by the unconstitutional breeding of the poor and feeble-minded, the spread of Negro blood through miscegenation, and the swamping of an intelligent native stock by the immigrating dregs of southern and eastern Europe.' He also reported that fair Nordic populations were at the top of the intelligence scale, the darker the skin, the lower the intelligence. *Gates, Jr.* p. 78. Where have we heard this in our time?

According to Harvard PhD, Lothrop Stoddard, we might fear white lands being taken over by colored armies, but the greater danger is with migrations by colored men into white man's land could be lost to the white world. The solution is the white civilization must stay separate and it must breed the best. *Gates*, p. 79.

Massacres

Individual atrocities in the decades after the Civil War are somewhat well-known—Ku Klux Klan and others running around burning churches, lynching Black men and women. Less well-known are white mobs massacring Black citizens and burning their homes and businesses.

Most sympathizers with the Confederate cause argue that idealizing the officers and soldiers must be preserved because that's history. It is obvious now that there is an almost universal embarrassment about another aspect of the history of enslavement and afterward. Finally, we are now getting a more complete history reported in newspapers, magazines, and on TV.

Tulsa, Oklahoma Massacre, 1921

The first atrocity of mass murder that became better known, happened in Tulsa in 1921. Mobs of white residents, many supported by city officials, attacked Blacks in the area of the city where most lived. The area was prosperous and known as "the Black Wall Street." The attack destroyed more than 35 square blocks of the city. They even used aircraft. Hundreds were hospitalized and 6,000 or so Black people were jailed for several days.

The City of Tulsa is now taking on the responsibility of finding a more accurate counting of the dead. Research is underway to investigate indications of mass graves near the Greenwood area. The massacre is now being investigated more thoroughly and estimates are that between 75 and 300 Black persons were killed.

But now we find that there were other massacres of Black people, some earlier than Tulsa, some later. From **bet.com, and presented on PBS** we learn of three such occurrences. The **Colfax, Louisiana Massacre of 1873**, resulted in about 150 Black men being murdered by white men trying to freely assemble at a courthouse. The exact number of deaths is not known because many Black bodies were thrown into what was called the Red River.

Wilmington, North Carolina Massacre 1898

Wilmington had a thriving Black population. There were several elected Black officials. "The threat of Negro rule" created illogical white racial resentment.

The media frequently reported erroneously, that "white womanhood" was threatened by black men. A white Wilmington newspaper printed a speech by a Georgia feminist that read, "if it requires lynching to protect women's dearest possession from ravening drunken human beasts, then I say lynch a thousand negroes a week ... if it is necessary."

By the election of 1898, Black men were prevented from voting thus, all Black elected officials had been defeated. However, white supremacists could not stop the economic power that Blacks had already created. Therefore, they destroyed Black Wilmington with terrorism.

The day after the 1898 election, whites announced the "white declaration of independence, destroyed the printing presses, forced out the mayor, and a mob of white men attacked Black residents.

There were reportedly 60 to 300 Black people killed by this act of domestic terrorism. For over 100 years, the power structure of Wilmington tried to erase the massacre from its history. Then in 2000, "the General Assembly established the 1898 Wilmington Race Riot Commission to develop a historical record of the event and to assess the economic impact of the riot on African Americans locally and across the region and state." The massacre is now in the state's historical record.

Atlanta Massacre 1906

Like many race massacres, the violence in Atlanta started with white women accusing Black men of rape. On September 22, 1906, Atlanta newspapers reported that four white women said they were assaulted by Black men—a claim that was completely unfounded.

The real situation was that whites felt threatened by upwardly mobile Black communities in Atlanta, that were taking jobs that white people thought should be theirs to fill. This bogus report of sexual assault drove as many as 2000 white men to the streets. The terrorists went into the Black communities to beat, stab and shoot any Black people in sight. PBS reports "a disabled man was chased down and beaten to death." Communities were destroyed and the unofficial death toll was up to 100.

Elaine, Arkansas Massacre 1919

The Encyclopedia of Arkansas calls the Elaine Massacre "by far the deadliest racial confrontation in Arkansas history and possibly the bloodiest racial conflict in the history of the United States."

Blacks outnumbered whites 10 to 1 and were demanding economic justice, as many of them were forced into sharecropping. A union was created to protect sharecroppers. This enraged the whites.

In September 1919, at a union meeting among Black workers, whites showed up to riot. As a result, one white man was shot and killed. Whites convinced themselves there was a threat of a "Black Insurrection." And as usual, reacted with violence.

Hundreds of white men attacked Black residents but many fought back—including Black veterans. Sadly, there were reports of over 200 Black people, including children killed.

Many who were not killed were arrested and tortured while in custody. They were forced to "confess" about an insurrection with twelve men receiving the death penalty. They eventually became known as the Elaine 12. With the help of the NAACP, their case went to the US Supreme Court in 1923, and they were exonerated.

This was one of the first times the NAACP won a case in front of the Supreme Court.

Rosewood, Florida Massacre 1923

Similar to the massacre in Tulsa, in 1921, a Black community was burned to the ground two years after a white woman named Fannie Taylor, claimed she was assaulted by a Black man on January 1, 1923. The first person killed was Sam Carter, a local blacksmith. He was tortured and his mutilated body was hung from a tree.

It was later found that Fannie Taylor had invented the story to cover up her affair with a white man. After Rosewood was destroyed, a grand jury and special prosecutor decided there was not enough evidence for prosecution of the white men who killed innocent American citizens.

In 1997, the late, great filmmaker John Singelton famously made the film Rosewood, starring Ving Rhames, based on the massacre.

What is wrong with white people?? Have we lost our soul?

Attempts to Recover

Many of us are generally aware that there are large populations of African Americans in northern and western cities—New York, Boston, Detroit, Cleveland, Chicago, and Los Angeles to name some. Was this always the way it was ever since these cities were established? No, there were, of course some enslaved people in the northern states, as well as free persons of color. But the Black populations of these cities swelled due to what is called one of the most massive migrations in history from the south to the north and west. This migration was not a mass march, but rather one family or individual slipping away with as little publicity as possible. The time period of this migration is termed by *Isabel Wilkerson* to be from 1915 to 1975.

The massacres described above, and the pervasive atmosphere which persons of African descent lived in, including 1) again being disenfranchised, 2) subject to the **reign of terror** by white hate organizations and politicians, 3) getting the message from the people they sharecropped for, the police and courts and the whole of white society, that black lives were worthless, 4) being confined to the bottom of the economic ladder, and 5) being forced into only menial and dangerous labor jobs and share-cropping, resulted in millions leaving the South and migrating to northern and western cities.

In the Jim Crow south, just thinking about migrating was dangerous. The white south wanted the cheap labor and share-cropping. Thus, many of the migrants had to carefully plan when and how to leave. The families that *Wilkerson* traces have these stories. One man, George

Starling, worked in orange groves picking oranges. The work was hard and dangerous. So, Starling decided to try to organize the workers to get better working conditions. When he was found out as the organizer, he was strapped down and beaten severely. He then escaped north on the railroad without the owners knowing he was leaving.

Another family, Ida Mae and George Gladney, were share-croppers. The owner was respected by George and Ida Mae—his treatment of them was better than others experienced. But the beatings they had witnessed of a falsely accused cousin, plus painful work of picking cotton as sharecroppers, convinced them to find a better life. In this case, George went to the landlord just before they left to inform him and express appreciation for his concerns for George and Ida Mae.

Of course, white Americans who decide to move from one part of the US to another, don't have to contemplate that if they are caught moving, or that their lives could be in jeopardy, due to the powers of their former employers or landlords. But during the Great Migration, this was a major concern for African Americans. It could be as risky as being a runaway slave before emancipation. Therefore, just as those recorded by *Wilkerson*, many slipped away in the middle of the night or maybe on a trip to town that just happened to be the time when a train was leaving for the north. Those who left were careful about who they told they were leaving. If their plans were thwarted and they had to return, their plight most likely would have been worse than before.

When the Great Migration started in the 1910s, white southern elites seemed to be unconcerned, and industrialists and cotton planters saw it as a positive, as it was siphoning off surplus industrial and agricultural labor. As the migration picked up, however, southern elites began to panic, fearing that a prolonged black exodus would bankrupt the South, and newspaper editorials warned of the danger. White employers eventually took notice and began expressing their fears. White southerners soon began trying to stem the flow in order to prevent the hemorrhaging of their labor supply, and some even began attempting to address the poor living standards and racial oppression experienced by Southern blacks in order to induce them to stay.

As a result, southern employers increased their wages to match those on offer in the North, and some individual employers even opposed the worst excesses of Jim Crow laws. When the measures failed to stem the tide, white southerners, **in concert with federal officials** who feared the rise of black nationalism, co-operated in attempting to coerce blacks to stay in the South. The Southern Metal Trades Association urged decisive action to stop black migration, and some employers undertook serious efforts against it. The largest southern steel manufacturer refused to cash checks sent to finance black migration, efforts were made to restrict bus and train access for blacks, agents were stationed in northern cities to report on wage levels, unionization, and the rise of black nationalism, and newspapers were pressured to divert more coverage to negative aspects of black life in the North.

A series of local and federal directives were put into place with the goal of restricting black mobility, including local vagrancy ordinances, "work or fight" laws demanding all males either be employed or serve in the army, and conscription orders. Intimidation and beatings were also used to terrorize blacks into staying. These intimidation tactics were described by Secretary of Labor William B. Wilson as interfering with "the natural right of workers to move from place to place at their own discretion." *Wikipedia, December 2020.*

There were certain characteristics of those that migrated. One, the life they were living was intolerable for them and they weren't going to take it anymore. Another, this took a lot of careful planning—including how to escape in the first place and then finding a place they would go. They had to have some idea of how they would make a living in their new home. Finally, they had the grit to make sure that whatever happened, so that they would not have to return to their oppression in the south. In summary, the migrants were those that would do whatever it took to succeed.

Migrants arriving in the north were faced with the decades of propaganda that was used to create the Restoration. Many northern white people had bought into this hate propaganda. Housing was not allowed in "white areas." Schools were segregated. Where companies had labor unions, Black people were prohibited from joining. Among other effects, this pushed Black people to the bottom of the wage-earning jobs. Riots and killings by whites occurred in Chicago when Black people crossed an imaginary line and swam in white areas.

Here is what life could have been like if the migrants were accepted as fellow humans rather than as the stereotypes that had been planted in the white people's consciousness over the centuries. The newcomers could have been invited into homes for overnight or even until they could find a place of their own. Migrant parents of school children could have been invited by white neighbors to go to school—where both Black and white children attended to get acquainted with teachers. Adults seeking a job could have been introduced to openings and when a job was secured, invited to join the union (if one was available). And public accommodations like swimming areas would have been open to all.

Black women were especially vulnerable. When living in the south, it was not unusual for women to work for wages or work along men in the fields so that the family could earn a living. In the northern cities the migrant women still had to work, but now their only source of income was menial jobs. There were no organizations nor governmental protections on worker rights or safety. There were already domestic white workers in these jobs, so for a Black woman to get a job, she had to hire out at a lower wage than the Irish, German, and Scandinavian servant girls. *Wilkerson.* pp. 333, 334, 335.

Wilkerson describes the "slave markets" in northern cities where domestic workers would go in hopes of getting picked up for the day. These were in no way "official" sites, they just grew over time as a place for the pick-ups. There were 25 such markets in New York City. The women negotiated individually with those picking up for as little as fifteen cents an hour (around $2.00 in today's dollars). There were no written contracts nor did the employers explain or commit to what the working conditions would be.

The women had no assurance of how long their day would be, whether she could take breaks, etc. From *Wilkerson* and other sources, including the recent novel, *The Help*, we have learned that the Black women were not allowed to use the bathroom in the employer's house, eat off the employer's utensils, etc. The domestic workers also were frequently in danger of sexual assaults by the white residents in the household. Again, we see that the plague of racism was alive and well in the north. *Wilkerson.* pp. 333, 334, 335.

There was also the matter of safety getting to and from work. A Black woman walking in a white neighborhood could be attacked; she was always viewed with suspicion and had to justify to anyone, including the police why she was in the neighborhood. The reverse was also true. If a white person saw a colored woman walking in the neighborhood, even if she was dressed to go to an office job, it was assumed she were available for scrubbing toilets, etc. *Wilkerson.* p. 335. Has this changed? No, I have heard from friends that they are questioned by police when in "white" neighborhoods.

One woman of color in Los Angeles said she thought getting her high school diploma would make a difference. She kept trying to find different work. Jobs on assembly lines, running elevators, clerking in stores, filing in offices, were typical jobs open to unskilled women in those days. "But everywhere I went," she said, "they wanted to keep me working as a domestic." *Wilkerson.* p. 334.

It is almost totally unknown today that in addition to immigrant populations of Black persons in northern and western cities, Black persons had moved to most parts of the US following emancipation, according to *Rothstein*. Most of us would be surprised to learn—as I was—of the thriving African American populations in places like Montana. **In 1890, there were Black persons living in every county of Montana.** *Rothstein, pp.*

41, 42. Rothstein doesn't say, however, in the late 1800s, tens of thousands of Texas long-horned cattle were driven from Texas into Montana and adjoining Alberta and Saskatchewan in Canada along famous trails. According to *Barton H. Barbour, et. al.*, a large proportion of the trail drivers—cowboys—estimated to be as much as fifteen percent were African American. *America West Chronicles, p. 182.* This may be why there was a widespread population of African Americans in all Montana counties, especially the rural ones.

By 1900 there was a thriving middle class of African Americans in Helena as well as laborers. The African Methodist Episcopal Church of Helena was prominent enough that it hosted its denominational western conference in 1894. There were Black businesses, a Black literary society that sometimes drew hundreds of participants to listen to all kinds of literary presentations. Then in 1906, Helena's prosecuting attorney announced that "it is time that the respectable white people of the community rise in might and assert their rights." Soon afterward, Montana banned interracial marriages.

By 1930, there were no Black people in eleven of the fifty-six counties. In Helena, the state capital, there were 420 Black people in 1910, 131 in 1930, 45 by 1970, and 113 in 2010. *Rothstein, pp. 41, 42.* This plague of racial fear and hatred promulgated by the power sources reviewed above, was spread to all parts of the US.

> My wife grew up in Helena in the 1950s. There was
> only one Black student in her high school.

In many locations, a response by Black people was to form their own social structures—churches, schools, colleges, self-help organizations, and fraternal organizations. This led to a flowering of writers, and musicians, etc. The Harlem Renaissance was important mainly in the 1920s. According to *Gates,* while the emergence of Blacks taking more control over their lives was highly beneficial, it created or reinforced the concept that not all Black people were like the propaganda and caricatures had shown them. Some referred to this as the "New Negro." It had the unintended consequence of admitting that the propaganda had some validity.

A further evidence of how widely fear and hatred of Black people had been infused in the white population was the practice of "sundown towns." In many parts of the US during this time, sundown towns meant that if you were Black you must leave town by sundown. There was no need to say what the "or else" was. *Rothstein, p. 42 and Loewen, pp. 122, 123.* These ordinances were almost always illegal, but that didn't seem to matter. Our moral compasses can be twisted and turned to fit our fears and hatred. Why were these new arrivals treated like this? The answer is found in the narrative provided above. The north and west had adopted the plague of racism, especially the propaganda put out during the Restoration period.

Now back to Ida Mae. In her new home of Chicago, Ida Mae found to her surprise that she was **encouraged to vote**. In the South, she and most other Black persons didn't know or care when or if elections had come or gone. If a Black person had attempted to vote, their livelihoods, even their lives would have been in danger.

But if Black persons knew anything about politics, it was that the Democratic Party controlled the South—the party that had restored white control after Reconstruction. It was just the reverse in Chicago. Now, this Democratic Party in Chicago was going all out to recruit the newly arriving Black persons to vote. Persons like Ida Mae were not only being recruited but given instructions on how to vote, shown the location of their polling places, what the ballots looked like, given sample ballots with Democratic candidates clearly marked so they would vote for these candidates. *Wilkerson,* pp. 304, 305

In 1940, the Democratic Party of Chicago had to do whatever was needed to keep the new arrivals from voting Republican—the party of Lincoln and Reconstruction. The goal of the northern Democrats was to get Franklin Roosevelt elected to a new term. These new Illinois residents were an incredible gift to the Democratic Party. Many of the new arrivals knew about the beneficial programs started with the New Deal so could be persuaded that their best interests were to vote for Democratic candidates. *Wilkerson*, pp. 304, 305.

"On election day, Ida Mae was not certain what to do. She had never touched an election ballot. She walked in, and a lady came over and directed her to where she should go. Ida Mae stepped inside a polling booth for the first time in her life and drew the curtain behind her. She unfolded the palm card she had been given and tried to remember what the lady had told her about how to punch in her choices for president of the United States." *Wilkerson*, pp. 304, 305.

Wilkerson goes on to record that Ida Mae, after doing what was unthinkable in her home in the South, was recognized as someone who talked easily with other people and went on to become a regular campaign worker in following elections. She could remember how hesitant and unfamiliar she was with voting the first time, so she could easily connect with them and show them how to go through the voting process. These simple acts were a direct challenge to the system that excluded Black persons from participating in society's decision-making.

That is only part of the story. Black voters in Chicago may have made the difference in Illinois going for Roosevelt in a very tight race. And Illinois going for Roosevelt was enough to give him enough Electoral College votes to win his third term.

> Ida Mae's is also is a story of power. Power can be wielded by guns, clubs, spreading falsehoods, etc., but also by simple acts of bravery and determination.

So, the North and West was already affected by the plague of racism when southern Black people migrated there. For white people in jobs requiring lots of physical labor, often these jobs also being the lowest paid, the migrants were competing with their jobs and livelihoods. It didn't take much for many white people to blame the Black migrants for their economic problems.

What many of the whites did not consider was that the white power structure that was holding down the pay of Black workers, was also holding down wages of white workers who had to compete with lower-earning Black workers.

Northern industrialists saw an opening here. In some of the labor disputes, Black people were hired as strikebreakers. This accomplished two goals for the industrialists. The strikes could be ended more to the advantage of the owners and secondly, feelings of animosity toward Black citizens could be heightened. *Wilkerson*, pp. 317, 318.**This is another case of the white power structure getting the lowest-paid whites to join the powerful against oppressed people, in this case, African Americans.**

Here's what President Obama writes after controversy over a statement he made during his first campaign for president. "... maybe I'm bothered by the care and delicacy with which one must state the obvious that it's possible to understand and sympathize with the frustration of white voters without denying the ease with which, throughout American history politicians have redirected white frustration about their economic or social circumstances toward Black and brown people." *Obama*, pp. 144, 145.

The act of migrating was a statement that, "we're not going to take this any longer." Most migrants had little knowledge of what to expect in the North. A large proportion found new obstacles to freedom and very limited economic and social freedom. Still, they migrated by the thousands hoping for a better life. No doubt they looked forward to a time when their children could expect a better life in the north. Many of them and their descendants did have a better life. Many contributed to the development of the rich Black culture, especially in literature, theater, music, and dance that we enjoy today. But, as will be covered later, all struggled and had to battle against the cultural and political forces in the north that kept many of them in economic and social poverty.

"Many Black parents who left the South got the one thing they wanted just by leaving. Their children would have a chance to grow up free of Jim Crow and to be their fuller selves. It cannot be known what course the lives of people like Toni Morrison, James Baldwin, Diana Ross, Aretha Franklin, Michelle Obama, Jesse Owens, Joe Louis, Jackie Robinson, Serena and Venus Williams, Bill Crosby, Condoleezza Rice, Nat King Cole, Oprah Winfrey, Berry Gordy (who founded Motown and signed children of the Migration to sing for it), the astronaut Mae Jemison, the artist Romare Bearden, the performers Jimi Hendrix, Michael Jackson, Prince, San "P. Diddy" Combs, Whitney Houston, Mary J. Blige, Queen Latifah, the director, Spike Lee, the playwright August Wilson, and countless others might have taken had their parents or grandparents not participated in the Great Migration and raised them in the North or West. All of them grew up to become among the best in their fields, changed them, really, and were among the first generation of Blacks in this country to grow up free and unfettered because of the actions of their forebears. Millions of other children of the Migration grew up to lead productive, though anonymous, lives in quiet, everyday ways that few people will ever hear about." *Wilkerson,* pp. 535, 536.

May I give the names of a few of those millions of others of the Great Migration or children of the Migration; my friends, Jane Burns, a school teacher and activist in the Student Non-violent Coordinating Committee when the late John Lewis was its leader; Rev. John Crestwell, a Unitarian Universalist minister; Shauntee Daniels, a heritage and cultural preservationist; Thornell Jones, a physicist, computer pioneer, teacher, mentor, Boy Scout leader, anti-racism activist; U. S. Navy Captain (Ret.) Stanley Keeve, Jr., commanded two warships as well as the Joint Base Pearl Harbor-Hickam, mentor; the late, Willie Kendricks, a war veteran and NAACP activist; the late, Henry Ledbetter, a nuclear engineer; and Dr. Candice Wanhatalo, a clinical psychologist. Migrations of African descendants from Puerto Rico to the northeast US, are my friends, Dr. L. E. Gomez, a physician; and Dr. Olga Pabon, a teacher and school administrator.

Only a Part of the Story

I had assumed that my friend, Yevola Peters was a part of the Great Migration having grown up in South Carolina. Mrs. Peters is a force for racial justice in Maryland. She was a school teacher; worked with the Community Action Agency, which was established by the federal government to close achievement gaps that disadvantage low-income and minority students; assistant to the County Executive; operates the Family Life Center in her Episcopal church; was resident counselor at a subsidized housing project; organized a community development corporation; and is still active in several justice organizations. When I asked permission to include her name, as a part of the Great Migration, I received the following, on which I made minor edits.

Yevola Smith Peters

I don't really view my heritage as part of the "Great Migration" since **my parents did not migrate from the South,** and in fact made a point of **<u>not migrating</u>**. Just a very brief history: Following the Civil War, my father's Grandfather, Peter Smith, and his brother, Phillip Smith, were given land in the Sandridge section of Dorchester County, South Carolina, as freed slaves. They accumulated more land and donated a site for a family/community church and school. Before they died, they handed down land to their children. My Father's father (Daniel, my Grandfather) was very business minded and accumulated more land, was a farmer and also operated a community store, and he very carefully deeded plots of land to each of his six living children before he died (and his children, including my father, did the same to make sure that their children took ownership of the land). Without going into details, after receiving his elementary education in Dorchester County, my father (born in 1904) was determined to go to college. He often related to us the story of his Grandmother, who told him that as a slave during her youth, she had her fingers chopped off with an axe by the wife of the slave-owner because the slave-owner's daughter was teaching her to read and write.

My father, after much struggle, convinced his father to send him to school in Orangeburg, South Carolina at Claflin College (a Historically Black College and University). He finished high school and college there. He met my mother at Claflin during his college years. He and my mother eventually became teachers at Claflin. My father taught chemistry and physics. During World War II, he was assigned to work as a research chemist with the Development Department of a chemical company in Charleston, S.C. and continued to teach at Claflin on a part-time basis. When the war ended in 1945, he was offered a position in a branch of the Company that was located someplace in New York (because of the segregation in South Carolina), and he turned it down to continue teaching at Claflin, even though the pay at the Chemical Plant would have been so much higher than he was making at Claflin. However, he did travel back and forth to New York to complete graduate studies at Columbia University while continuing teaching at Claflin.

My point being that there were Blacks throughout the South who **refused to "migrate"** and although confronted with Jim Crow, they stayed the course and were very active in the Civil Rights movement. Now while I did have a few aunts and cousins who migrated, I just wanted you to be aware of the **"refusal to migrate"** movement that also took place among Blacks. (I recall having had a high school teacher who use to say in disgust about "migration", that "too many 'Negroes' would rather be a lamp post in New York than be a Doctor in the South.")

So, there was an effort being made when I was growing up to slow down the migration and to build "Black Progressive Communities" and an "overcome" movement in the south. Sadly, as I look at too many of our youth and families today, especially in our subsidized housing communities, I wonder about the results of "desegregation" on many of our families as I compare the successful outcomes of the numbers of "share-holder" families that I grew up with in segregated South Carolina. Values and goals are so different. **In fact, I just received a tribute to my mother from one of her former students** who is now living in Maryland and retired from Morgan State University. I am sharing this with you just so you can hopefully get a sense of the nurturing that took place by our teachers during the period of segregation. (see *Dr. Payton*, below)

After having to attend Claflin for at least one year, I decided it was time for me to leave home and broaden my experiences. But after having been accepted to Boston University, I selected staying below the Mason-Dixon line, coming to another HBCU, Morgan State College in Baltimore, as a transfer student in 1953. (I did go to BU for graduate school immediately after graduating from Morgan in 1956.) While I had expected to return to South Carolina, I met my husband at Morgan, who grew up in Mineola, NY (his heritage was the Shinnecock Indian Tribe on Long Island). We ended up in Maryland because that is where he first applied after graduation and began teaching in 1956 (Queen Anne's County) and we got married in 1957 following my graduation from BU. Otherwise, I probably would have been in South Carolina teaching and whatever else I was called to do!

So, my being in Maryland was not because of the "Great Migration". I needed to make that point! In fact, my sister who is 12 years younger than I spent many days during the 1960s in jail in Orangeburg, SC, as a high schooler, marching and working with my parents and many others in the civil rights movement. She and her husband, after her husband served many years in the Army and retired as Colonel, are now living in Georgia! Before my brother died at 51 years of age in 1984 (he was 2 years older than I), after receiving his doctorate from UCLA and spending several years as a research chemist in California, he taught for many years (up to his death) in the graduate school of VPI in Blacksburg, Virginia. So, as you can see, I have a different perspective of the "Great Migration".

I just needed to emphasize that there was not just **one** direction taken by all African Americans. **There was indeed a "Great Migration" for many.** And then there were many, like my family, who did not migrate but settled throughout the south and worked to **change** the south. While my father's family became land owners, my mother's parents were sharecroppers until my mother went to college, married my father and bought them a home in Orangeburg, S.C. and focused on helping African Americans to own their own land and become economically sufficient. And while my mother's four siblings decided to **migrate north** (New York and Connecticut), there were so many African Americans who **did not** migrate and become successful in the South, and I did not want that point lost. **My point is, yes, there was a great migration that was beneficial to many African-Americans, but that was not my history. Just like W.E.B. DuBois and Booker T. Washington had different views, there was not just one road taken by African-Americans to overcome the effects of slavery.** *Used by permission, Yevola Smith Peters*

In Loving Memory of and Tribute to Mrs. Katie Pugh Smith

Story by Dr. Cecil W. Payton

As young African American males growing up in the 50s and 60s in the tiny town of Orangeburg, South Carolina, African American students were naturally were relegated to attending segregated schools based on one's skin color.

I remember well how we were bused past all the white schools to all the black schools that were not nearly as well equipped. That did not, however, deter us from seeking the best education that we could get. Although our schools were not well-equipped, we had some of the best, highly qualified Black teachers who really cared about the students and went above and beyond the call of duty to ensure that we were fully prepared for the next chapter in our lives.

One such teacher was the late Mrs. Katie Pugh Smith [mother of Yevola Smith Peters], a loving and caring teacher who had such a profound effect on my life. She and her husband, Hampton D. Smith were both educators, he a professor at Claftin College (now university) and she an elementary/middle school teacher in the Orangeburg County Public School System. In addition, their home was on the same street as my family's, only about a half mile apart. I remember vividly how they would wave in their car as they passed by our home every day on their way to work. I was fortunate to have Mrs. Smith as my sixth and seventh grade teacher.

Initially, she was to have been only my sixth-grade teacher, but she was so impressed with our class that she asked to move up one grade so that she could be our seventh-grade teacher also. Of course, we were delighted because she was such a wonderful teacher who always encouraged us to do our best. She truly believed that we could be anything we wanted to be and that would always find something extra to learn.

One of the things that so endeared me so much to her was the time when I was the only one in a class of about 30 students who got all 100 words spelled correctly on a spelling test. She was so proud of me that she had me stand in front of the class as she shared my test result. The excitement and enthusiasm in her voice was so exhilarating to me that I still remember the moment as if it were only yesterday. That moment instilled in me the confidence I needed to succeed. Even today, I can hear her voice as she said, "Cecil, I am so proud of you."

In addition to being great in the classroom, Mrs. Smith was an avid outdoor person. She would take us on field trips to explore nature. On one particular trip, we all had to remove pine seedlings from a tree farm and plant and nurture them in our respective yards at home. Having grown up on a farm, I was so excited that I three pine trees at my home.

As those trees grew over the years, they continuously reminded me of Mrs. Smith who passed away about 35 years ago. It was only about five years, however, ago that we had to have the last of the three trees removed from the family's estate for fear of it being struck by lightning. However, that site is marked by a ring of beautiful azalea plants that our mother planted years ago.

Yes, Mrs. Katie P. Smith was very special to me. I only wish the she could have lived long enough to witness what I have become.

Cecil D. Payton, PhD - The Kid from the "Wrong Side of The Railroad Tracks" *Used by permission, Yevola Smith Peters*

Mrs. Peters' personal history emphasizes that historical changes were made by African Americans who stayed in the South. Remember, the Civil Rights Movement of the 1950s and 1960s came from the South. No doubt there was a lot of assistance from some leaders who were living in the North, but without the leadership of those and their descendants who did not migrate, it is doubtful it would have occurred.

Peters' story shows that after the War and Reconstruction, there were African American families in the South who worked to get and to provide education for their children and used their energy and business skills to acquire property so that they could provide for their families and pass along some wealth to future generations. Below are a few of the leaders of the Civil Rights Movement who grew up and stayed in the South to get civil and human rights for those in the South, but extended that to the whole nation and to the wider world. It is notable that most of these men and women had college degrees enabled by their families.

Ralph Abernathy – born and raised in Alabama

James Farmer – born and raised in Texas

Fannie Lou Hamer – born and raised in Mississippi

Martin Luther King, Jr. – born and raised in Georgia

John Lewis – born in Alabama, moved to Tennessee and Georgia

Rosa Parks – born and raised in Alabama

Hosea Williams – born and raised in Georgia

Andrew Young –born and raised in Louisiana

Whitney Young – born and raised in Kentucky

A more complete history of African Americans would include those that have resided outside the South for generations. In Maryland, which is not considered part of the South because it did not secede, Black families suffered under most of the injustices that those in the South experienced, including lynching as a common practice.*See Alexander. In spite of injustices, some succeeded in great accomplishments. These include those that rose to become community leaders, teachers, and politicians. My friend, the late Dr. Marlene Browne come from generations residing in the North. She grew up in Rhode Island, became a professor at Howard University and the US Naval Academy. She was also an accomplished violinist.

America Goes Backward

But to our nation's great shame, many Black parents who left the South, as well as those who stayed, did not get what they wanted for their children—to grow up free of Jim Crow. The plague of fear and hatred from white people increased with fury from the Restoration period continued with a new tactic by every level of government, city, county, state and federal and pushed on governments by powerful private groups. A new scheme was to institute through governments, the practice of separating residential communities along racial lines. Many whites argued that this was just a natural thing that happens, "people want to be with their own kind." Those most affected, the Black population, were not asked for their views on the matter.

The full force of the federal government was put behind this policy. By getting involved with house mortgages, the federal government with the cooperation of the real estate industry, promulgated red-lining. How this worked (works) is to designate areas of municipalities as either Black or white. Mortgages for Black home-buyers would not be approved if seeking to buy in a white area. Furthermore, higher interest charges were placed on mortgages of Black buyers than was done for white buyers.

World War II, brought the practice of separation of housing according to race to new depth. *Rothstein* has many accounts of how this worked in practice. In Richmond, California, the war industries brought an influx of workers who obviously needed housing. The federal government came to the rescue by putting up public housing. It was officially segregated by race.

The African American section was poorly constructed and intended to be temporary. That for the white area was stronger and closer to already established white areas. Not only was housing segregated by race, but the local housing authority established rules that separated Black and white people in activities such as use of recreational facilities, separate Boy and

Girl Scout troops according to race, and attending movies. This housing pattern exists to this day. *Rothstein,* p. 5.

In this instance, the federal government would not insure bank loans for potential Black buyers, so public housing was the only option. Many families had to double up on housing. Even worse, some Black workers lived in cardboard shacks, barns, tents, orange crates, or even out in the open. *Rothstein,* p. 6, 7.

One might think that the nation being in danger of losing a war to Germany or Japan or both, that governmental officials would be more concentrated on preventing defeat in war than on directing citizens how to live their daily lives.

Even though Franklin Roosevelt is known as one of the great liberators for the common citizen—his Four Freedoms speech—freedom of speech, freedom of religion, freedom from want, and freedom from fear, that "everyone in the world ought to enjoy," his practices were short of these ideals.

As early as WW I when Roosevelt served as Navy Secretary under Woodrow Wilson, Roosevelt went along with Wilson's efforts to separate the races and move Black employees of the federal government to lower-level non-supervisory ranks. As president under the New Deal, he frequently gave in to the demands of white congressmen that separated races and eliminated Black people from benefits that were being created for white people. Passage of the Social Security program in 1935, was achieved by accepting the demands of southern politicians to restrict coverage of some groups of citizens, including farmers and farm workers. (These were later covered due to the effort of the Eisenhower Administration.)

Whether FDR would like to have advanced the civil and social rights of persons of color is up for debate. It is true that, since a big part of the Democratic Party at that time were Southern politicians and voters. To get some things done, other goals had to be abandoned. Not much resistance is apparent from him based on the following.

The most specific racist actions of the federal government since the Wilson Administration was to legally mandate that white people and Black people must live in different neighborhoods. A part of this almost universal practice was that the housing for Black workers or residents was always inferior to that specified for white people. Here is some of those cases.

For construction of the TVA system of dams and hydro-electric generators, the government built a village for the white workers. Black workers were housed in barracks farther away from the job. With the Civilian Conservation Corps to create work for jobless youth, some localities refused to allow CCC camps for African Americans and the director of the CCC established this as national policy. *Rothstein,* p. 19, 20,

Similar policies were adopted by the Public Works Administration. This program was engaged in "urban renewal." Urban renewal went a long way toward established housing segregation that is with us today in almost every US city. The typical project was to demolish sub-standard housing, frequently where a large proportion of the population was African American.

Then the area was cleared and new modern construction built to be occupied by white families. Where before, both Black and white, as well as identified ethnic groups lived in some of the neighborhoods the authority prohibited this after the renewal. The authorities often claimed they were respecting the population make-up before the projects occurred, but they sometimes created racial segregation where none had existed. Cities where these projects were established include, Cleveland, Detroit, Indianapolis, Toledo, and New York. *Rothstein,* p. 22, 23.

Public housing was then built for non-white families. These were often either high rise buildings with hundreds of families in each. The other was apartment complexes—still with the families concentrated in relatively small spaces. Amenities, such as open space, recreational facilities, shopping, etc. were non-existent or some distance away. And the common theme was a distance from white residences and city amenities. *Rothstein,* p. 22, 23. This is the case in Annapolis Maryland.

"It would be going too far to suggest that cities like these would have evolved into integrated metropolises were it not for New Deal public housing. But it is also the case that the federal government's housing rules pushed these cities into a more rigid segregation than otherwise would have existed. The biracial character of many neighborhoods presented opportunities for different futures than the segregated ones that now seem so unexceptional." *Rothstein,* p. 24.

Civil Rights Era

After the Redemption and many long years of resistance primarily led by Black people, we came to the 1950s and 1960s—the Civil Rights era. We were going to end racism. The Supreme Court and the federal government set out on a new path of racial justice. We were done with the Reign of Terror. We had a War on Poverty. Black people were increasingly elected to local, city, and state offices. Secondary schools and colleges were being integrated or at least Black persons were being admitted. Black people were starting to consider that they or another Black person could be president.

Well … that's not what happened. Analysts, countering the "science" of earlier decades, began doing serious scientific studies in the past few decades with the goal of understanding the social and economic disadvantages of African Americans. The most well-known is the Moynihan Report published in 1965. Moynihan has a Ph. D. degree in history from the London School of Economics.

For those in power who are seeking to avoid responsibility for racial oppression, they can draw on statements from the Moynihan Report such as: "At the heart of the deterioration of the fabric of Negro society is the deterioration of the Negro family. It is the fundamental source of the weakness of the Negro community at the present time." "The structure of family life in the black community constitutes a 'tangle of pathology... capable of perpetuating itself without assistance from the white world,' and that 'at the heart of the deterioration of the fabric of Negro society is the deterioration of the Negro family. It is the fundamental source of the weakness of the Negro community at the present time."

Moynihan's emphasis on the disadvantages of being a single Black mom in our society can lead to the admonition to, "go get married and don't have so many children." This is called **blaming the victim.**

However, digging deeper into the Report, in addition to providing substantial data and analysis on the status of Black people, especially Black families, Moynihan states, **"It is more difficult, however, for whites to perceive the effect that three centuries of exploitation have had on the fabric of Negro society itself. Here the consequences of the historic injustices done to Negro Americans are silent and hidden from view. But here is where the true injury has occurred: unless this damage is repaired, all the effort to end discrimination and poverty and injustice will come to little."**

What was needed was a national effort. "Such a national effort could be stated thus: **"The policy of the United States is to bring the Negro American to full and equal sharing in the responsibilities and rewards of citizenship. To this end, the programs of the Federal government bearing on this objective shall be designed to have the effect, directly or indirectly, of enhancing the stability and resources of the Negro American family."** *Moynihan*, p. 40.

There was a lot of reaction to the Moynihan Report. Both white and Black reviewers were both severe critics and supporters. What is evident now is that the high hopes of the War on Poverty and related Great Society programs have largely been dashed.

Very soon after gaining some power for racial justice in the 1960s, the white power structure started campaigning to reduce or eliminate a lot of these efforts. Arguing, "the War on Poverty is a failure." "Head Start is a failure," etc. The white power structure saw that they had to re-create what existed nearly a century earlier—the equivalent of the Redemption where Black people were "put in their place." Affirmative action was attacked, arguments were made that this federal rule resulted in white people being denied access to jobs or education to make room for less qualified Black people.

But a more sweeping initiative to undo the advances of the Civil Rights ere was the War on Drugs. This brought the full force of the federal government to the war. The War on Drugs enabled the goal of again depriving Black people their place in society, but this time it was done without naming race. The main vehicle was by establishing much harsher penalties for possession or use of crack cocaine than was the case for other forms of cocaine. The use of crack cocaine was much more common among Black people than white people.

The most thorough study of this period—of this strategy—was done by Michelle Alexander in her book, *The New Jim Crow*. She calls this new war the "James Crow" system to replace "Jim Crow." This strategy did not rely so much on hate groups going around burning crosses and taking the law into their own hands. No, the new system was being engaged by lawyers—James Crow, wearing suits and ties and joining the country club—and making the laws. Worse yet, by actions of Republican presidents and Congress members, they have been installed in offices especially the federal judiciary, as will be developed more fully in Topic V. This new effort is the equivalent of the <u>Redemption</u> described above.

For Black people to take part in the advantages of living in the United States, they have had to create or accept a "double consciousness." **"the one projected on the Black community ... by its own members" to counter the one projected on the Black community "by the dominant culture."** As Du Bois wrote in the *Souls of Black Folk* (1903): "this American world ... yields the Negro no true self-consciousness, but only lets him see himself through the revelation of the other world. It is a peculiar sensation, this double-consciousness, this sense of always looking at one's self through the eyes of others, of measuring one's soul by the tape of a world that looks on in amused contempt and pity. One ever feels his two-ness—an American, a Negro; two souls, two thoughts, two unreconciled strivings; two warring ideals in one dark body, whose dogged strength alone keeps it from being torn asunder." *Gates*, p. 198.

This is still with us today. In my experience, I discern the frustration of Black persons who have "made it" professionally and economically and yet feel the crush of racism keenly in their everyday lives. They want to be wholly who they are, yet are constantly reminded that they must "fit in" and accommodate to the white culture.

The Plague

Now, we see that this plague that came over Europe and North America is even more vicious than we thought. We have learned recently of flesh-eating infections. **The plague of racism is soul-eating. It has eaten at the soul of America.**

Fortunately, there is a cure. There will always be some scars and plaque (pronounced plack) left from the infection but the soul can be cured.

Although there has always been a Resistance to the enslavement of persons of African ancestry, we are blessed in our generation to have ever-expanding resources to once and for all time, rid ourselves of this plague.

First, let's summarize the Resistance noted in the three Parts so far.

*Captive Africans jumping overboard during the Middle Passage

Enslaved Africans who had been purchased for forced labor primarily in the south, running away, disobeying masters, work slowdowns, etc.

*Bacon's Rebellion, 1676-1677, in which the black slaves and white servants joined forces.

*In the 1880s, George Washington Williams, Frederick Douglass and other African Americans countered much of the narrative of Black inferiority being published in popular magazines and journals, arguing that the nation should look to history, not to science.

*In response to being excluded from the dominant culture, Black people formed their own social structures—churches, schools, colleges, self-help organizations, and fraternal organizations, leading to a flowering of writers, musicians, etc., the most well-known being the Harlem Renaissance.

*Attacks most likely led to Black people organizing to counter the image and was important in the NAACP gaining some public support

*In 1940, Ida Mae Gladney votes for the first time, then becomes a worker for the Democratic Party in Chicago and went on to become a regular campaign worker in following elections, encouraging and instructing other Black people in voting.

(A poem about others in the Resistance appears at the end of this Topic.)

Today's resources include a large body of writings, videos, workshops, and lectures, and yes, spiritual practices, by both persons of color and White persons on understanding racism and what can be done to work toward its elimination. Indeed, the sources drawn from to prepare this Topic have this element.

A common theme is that, as white persons, we do not have to think about being white. Persons of color, on the other hand, are aware of being brown or Black every part of their daily lives. Our brothers and sisters of color must be concerned about how they will be received at work, as students, how they will be treated as learners, how they will be perceived as trouble-makers, how their future will be presented to them. They and their parents must always breathe a sigh of relief when they return home safely without being harmed by police. Persons of color on the job often must bear being passed over for more responsible, higher-paying jobs, thus depriving them of the income they should have gotten to provide for their family and to build wealth to pass on.

When this information is provided to white persons, for some it is the beginning of contemplating whether what they have been believing, thinking and doing may need to be re-considered. This can happen to you. You are then on a path for a better future.

Here are some main steps that you can take:

1. Educate yourself about racism by a variety of ways. The references at the end of the Topic are a place to begin. Do lots of reading, search out and join discussion groups seeking to understand racism, find out what is going on politically at your local, state, and federal government level, get to know **and listen to** a variety of Black people, those struggling for daily survival or in prison, those with low-level jobs but are surviving month to month, and Black professionals

2. Get to know one or more Black persons on a deep level, develop a trusting relationship so that the two of you can discuss hurtful topics about racism

3. Be open to discard long-held beliefs about persons who are not white —be willing to cast aside the stereotypes that have sustained you over the years. Study history in a new light, be willing to ask questions and challenge what has been and is being taught. Go beyond the daily news to get a more complete view of important events.

4. Ultimately—and this can happen at any time, but must happen if we are to succeed—engage your soul. You may be surprised by what you find. The soul can be repaired. What I found is that I can no longer accept that Black and Brown sisters and brothers in our society are oppressed. Curing America's soul happens by many many individual persons curing their soul.

You most likely will be upset by what you read in this Topic and have a great urge to disagree with it. What I will say is that if you had had the experiences that I have had over the past 25 years of getting to know persons of color, engaging in discussions and political actions, and reading on this topic, you would come out where I am.

One more thing. Those of us who believe we are working for racial justice, easily get into the mind-set of reading about injustices and looking down on all those "bad" people. This freezes our ability to do anything about it. Here is what Rev. Dr. Martin Luther King wrote in his *Letter From Birmingham Jail.*

"I must make two honest confessions to you, my Christian and Jewish brothers. First, I must confess that over the last few years, I have been gravely disappointed with the white moderates. I have almost reached the regrettable conclusion that the Negro's great stumbling block in the stride toward freedom is not the White Citizen's Council-er or the Ku Klux Klanner, but the White moderate who is more devoted to "order" than to justice; who prefers a negative peace, which is the absence of tension to a positive which is the presence of justice; who constantly say, "I agree with you in the goal you seek, but I can't agree with your method of direct action;" who paternalistically feels that he can set the time-table for another man's freedom; who lives by the myth of time and who constantly advises the Negro to wait until "a more convenient season." Shallow understanding from people of goodwill is more frustrating than misunderstandings from people of ill will. Lukewarm acceptance is far more bewildering than outright rejection."

White power tells Black people, "you can't live
in 'our' neighborhood." Is that you?
White power tells Black people, "you can't send
your kids to 'our' schools." Is that you?
White power tells Black people, "our taxes
should go to 'our' schools." Is that you?
White power tells Black people, "you can't
vote in 'our' elections." Is that you?
White power tells Black people, "you can't be
ministers in 'our' churches." Is that you?
White power tells Black people, "you can't be scientists,
engineers, philosophers, managers, supervisors, corporate
officers in 'our' institutions." Is that you?
Yet if a Black person refuses to stand and salute the
flag, he or she is accused of being un-American.

Before I had read several of the books listed in the references, I had an unusual (for me) experience. I often wake up in the middle of the night and don't get back to sleep. I was in what is called a "limbo condition," where you are not fully asleep but sometimes dreaming. In this state, you can dream, but to some extent control the thoughts. In that condition, the following came to me. It wrote itself. As soon as I was awake, I wrote it down. The only changes I made were to correct some of the names that were wrong.

Black Lives Matter
By Darrel Nash
2017

What's all this Black Lives Matter stuff?
Where did it come from?
Was it just plopped down in the middle of us?
　　　Well, let's see.
A Ferguson policeman killed Michael Brown
after an altercation. His body was left lying
in the public square for hours because
"this is a crime scene."
　　　Large groups took to the streets
　　　in protest, because Black Lives Matter
　　　and the term becomes popularized
A self-appointed white man shoots
and kills Trayvone because he is
taking a short cut through "our
neighborhood."
　　　Large groups took to the streets in
　　　protest, because Black Lives Matter
A thirty years or more War on Drugs
puts millions of Black people in
prisons for using crack cocaine.
　　　Campaigns and political action
　　　takes place around the country to
　　　find alternatives to prison and treat
　　　all offenders the same regardless
　　　of type of cocaine, because Black
　　　Lives Matter

145

White men beat a young Black man to
death because he was accused of
whistling at a **white** woman

> *Emmett Till's mother opens*
> *the casket at his funeral so*
> *that all could see what* H A T E
> *does, because Black Lives Matter*

White police use fire hoses and attack
dogs to stop demonstrators from
marches for justice

> *Martin Luther King, John Lewis*
> *and many many others proclaim*
> *that we have come to cash the check*
> *promised by our Founding Fathers,*
> *that so far has been marked*
> *"insufficient funds" because*
> *Black Lives Matter*

Black men and women are denied
employment to other than menial
and back-breaking jobs

> *A. Philip Randolph and others formed*
> *the Brotherhood of Sleeping Car Porters*
> *because Black Lives matter*

Black men and women were prevented
and discouraged from joining and
assisting in the country's defenses
because the **white** power structure claimed
Black people were not brave and maybe
didn't support the US
Black soldiers fought in the

> *Revolutionary and Civil Wars,*
> *the Buffalo Soldiers and the*

Tuskegee Airmen all served
with distinction and bravery under
the most demanding and dangerous conditions.
After many decades, their services
are being recognized because Black Lives Matter

A generations-long reign of terror was carried out
where Black men are lynched and Black churches
burned
Even in these times there were barely
audible but brave voices in both the
South and the North and both Black
and white saying, Black Lives Matter

After legal enslavement was ended **vile,
vitriolic, lies** were promulgated
By Whites in the North and South
that the Negro was best enslaved
because he was slothful, ignorant
and not able to take care
of himself

Booker T. Washington spent his life
working and urging Black
people to get educated and develop
skills and talents that were better
than anyone else's, because
Black Lives Matter

Southern states secede from
the Union to protect slavery

The secession is defeated
and the Constitution is amended
to end slavery because Black Lives Matter

The economy of the south is
dependent on chattel slavery;
plantation owners oppose ending
slavery, and many white persons in the
north are opposed to ending slavery
because their businesses profit by it

> *Frederick Douglas, John Brown,*
> *the Friends Society and many others*
> *work for abolition of slavery*
> *because Black Lives Matter*

The white power structure of the Southern states,
while strongly defending "states rights" get
Congress to enact the Fugitive
Slave Act requiring any state to
return run-away slaves to their "owner"

> *Harriet Tubman and others form the*
> *Underground Railroad to ferry slaves*
> *to northern states and to Canada*
> *because Black Lives Matter*

George Washington, Thomas
Jefferson, George Mason and many others favor
ending slavery but "not right now."

> *But George Mason, called "the father of*
> *the bill of rights" said in his address to*
> *the Virginia Ratifying Convention,*
> *"As much as I value an union of all*
> *the states, I would not admit the*
> *southern states into the union,*
> *unless they agreed to the*
> *discontinuance of this disgraceful*

trade, because it would bring weakness
and not strength to the union."
Because Black Lives Matter

An early draft of the Declaration of
Independence lists fostering the slave
trade among the grievances against
Britain because Black Lives Matter

Congress removed Jefferson's assertion that
Britain had forced slavery on the colonies,
in order to moderate the document and
appease those in the white power structure
in Britain who supported the Revolution.

So, I repeat, What's all this Black
Lives Matter stuff? Where did it
come from? Was it just
plopped down in the middle of us?
What do you think?

References for Topic III

Alexander, Michelle, The New Jim Crow, Mass Incarceration in the Age of Colorblindness, The New Press, 38 Greene Street, New York, 10013, ISBN 978-1-59558-643-8, 2012.

Allard, Linda, ed., The Journals and Miscellaneous Notebooks of Ralph Waldo Emerson, Cambridge, Harvard University Press, 1976.

Barbour, Barton H. Ph.D, et. al., America West Chronicles, Publications International Ltd, 8140 Lehigh Avenue, Morton Grove, Illinois, 60053, ISBN 978-1-68022-833-5, 2007.

Bowens-Wheatley, Marjorie and Jones, Nancy Palmer, (eds.), Soul Work, Anti-racist Theologies in Dialogue, Skinner House Books, 25 Beacon

Street, Boston (since moved to 24 Farnsworth Street, Boston 02210-1409,) ISBN 1-55896-445-2, 2003.

DiAngelo, Robin, *What Does it Mean to be White, Developing White Racial Literacy,* Peter Lang, 29 Broadway, 18th Floor, New York 10006, ISBN 978-1-4331-3100-3, 2016.

DiAngelo, Robin, *White Fragility, Why it's So Hard for White People to Talk About Racism* Beacon Press, Boston, ISBN 9780807047415, 2018.

Gates, Henry Louis, Jr., *Stony the Road, Reconstruction, White Supremacy, and the Rise of Jim Crow,* Penguin Press, New York, ISBN 9780525559535, 2019.

Gilman, William H., ed., *Selected Writings of Ralph Waldo Emerson,* New York: New American Library, 1965.

Irving, Debby, *Waking Up White, and Finding Myself in the Story of Race,* Elephant Room Press, Cambridge, Massachusetts, ISBN 978-0-9913313-0-7, 2014.

King, Martin Luther, Jr., Martin Luther King, Jr. Research and Education Institute, April 16, 1963.

Lewis, John, *Walking with the Wind, A Memoir of the Movement,* Harcourt Brace & Company, 6277 Sea Harbor Drive, Orlando, Florida 12887-6777, ISBN 0-15-600708-8, 1998.

Loewen, James, *Lies My Teacher Told Me, Everything American History Textbook Got Wrong,* The New Press, 120 Wall Street, New York 10005, 2019.

Mann, Charles C., *1493, Uncovering the New World Columbus Created,* Vintage Books, Random House, Inc., New York, ISBN 978-0-307-27824-1, 2012.

Morrison-Reed, Mark D., *The Selma Awakening, How the Civil Rights Movement Tested and Changed Unitarian Universalism,* Skinner House, 24 Farnsworth Street, Boston, 02210-1409, 2014.

Moynihan, Daniel Patrick, *The Negro Family: The Case For National Action* (known as the Moynihan Report), Office of Policy Planning and Research, United States Department of Labor, Washington, DC, 1965.

Nash, Darrel A, *A Perspective on How Our Government Was Built, And Some Needed Changes,* Rose Dog Books, 585 Alpha Drive, Suite 103, Pittsburg PA 15238, ISBN 978-1-4809-7915-4, 2018.

Niven, John, *John C. Calhoun and the Price of Union,* Louisiana State University Press, Baton Rouge, ISBN 0-8071-185-8-3, 1988.

Obama, Barack, *A Promised Land,* Crown, Random House, Penguin Random House, LLC, New York, ISBN 978-1-5247-6316-9, 2020.

Porte, Joel, ed., *Emerson in His Journals,* Cambridge, Harvard University Press, 1982.

Roesch, James Rutledge, *From Founding Fathers to Fire-Eaters: The Constitutional Doctrine of States' Rights in the Old South*

Rothstein, Richard, *The Color of Law, A Forgotten History of How Our Government Segregated America,* Liveright Publishing Corporation, New York, 10110, ISBN 978-1-63149-453-6, 2017.

Tatum, Beverly Daniel PhD, *Why Are all the Black Kids Sitting Together in the Cafeteria?, and Other Conversations About Race,* Basic Books, Hachette Book Group, 1290 Avenue of the Americas, New York, NY 10104, ISBN 978-0-465-06068-9, 1997,2017.

Washington, Booker T., *Up from Slavery,* Dover Publications, Inc. New York, ISBN-13: 978-0-486-28738-6, 1995.

Wilkerson, Isabel, *The Warmth of Other Suns, The Epic Story of America's Great Migration,* Random House, Inc. New York, ISBN, 978-0-679-76388-8, 2010.

Zinn, Howard, *A People's History of the United States,* Harper Perennial Modern Classics, New York, ISBN 978-0-06-196558-6, 2003.

Additional Reading

Bowens-Wheatley, Marjorie and Jones, Nancy Palmer, (eds.) Soul Work, anti-racist theologies in dialogue, Skinner House Books, Boston, ISBN 1-55896-445-2, 2003.

Boyle, Gregory, Tattoos on the Heart, The Power Of Boundless Compassion, Simon and Schuster, Inc., 1230 Avenue of the Americas, New York, 10020, ISBN 978-1-4391-5315-4, 2010.

Bryant, Howard, Full Dissidence, Notes From An Uneven Playing Field, Beacon Press, Boston, ISBN 9780807019559, 2020.

Dyson, Michael Eric, Tears We Cannot Stop, A Sermon to White America, St. Martin Press, 175 Fifth Avenue, New York 10010, ISBN 9781250135995, 2017.

Lewis, John, Walking with the Wind, A Memoir of the Movement, A Harvest Book, Harcourt Brace & Company, San Diego, New York, London, ISBN 0-15-600708-8, 1998.

Moore, Wes, The Other Wes Moore, One Name, Two Fates, The Random House Publishing Group, New York, ISBN 978-0-385-52820-7, 2010.

Morrison-Reed, Mark, The Selma Awakening, How the Civil Rights Movement Tested and Changed Unitarian Universalism, Skinner House Books, Boston, ISBN 978-1-558-96-733-5, 2014.

Oluo, Ijeoma, So You Want to Talk About Race, Seal Press, 1290 Avenue of the Americas, New York, 10104, ISBN, 978 1 580 05677 9, 2018.

Patel, Eboo, Sacred Ground, Pluralism, Prejudice, and the Promise of America, Beacon Press, Boston, 2012.

Sterling, Dorothy, Black Foremothers, Three Lives, The Feminine Press, Box 334, Old Westbury, New York, 11569, ISBN 0-912670-60-6, 1979.

Wideman, John Edgar, Two Cities, (A Love Story), Houghton Mifflin Company, 215 Park Avenue South, New York, 10003, ISBN 0-395-85730-9, 1998.

Topic IV

American Oligarchy

We must make our choice,
We may have democracy—or we may have
wealth concentrated in the hands of a few
But we can't have both – *Louis Brandeis*

We need a civic society—not a business society.
One where we are concerned for the
welfare of each other. – *Jazz musician Wynton Marsalis*

Taxes are "the price we pay for civilization." – *Oliver
Wendell Holmes, Jr.*

Democracy Dies in Secrecy – *Washington Post*

Introduction

Topics IV and V fast forward to more modern times. These are two of the
efforts from the last and current centuries that uses the time-tested activity
of taking away power from the majority of US citizens and concentrating
it among powerful groups. Topic IV is to weaken governments by getting

control of the society by the super wealthy; taking advantage of the long-term aversion to taxes for many in society. The other is to get control of our court system by one organization so that only its viewpoint is considered valid.

Topic II covered the long-lasting distrust of citizen participation in our political decisions going back to colonial days when white male property owners were considered the only part of the population qualified to make decisions for the rest. You may think those days are past, but read on.

So, from Topic II we see that from the colonial period onward and into the Confederation and finally ratification of the Constitution and adoption of the Bill of Rights, the power groups were opposed to paying taxes. A large portion of that Topic was devoted to the attitude toward taxes because this affliction is still with us. Topic IV will show how our attitude toward taxes was maintained and re-invigorated in the twentieth century and is with us today. It is more dangerous than ever. As you have read, my view is that if you want something, you should pay for it. Regarding taxes, we pay for the public good—not for individual goods that we ourselves need. A public good is something that is for the good of our society, such as a fair justice system and an educated population.

I always go back to what James Madison wrote in Federalist Paper No. 45: "...We have heard of the impious doctrine of the Old World, that the people were made for kings, not kings for the people. Is the same doctrine not to be revived in the New [World] in a different shape— **that the solid happiness of the people is to be sacrificed to the laws of political institutions** of a different form? ...It is too early for politicians to presume on our forgetting that **the public good, the real welfare of the great body of people, is the supreme object to be pursued, and that no form of government whatever has any other value than as it may be fitted for the attainment of this object.**"

The great question is how can the government know what the great body of people want? The obvious answer is the great body of people must have the right and then exercise that right to vote. Regarding public goods, if the **great body of people** is well-represented by elected officials and a health care system sponsored by the government is chosen, then this system should be paid for through the taxing system. And it follows that if government is going to finance this system, then taxes should go up to cover it.

This Topic (Topic IV), while showing threads going back to the early days of the Revolutionary period, reports on a new development being imposed on our country. In a <u>democracy</u>, those wanting to influence and shape public policy, do it in open forums, making speeches open to all, writing articles for newspapers and magazines that most of the citizens might read, etc. The voting public listens, and debates what is being presented. Some of us may want more government programs and involvement, some want less, so vote according to our preferences. But after the arguments, and campaigns and voting, we can all say, well, that's what the majority wants, so that's what we will have for now. Then, again in a democracy, if we want changes, we contact our elected representatives **and we are heard**. If we are not happy with the way they are voting, then we work to get someone else elected next time and the process keeps going.

What is being (or has been) imposed on us is something else. Instead of the open debates that take place in a democracy, we have a power that depends on secrecy, stealth, and money. Instead of citizens trying to influence government, this power is trying—and to a large extent succeeding—in running our society outside of government. This power is deciding how our tax system is made, how our environment is protected, whether our public education system will survive and on and on.

It is important to understand that there are two things essential for an **imposed** system to operate, secrecy **and** money. Groups may meet in secret to plan government takeover. But unless they have huge sums of cash, it doesn't get very far. But with a ready supply of money, this power can plan and carry out a grand design that can be implemented over a long period of time. Temporary setbacks can be used to evaluate what didn't work and then do some redesigning to be more effective in the future.

I will name names as the Discussion develops, but keep in mind one in particular—Charles Koch.

The remaining sections draw heavily from *MacLean, Mayer, Leonard, Schulman,* and *Fang.*

Republicans Move to the Right

After the Great Depression and World War II, there was a general consensus among both major political parties that the government had important roles to play to assure and enhance the welfare of the nation. But pushback began in this post-war period. Most well-known was the 1964 campaign of Barry Goldwater. He wanted to cut way back on the size and involvement of government. Among his campaign proposals was to sell off the TVA, the government system of dams on rivers in the southeast for flood control and electricity generation.

Opposition to Black people gaining power disguised as states' rights was the engine for the movement of the Republican Party to the right starting in the 1950s. While there were many in the party who pined for the "good ole days" before the New Deal, it was, before the time of Goldwater the party of Eisenhower and Thomas Dewey. These politicians accepted as done deals many of the New Deal programs like Social Security.

An economist, G. Warren Nutter was given "major staff responsibility for every one of the Goldwater campaign's important speeches," and control over communications from the Republican National Committee. Nutter claimed that he wrote the platform plank on civil rights. Except now civil rights meant for them states' rights. This left no doubt that the party had thrown overboard being the Party of Lincoln. Moderate mostly northern Republicans were shocked by the change. Few in the Party supported full equality of Blacks, but they were also opposed for now being allies with the South. "For those of us who revere the memory of Abraham Lincoln," a New Jersey woman on the Republican National Committee complained, "this is difficult to swallow."

Goldwater's campaign and speeches left no doubt about his dream for America. Advocating to eliminate or privatize popular features of the New Deal, such as Social Security and the Tennessee Valley Authority system did not set well with many voters. So, was Goldwater's honesty what brought him down? The lesson learned from Goldwater's campaign was that advocates of small government, opposition to Black people gaining power and in favor of huge tax cuts for the wealthy learned to be more secretive.

Milton Friedman, a University of Chicago professor took on the task of explaining Goldwater's positions. He explained that all these New Deal programs had destroyed the people's individual responsibilities— weakened the fiber of the people. I have to ask if Freidman did as "scientists" did in Topic III which was to decide on what outcome he wanted and then conduct the studies that was support this conclusion. Especially in social sciences, there are multiple factors that influence the conditions of people. Unless all or most of the important factors are taken into account, the conclusions may be faulty.

Freidman made sure that listeners understood that in his view, the practices of keeping Black people down should continue. He said the Civil Rights Act forced everyone to conform to the values of some, which violates the liberty of those that oppose reform.

> I respond that some values should not be subject to popular vote or preference. One such value is justice. Each person in our society should receive the same chance for a fair jury trial, access to competent legal counsel, access to the same jobs as everyone else, the provision of an education that will enable the person to function in society, recognition of a person's

skills, talents, dreams, etc. regardless of the person's ancestors, their choice of a family, and where the person lives and has lived, to name a few.

Our nation's values were expressed in the Declaration. All [persons] are created equal and they are endowed by their creator with certain inalienable rights, among which are life, liberty, and the pursuit of happiness. And I like to believe that most or all of our religions affirm something similar to the Book of Jeremiah where we see that we are to seek justice, love mercy, and walk humbly with our God.

Friedman urged reliance instead on "free market principles": prejudice would cause lower wages for black workers, which in turn would reduce production costs for those who employed them, so more employers would hire African Americans, he said—and presto, "virtue triumphs."

Support for Goldwater on the intellectual side, was also led by *National Review* editor William F. Buckley Jr. His views were that we must have a much smaller government, one that doesn't interfere in [white, straight, male] people's lives. These views became more and more accepted by Republicans and were brought to fruition by the election of Reagan. Since then, "liberal Republicans" have disappeared from politics. This could be viewed as just that the population agrees with this view of government and therefore following Madison's ideal this should bring us what we as a nation desire.

Unfortunately, from there it has gone to where now we are in real danger of losing anything that can be called a democracy. [Remember that Madison's ideal that **the people** should decide what government should do assumes that **all** people have access to influencing their preferences.]

The Marriage of Academia With Right-wing Politics

The Supreme Court ruling, *Brown v. Board of Education of Topeka*, 347 U.S. 483 (1954), had a profound effect on schools throughout the nation, but especially in southern states. Recall from Topic III that much of the country had re-established white domination by replacing Reconstruction with Redemption. Now the Supreme Court ruling meant that the rights of African Americans had to be taken into account, at least in the area of education.

The ruling overturned the Court's ruling in 1896, *Plessy v. Ferguson*, 163 U.S. 537 (1896), that upheld the constitutionality of racial segregation laws for public facilities as long as the segregated facilities were equal in quality. The *Brown* decision found that in the field of public education the doctrine of "separate but equal" does not produce equality. Separate educational facilities are inherently unequal. Recall the story of Dr. Payton above on being bussed past the better equipped white-only schools.

Brown v. Board of Education upset particularly the Southern states. The Federal government had largely left states alone for decades, especially anything to do with civil and political rights of its oppressed citizens. Southern states, especially, decided rather than comply with the ruling, they would make another effort to continue the oppression of African Americans. With *Brown*, politicians like US Sen. Harry Byrd, Democrat of Virginia went into action.

Byrd was the political boss of Virginia. (As covered in Topic III, nearly all elected officials in the South at the time were Democrats—the party that was able to replace Reconstruction with Redemption in the 1870s.) Byrd's most well-known action to nullify the mandate of *Brown* was to create "massive resistance" to school integration in Virginia by closing all public schools and setting up private schools to be attended by only white students. Churches and other organizations went to great expense into creating private schools which were beyond the Court ruling.

Byrd found a supporter in James Kilpatrick, editor of the *Richmond News Leader*. As Kilpatrick looked for a respectable way to fight *Brown*, to lift the cause above "the sometimes sordid level of race," he found John C. Calhoun's theory of states' rights, primarily the right of nullification, to fit his needs. (Remember Calhoun from Topic III.)

After Eisenhower called in the National Guard to protect the students wishing to go to Central High School, *National Review* editor William F. Buckley Jr. joined in the opposition to *Brown* and its implementation. Buckley showed his true colors by defending the governor's actions, telling his readers that Faubus was just using his state power to prevent the unconstitutional action of the Supreme Court. We now have armed federal troops patrolling our once tranquil towns. He said, these nine justices of the Supreme Court had created a situation that could "be settled only by violence and the threat of force." (Notice how the practice of demonizing a part of the Government if it acts against your preference was also used then.) Buckley said, the NAACP was exaggerating the mistreatment of the black students. What were "ugly epithets," spitting, and being "pushed around" compared with "the picket-line practices of monolithic labor unions"?

(You guessed it, Buckley was also opposed the labor unions.) He said the "line of bayonets in Little Rock" was hidden under "the maternal skirts" of "Mother Welfare State." All these evils, civil rights, labor unions, and social insurance was leading to the "army of occupation ... enforcing unconditional surrender." *MacLean*, p. 55. (What a reach! Remember from "Opening Salvo" that one way of being untrue is to connect two things that don't have any relationship.)

In a recently published book by Stuart Stevens, he reports that Buckley viewed the Negro as never having the ability as high as the white race and that the two races should never be together. Modern writers, such as Washington Post columnist, George Will who consider Buckley the hero of conservatives, never mention this aspect of Buckley's philosophy.

Another Virginian joined the resistance battle—Colgate Darden, president of the University of Virginia. Darden had recently hired an economist by the name of James McGill Buchanan, October 3, 1919 –

January 9, 2013. Both men saw the desegregation ruling as way more than a change of who goes to which schools. They saw a challenge to the whole southern society. For decades, the Supreme Court could be counted on to not interrupt the social systems of the country established by White people in positions of power. If the Court could find schools in violation of the equal protection provision of the Fourteenth Amendment, who knows what other aspects of White supremacy society may be in danger of a ruling based on equal protection. *MacLean*, pp. xv, xvi.

After his formal education, James Buchanan was on the staff of various universities and in 1965, was appointed as chair of the economics department at the University of Virginia. *McLean*, pp. xv and xvii. Buchanan provided intellectual cover for the political group opposed to *Brown* by arguing for a concept called "public choice." In its most extreme version, this field of thinking, covered more fully below, is that a person should not have to pay any tax unless he himself had approves of it. (Buchanan will appear again later in this Discussion.)

The connection to this concept is that those that were opposed to *Brown* could argue that since Black citizens did not pay as much in taxes as white people, the government was not obligated to provide public education to black children.

Buchanan and fellow economist, G. Warren Nutter (the Goldwater campaign staffer) then co-founded the Thomas Jefferson Center for Political Economy at the University of Virginia. They purposely made the Center a platform for establishing and promoting a specific point of view and would not allow other viewpoints to be considered or studied. From the beginning, they knew that this was risky in a university setting. **Nutter told Milton Friedman that the obvious danger of a university providing a "political rallying point for only one point of view," is that it may slip from scholarship to propaganda.** *MacLean*, pp. 95, 96.

Buchanan used his status as an economist to argue for a definition of incentives to review government programs so that we could return America to "the free society" it had once been, only some of which the society of Virginia of the 1950s had managed to preserve, according to Buchanan.

In Buchanan's view, this free society is one where the individual is free to use his knowledge and power solely for his own benefit. In this view, the government should not be taxing individuals to pay for the increasing package of public goods and social programs. He promoted the notion that tax policy ought to be arrived at through **unanimous** consent. *MacLean*, pp. xxiii, xxiv.

It is useful to think about "public goods" compared to "private goods." Buchanan was opposed to the government providing all public goods. What are public goods? Are there some goods, some services, that can only be provided by a level of government? **Definitely, yes!** One that should be obvious is a justice system. Does anyone want our court system run as a private enterprise? Think about your list of the essential pubic goods that our society should not be without. In a couple of pages, you will see my list.

This "free society" in Buchanan's view was when the federal government as well as state governments were weak. This was when the powerful could make money in any way they wished and the governments had very little power. This time was from the days of the Confederation of the United States to before Teddy Roosevelt's Progressive Era. It later resumed afterward until the Great Depression. Those in power kept taxes very low, disregarding the needs of those without political power.

Buchanan saw a danger that the federal government was more concerned about the needs of those without power and was forcing wealthy individuals to pay for public goods and social programs that the wealthy had not approved of. If people wanted better schools, newer textbooks, and more courses for black students that might help children, for example, their parents and others who wanted to chip in should pay for them. The government shouldn't be involved in forcing those like him to pay for things they didn't want to. This was theft in Buchanan's view, taking what some people had earned to pay for the benefit of others.

In this view, even if an expenditure makes the nation as a whole better off, there is no such thing as a **public good** that all taxpayers should contribute to. The extreme conclusion of their argument was that no tax should be enacted without unanimous consent of all the persons being taxed—obviously a recipe for no taxes.

Buchanan believed that his views were so important that essentially our Constitution should be thrown out or at least we should go back to earlier times when only white male property owners could vote. To preserve the wealth of those that were already rich, he advocated for restricting voters to only the wealthy. This way those that wanted to take some of rich people's money for "public goods" wouldn't be bothering the politicians. *The reference for MacLean's views is "Henry Manne to Buchanan, "Draft Program Synopsis for Mont Perlerin Society Meeting in Washington, DC, September 1998," BHA. MacLean* p. xxvii.

MacLean writes that Charles and David Koch saw how they could use Buchanan as a respected professional to help push their agenda. Buchanan could help them rescue the government for capitalism. The Kochs also knew the importance of secrecy so that those snoopy journalists wouldn't know what they were doing. *MacLean*, p. xxviii.

James Kilpatrick, the Richmond editor, wrote a book called, *the Sovereign States.* This was praised by persons across the nation who favored "economic liberty." Kilpatrick went back to Jefferson and Madison arguing for nullification, and John C. Calhoun's claim that the states had a "right of interposition"—or veto of federal actions and that the Supreme Court has been misinterpreting the Constitution's Commerce Clause to enable federal regulation, thus, the Wagner Act, the Social Security Act, and the Fair Labor Standards Act were as unlawful as *Brown*.

Harry Byrd's friend T. Coleman Andrews agreed. He said the choice was between "collectivism and slavery versus capitalism and freedom." His idea was that since Black southerners had not paid equal taxes as the white people, their pushing for equal educational resources was making the white people pay for the education of Black children. In his view, this was a "dangerous trend toward socialism."

This argument in itself is ludicrous! The Southern power structure had made sure that they kept all the wealth and earning power—keeping many Blacks in poverty. How were the oppressed supposed to pay for an adequate education?

T. Coleman Andrews was commissioner of the Internal Revenue in the Eisenhower Administration but resigned because he thought the graduated income tax was "discriminatory" and a "devouring evil" tantamount to "slavery." In an interview with *US News and World Report,* he said that for government to be "confiscating property" from citizens on "the principles of the capacity to pay is socialism." *MacLean,* p. 53. It is interesting how the powerful charge socialism whenever a government program is planned or implemented that they don't like.

Early on, some University of Virginia officials began to get very concerned about what Buchanan and Nutter had created. They got an awakening when in 1960, the Ford Foundation rejected a major application from the department because of the finding of dogmatism.

In June 1963, at the University of Virginia, the dean of the faculty alerted the president to "a condition in Thomas Jefferson Center's faculty within the Department of Economics." After a review of the Center, they concluded that indeed only one set of research findings was acceptable.

As in Topic III, we had in Buchanan a person who was using his prestige as an economic "scientist" to push his agenda. Buchanan did not do research to reach his positions, but rather used his imagination about how he would like to world to operate. He projected to the academic world that his creative mind enabled him to find that the world of economics did not operate the way generations of scholars in social sciences, humanities, and law had found. I find it hard to think that academics and scholars would accept his view of the world without demanding some scientific studies for support.

The long-standing view of the majority of economists is that the market, left to itself, does not produce all the goods and services that a society needs to function. Those associated with Buchanan's position argue for "free markets." "Let the market decide," etc. The term used for let the market decide is called, "*laissez-faire economics.*"

Founders of the discipline of modern economics, among them Richard T. Elly and John R. Commons, have demonstrated that market power shapes markets—not an impersonal invisible hand. Ely, a leader in the 1885 founding of the American Economic Association, was blunt about. He said, "no one who claimed the mantle of science should advocate "doing nothing while people starve." That "the market" will tell us what people want is just an opinion—not reality.

> There is probably no idea more misused than that we live in a market economy and that if we let the market decide, it will automatically produce the goods and services that we want. Many politicians and owners of a large business know a great deal about how the market works, but when they are fighting some government regulation on an aspect of their business argue that "the best and American way is to let the market decide."
>
> No, that is not the best and the American way. What those who argue that this is the right way things work, misuse the work of Adam Smith, a British economist who did his scientific work around the time of the American Revolution. Those that like what Adams wrote find in his writings that there is an "invisible hand" that works automatically to provide the goods and services that people want. Following is more what the actual market is like.
>
> On Competition and Government Responsibilities

Here is some basic economics that is covered in maybe Econ 102, or perhaps Econ 103.

Let's start with the Invisible Hand of the Market. This term is attributed to Adam Smith in his book, *An Inquiry into the Nature and Causes of the Wealth of Nations*, published in 1776. Smith describes a situation where there are many small buyers and many small sellers in a market, one of his examples was pins. In this circumstance, if one seller is charging a higher price for an identical product as the other sellers, this guy won't sell any pins, so he has to lower his price. This may get other sellers to lower their price. But this doesn't go on forever. At some price, a seller says, if I lower it any more, I won't cover my cost of producing my pins and getting them to the market place, so he doesn't lower the price. Only those producers that can produce and market their pins at this price will stay in business.

There are other assumptions that go along with this, one being that everyone's pins are exactly the same. Another is that none of the buyers have a favorite seller—they only look at the price. Or that there are no side deals made by a buyer or seller. Presto—the Invisible Hand.

Economists following Smith and other early analysts called this market condition *pure competition* or sometimes *perfect competition.*

How often do these conditions exist in the real world? <u>Never</u>. It is something like doing gravity experiments in a perfect vacuum. There may be some useful information gotten or it may be a good thought process, but in the everyday world, these conditions don't exist.

166

Now, we have to describe real world conditions of buying and selling. We start with definitions.

Monopoly: only one buyer

Monopsony: only one seller

Oligopoly: few sellers

Oligopsony: few buyers.

In no case where one or more of these conditions exist, is there an "invisible hand." In the case of the "monopoly and monopsony" people with power are dictating what price and quantity can be bought and sold.

In the case of the "oligopolist and oligopsonist" a few powerful people are in fierce battles with each other to arrive at a price and quantity that can be bought and sold. There can be all sorts of combinations here. The powerful may form alliances and gang up on others in this market to try to get some competition eliminated, and all sorts of other situations. This is a lot like our society in America today.

In the real world of our economy, there are a host of actions that marketers use to get the customer to buy their product. One is to argue that their product is superior to all similar products on the market, and that's what we see plastered all over our TV and newspaper and magazine ads. Another is to get on the good side of politicians that can make a difference and get the politicians to support their company, either with words or money.

Associations of producers may also do this. Another strategy is to get the relevant governmental unit to draw boundaries where only one company can operate. This is the strategy of electric and other public utilities, developed by Thomas Edison. A good one is to make your company essential to a unit of government. This is what defense, space, and similar companies do. The examples could go on and on.

The essential nature of all these situations is that it is extremely difficult to evaluate what a market price will be.

When politicians or business people say that "the market decides best," or similar words, you know that they are either ignorant or lying. My supposition is that almost all politicians are not that ignorant, so that leaves lying as what usually happens.

But there is more. The market and Buchanan's "public choice" does not produce for the nation 1) an educated population that John Stuart Mill (1806 – 1873) pointed out is necessary for a democracy to work, 2) a justice system that assures everyone regardless of income or racial and ethnic categories has adequate defense and a neutral jury, 3) a mail delivery system that is accessible to the whole country, especially in low population areas, 4) adequate housing including for those below a certain income level, 5) same for adequate nutrition, same for health care and facilities, 6) a system for people at the lower levels of income, that provides a means for putting away enough money for old age, 7) streets and highways available to all, 8) protection against, businesses that cheat and produce unsafe products, 9) protection against, industries that exploit our natural resources without regard to long-term needs and/ or pollute our air water, oceans, and ground water, and 10) protection against, insurance companies and financial institutions that sell worthless products and services or that are more expensive packages than the customer needs—to name the major ones.

A significant part of the population, when reading these observations immediately jump to, "this is socialism." I ask that you react with thinking, rather than emotion. The word "socialism" has been thrown around so much in daily usage that there is no common definition or understanding of what it is.

More generally, is the moral issue. As I have maintained, our Constitution is more than a contract, it is a covenant between the government and the people and among the people. "We the people of the United States in order to form a more perfect union …" means we have responsibilities to each other.

The University of Virginia was no longer a welcome place for James Buchanan and his allies. But Buchanan did not change his views. Instead, he found a welcoming place at the economics department at George Mason University in northern Virginia in a suburb of Washington DC. He kept on teaching his "public choice" ideas. At George Mason, a Richard Fink* had moved a program at Rutgers University called the Center for the Study of Market Processes to George Mason. George Mason was chosen because the Koch family had given more than thirty million dollars to the university. Fink's Center was eventually renamed the Mercatus Center. The controversy at the University of Virginia resulted in James Buchanan leaving there and moving to George Mason University's economics department in northern Virginia where he introduced and continued his teachings on "pubic choice" theory. James Buchanan found his home at the Mercatus Center. *Fink was a long-term associate of Charles Koch.

George Mason is where the Koch brothers' goals made a major political advance. It was able to begin the push to reduce tax rates and therefore taxes on the super-rich that were first implemented in the Reagan administration. (Corporate tax rates which were very high in the 1950s and lowering them probably did have the effect of improving the economy.) Paul Craig Roberts, an adjunct professor at GMU, did the work on the first tax cut bill of the Reagan era, which was introduced by his former boss Congressman Jack Kemp.

George Mason University was performing "beyond its weight" so to speak. A big reason was the unlimited funding from Charles Koch into Mercatus and other programs at the university. It concentrated in this one location advocates of conservative economics, who drew their concepts from Austrian economics. The Center became home to free-market economists Nobel Prize winner Vernon Smith and Tyler Cowen, an author and *New York Times* contributor who was one of the students that also had moved with Fink from Rutgers to George Mason in 1980. The Mercatus Center became a center for proposing deregulatory policy which is going strong today. The Center went beyond economics; it recommended 14 of the 23 federal rules targeted on the incoming Bush Administration's regulatory "hit list." *Schulman*, pp. 229, 260, 261, 262.

> A favorite whipping-boy of conservatives is federal regulations. Here is how we get regulations. Regulations are initiated by the various federal agencies that operate under duly passed laws. (There are possibly other sources.) Officials in the agencies often use regulations to inform the public how they will carry out the laws that they are responsible for. Once a regulation is finalized, it has the force of law but Congress always has the power to end the regulation. As a retiree from a federal regulatory

agency, I have experience in how a regulation takes on the force of law.

Creating a regulation is a months-long even years-long process. First a proposed regulation is prepared and published in the *Federal Register*. Accompanying the proposed rule is a provision that members of the public or organizations may submit comments—favoring, opposing, clarifying, or perhaps pointing out technical errors and faulty assumptions. After the time period for public comment is ended, typically about 60 days, the agency who submitted the proposed rule <u>must</u> respond to all the comments. These can be for clarification, showing why the comment is erroneous or otherwise does not need to be considered further, or that the commenter is correct and the rule should be changed accordingly.

Then the regulation, as modified by responding to the comments is published as a final regulation again in the *Federal Register*. This then has the force of law unless Congress votes to end the regulation. [This description held until the Trump Administration.]

There is no doubt that this human process has errors and bad regulations are sometimes issued. And more importantly, there is a massive volume of regulations. It would be well if there was a constant review to determine if regulations should be terminated or revised for today's situation. But these considerations are no justification for arguing that there are too many regulations, or a favorite argument of conservatives such as George Will, that Democrats can't wait to put in more regulations. Today's society is way more complicated and the government is

doing way more due to legislation and court rulings,
so more regulations are needed.

Buchanan's most famous work, co-authored with Gordon Tullock, was *The Calculus of Consent*, 1962), for which he received the Nobel Memorial Prize in Economic Sciences in 1986.

Calculus illuminates the positions mentioned above that by allowing everyone to vote on how the government raises and uses taxes means that we have over-investment in the public sector. All the coalitions of voters, politicians, and bureaucrats gang up to get the rich people's money. This taking of money out of the hands of businesses and industries result in lower economic growth, thus taking the money away from its most productive uses.

Buchanan said those who failed to plan and save for the future, "are to be treated as subordinate members of the species akin to…animals who are dependent." Tyler Cowan who followed Buchanan and directed the Mercatus Center, says that if we "rewrite the social contract" people will be expected to fend for themselves much more than they do now." Some will flourish, others will fall by the wayside. As more people escape from poverty, it will be easier to ignore those left behind—apparently thinking this was a worthy goal. *MacLean*, p. 212.

Buchanan's writings were abstract thought experiments, not from any research on political practice. **Others noted that "the major deficiency" of the Virginia school and later George Mason was "the failure to search for empirical tests of the new theories."** The lack of proof, however, did not stop Buchanan and Tullock from offering what they considered the only right solution: to stanch the flow of money, change the incentives.

Majority rule, they said, ought not to be treated as a sacred cow. It was merely one decision-making rule among many possibilities, and rarely ideal. It tended to violate the liberty of the minority, because it yoked some citizens unwillingly to others' goals. Any collective with

the power to enlist the state for its members' benefit, Buchanan and Tullock insisted, was illegitimate in "a society of free men." The only truly fair decision-making model to "confine the political exploitation of man by man within acceptable limits" was unanimity; give each individual the capacity to veto the schemes of others so that the many could not impose on the few. Only if a measure gained unanimous consent, they argued, could it honestly be depicted as "in the public interest." *MacLean*, p. 79.

The opponents of how the government works, sometimes say, "why isn't the government run like a business?" I agree with that, but not with the usual arguments that government is incompetent and inefficient. My reason for saying the government should run more like a business is that it should govern for the long-run. In the case of government, this should go out fifty years or more.

Examples that could be pursued are, how much higher would national income be in 30 or 50 years: 1) if all residents have access to adequate medical services and facilities and as a result are healthier, 2) if everyone has access to a quality high school education so that they could succeed in college or a meaningful career, 3) if a college education for those that want it that among other things, creates a marketable skill commensurate with their education upon graduating from college, 4) if a robust system for people during their earning years had access to adequate training to acquire new marketable skills, 5) if all lived in a community or in an area of decent and adequate housing that has the comforts of the home that we all have come to expect 6) if all lived in a safe neighborhood free of intruders and police forces that act like an army of occupation, 7) if all lived in an area free of toxic air and water pollution, (as it is now, the powerful see to it that their living space is clean—leaving those without power to live next to chemical plants, oil refineries, etc.).

All these programs, in addition to providing additional income and other support to individuals and the nation, most likely would significantly reduce the social ills of broken families, addictions, crimes, poor health, mental illnesses, etc.

In Topic III, I express my strong opinion that much of the propaganda to try to dehumanize the descendants of enslaved Africans was said to be science, but did not use the scientific method to make their conclusions. Similarly, Buchanan developed his economic philosophy on supposedly scientific "abstract thought experiments, not from any research on political practice." This is the reason I am so saddened that the Nobel Committee made the award to Buchanan.

As a trained economist, I have felt over the years that Nobel prizes for economics are way overdone. Often there are no good candidates for such prestigious awards. It was right that the early awardees were recognized for their years of intellectual thought and research. This same level of achievement should still be applied in order to receive the award, rather than just choosing a few to recognize each year.

The Mercatus Center, as well as the Institute of Human Studies were both a part of George Mason University. The IHS was founded by F.

A. "Baldy" Harper, a free-market fundamentalist who had been a trustee at the Freedom School, where he had written essays for *The Freedman*. He compared labor unions to a bank robber. He said shorter work weeks were a source of crime, and that "compulsory 'unemployment' such as child labor laws," and "mandatory schooling "during teen-age years, are an important cause of juvenile delinquency." *MacLean*, pp. 130, 131.

The Mercatus Center and IHS trained students and other staff to work against *Brown* and other conservative causes. These people went out to work for other organizations that often had close ties with the Koch brothers and their large base of wealthy donors. The Koch brothers saw Buchanan's work as an intellectual basis for their goal of transforming governments into forces that "would save capitalism from democracy.

Huge contributions by Koch to George Mason University mostly to the Mercatus Center as well as strict controls over the programs made it next to impossible for the Mercatus Center to be an independent intellectual center, as universities are expected to be. Clayton Coppin, who taught history at George Mason and compiled the confidential study of Charles's political activities describes Mercatus outright in a report as "a lobbying group disguised as a disinterested academic program." Coppin also pointed out, as is the practice of the Kochs, that Charles could donate to an educational organization and get a tax deduction while all along the group was more like a lobbying organization of the Kochs.

According to *Mayer* and *MacLean* Buchanan's star fell as he and David Koch parted ways. *MacLean* found loads of Buchanan's writings in an abandoned building on the George Mason campus.

The above reviews only a part of George Mason University. I have been informed that other parts of the university have produced experts and scholars that have been of value to our society, especially for filling important positions in the federal government.

Brief History of the Koch Family

The Kochs are such an overreaching part of the history of how our democracy is now at risk, that it is important to pierce into how they came to their dark views.

The Koch brothers got their start—both their money and their dark view of democracy and the US government from their father Fred Koch. Fred was very inventive and found an improved way of extracting gasoline from crude oil. Then he was sued by the big oil companies for patent infringement. Fred won the case and developed a hatred for what he saw was the big business/government arrangement at the time.

The Soviet Union was just getting into the oil business and hired Koch to go there and help them use his process. But working in the Soviet Union he saw how the Communist system worked and developed a hatred for it.

Later, he was hired by the Third Reich of Germany in 1933. Hitler wanted to become self-sufficient within Germany and wanted to have his own oil refineries. Under Fred Koch's direction, the sought-after refinery was completed in 1935. Significantly, it was one of the few refineries in Germany that could "produce the high-octane gasoline needed to fuel fighter planes." "Naturally this company would do most of its business with the German military." Thus, the American venture became "a key component of the Nazi war machine."

In working with the Nazis, Fred decided that fascism was a better form of government than US democracy. He wrote that he favored it over America under the New Deal and that the only sound countries are Germany, Italy, and Japan. "The laboring people of these countries are proportionately better off than anywhere else in the world. When you compare the state of mind in Germany today with what it was in 1925, you begin to think this course of idleness, feeding at the public trough, dependence on government, etc., with which we are afflicted is not permanent and can be overcome. *Mayer*, pp. 36, 37, 38.

Fred Koch was an original member of the John Birch Society. He attended the founding meeting held by the candy manufacturer Robert Welch. The organization drew like-minded businessmen from all over the country. Members considered many prominent Americans, including Dwight Eisenhower as Communist agents. *Mayer*, p. 47.

Fred's sons, especially Charles and David built on Fred's opposition to the government by deciding to make their own rules. In one of several cases, Koch Industries as purchasers of oil owned by Native tribes in Oklahoma was accused of stealing some of the oil.

The theft was very low tech. After loading into their truck, they would insert a long stick into the tank and measure how much was left. By under-counting (mis-measuring) what was left, they were able to take more than they reported, thus cheating the owners out of revenue. They were able to do this because there were no auditors going around to determine if Kochs had reported their purchases correctly. This is also called "the honor system." In this case, native American owners of the oil had the "honor" and Kochs had the "system."

"Everyone operating on Indian territory told us one thing and one thing only? 'We're not stealing oil, but we'll tell you who is; Koch Industries." "And they all told me that Koch was taking one to three percent." And I said, "why don't you do something about it?" And first of all, they said, "It's more trouble than its worth." *Leonard*, pp. 14 - 17.

Under oath before a US Senate committee, Charles Koch admitted taking about $31 million in crude oil over a three-year period, claiming it was an honest mistake—that "oil measurement is a very uncertain art." But the committee showed that none of the other oil companies making these purchases had substantial problems with measurement. In fact, it was other oil companies that turned Koch Industries in. *Mayer*, p. 159

From the family's private letters and interviews with the Kochs and their intimates, Clayton Coppin, who had been with the company, saw that Charles Koch's strong political views came from his father. In an unpublished report called, "Stealth," Coppin concluded that Charles' hatred of government was so intense that it could only be understood from his childhood conflict with authority.

From his earliest years, he writes, Charles' goal was to achieve total control. "Charles did not escape his father's authority until his father died.". After that, Charles went to great lengths to ensure that neither his brothers nor anyone else could challenge his personal control of the family company. "He was driven by some deeper urge to smash the one thing left in the world that could discipline him—the government." *Mayer*, p. 65, 66.

By the late 1960s, Charles was digging into the writings of anarchists, Ayn Rand disciples, laissez-faire economists, and disaffected Student for a Democratic Society members. These enhanced his views that government should essentially protect private property and do little else. *Leonard*, p. 5.

As far back as 1976, Charles began **planning a movement** to accomplish his drive. Coppin's searches found the path of Charles's political evolution. In 1978, Charles declared, **our movement** must destroy the prevalent statist system. In an article in the *Libertarian Review*, Charles wrote that those outside the government need to organize. "Ideas do not spread by themselves; they spread only through people, which means we need a movement." "Our movement must destroy the prevalent statist paradigm." *Mayer*, p. 66.

Koch made an early connection with Robert LeFevre. In 1957, LeFevre started a group called the Freedom School. This school was closely aligned with the John Birch Society. Charles learned from the John Birch Society that marketing was very important. Later as he was building his political organization, he provided the most plush accommodations and sumptuous food at his conventions. He also learned the importance of secrecy. These concepts were used to influence a wide range of politics and policies that are with us today. Staying out of the limelight, Koch and associates have managed to make major changes our political landscape without the public (and many journalists and academics) being aware of what they were doing. LeFevre favored the abolition of the state because it was a disease, but to hide what he was saying he called it "autarchist." *Mayer* p. 52, 67.

Taxes and Taxation

Before the Sixteenth Amendment, poor people shouldered more of America's tax burden relative to their income than the rich. That's right— on the poor. Alcohol and tobacco had some of the highest sales tax rates. Rural areas, **including estates**, had lower property tax rates than urban areas. High taxes were levied on widely consumed products such as alcohol and tobacco. "From top to bottom, American society before the income tax was a picture of inequality, and taxes made it worse," writes Isaac William Martin, a professor of sociology at the University of California at San Diego.

In his history, *Rich People's Movement: Grassroots Campaigns to Untax the One Percent*, Martin says that the passage of the income tax law in 1913 was regarded as a calamity by many wealthy citizens. Since then and to this day, there has been vigorous attacks on income taxes. A favorite target is, as most of us know, is the progressive part. Meaning that as an income goes up, the higher portions are taxed at a higher rate than at lower income levels.

Andrew Mellon among others of the ultra-wealthy—he among others are characterized as being "the robber barons"—fought tooth-and-nail against progressive income taxes. Since then, the ultra-wealthy have used all means to characterize income taxes, especially graduated income taxes as harming the ability of the country to grow and prosper. Mellon was Treasury secretary under Presidents, Harding, Coolidge, and Hoover. We can thank him among others for ending the Progressive Era of Theodore Roosevelt among which were his battles to repeal income taxes. The favorite argument is that companies must make big profits so that they can pay their workers. Otherwise, they will not be able to hire workers. In the Reagan era, this was called trickle-down economics.

Following in his footsteps, Richard Mellon Scaife, an heir to the Mellon fortune, estimated that he contributed up to $1billion (adjusted for inflation) from his family fortune to philanthropy. But don't think his "philanthropy" went to helping those in need or for supporting public causes, like education and health. No, an estimated $620 million went into extreme right-wing political causes. In 1999, *The Washington Post* called him the top financial support of the movement that reshaped American politics in the last quarter of the 20th century." Scaife, was an early admirer of William F. Buckley, Jr.

Another of the ultra-wealthy is the DeVos family—the founders of Amway. (Betsy DeVos, President Trump's Secretary of Education is married to former Amway CEO Dick DeVos.) The family also contributed to conservative political causes and became a big contributor to the Koch donor network (see below). The family's political views were more reactionary than the Kochs, but they readily contributed to the Koch network as a way to fight against regulations and taxes. *The above based on Mayer, pp. 73, 78, 79, 84, 283, 288.*

This anti-taxing rhetoric strengthened in the latter part of the twentieth century and has come to full force in the twenty-first century. Modern versions of anti-taxing are 1) Grover Norquist champions the idea that there is some percent of the national economy that is the **right** amount for government to take—his preference 20 percent that was the case around 1900, 2) the more general argument that "taxes are too high," 3) that the Sixteenth Amendment (allowing federal income taxes) is illegitimate, 4) progressive income taxes are unfair.

> There is no obvious proportion of the national income that governments should take as taxes. What is the right portion? Obviously, no taxes would mean no government. And government taking one hundred percent would mean that individuals and businesses would have no choice in what resources

to use or what products and services to buy. Backing away from these two extremes, there is a wide range of the proportion of national income paid in taxes that could satisfy Madison's **public good, the real welfare of the great body of people,** and still have a thriving nation and economy. We can look to other countries for examples.

Regarding the progressive income taxes of the federal government and many states. Whether those with high incomes should be taxed at a higher marginal rate than low-income people is a case of there being no right or wrong answer—only a value judgement, such as "all people are created equal." One viewpoint is that since everyone shares in the benefits of government, then everyone should pay the same percent of their income, or more extreme, everyone should pay the same amount. Another viewpoint, the one I go by is expressed by the phrase, "from those that have more, more is expected."

Millionaires and billionaires should be paying way more in taxes than they now do. This is a part of my belief that we have covenanted—by way of the Constitution—to be one nation. This means that each of us has responsibilities to all others, and to the well-being of the nation. Am I my brother's keeper?

On taxes, James Buchanan, as discussed above, was more extreme than Norquist. Following a Swedish political economist by the name of Kurt Wicksell, Buchanan adopted the idea that the only legitimate taxes are those that are reached by **unanimous** consent of all taxpayers. *MacLean*, p. 79. This ridiculous notion, of course would mean that no taxes would ever be approved. The Koch brothers have a similar philosophy. In their case, rather than fight for the concept openly, they devised ways to manipulate the tax system so that they pay minimal taxes.

Since our tax system could not be changed easily, Koch and others used their knowledge and power to bend the current tax laws and regulations to get around paying taxes and then misusing the regulations to fund their pet projects. A primary practice, is to create philanthropic organizations and thus quality as a 501 (c) (3) organization that is not taxable. Then they create a sister organization, a 501 (c) (4).* The next step is to donate funds from the (c) (3) organization to the (c) (4) organization. With a (c) (4) designation, organizations are allowed to contribute to political causes. *IRS Regulation 1.501(c)(4)-1(a)(2)(i)IR. It is easy to see why there was such an uproar during the George W. Bush and Obama administrations against the Internal Revenue Service by those using this subterfuge. IRS employees were accused of conducting way more investigations of right-wing organizations than they did of others. *Mayer*, pp. 189, 190, 200.

President Reagan took up the mantle of Norquist arguing that taxes are too high. He started the huge tax reductions on the wealthy and every Administration since then has followed—sometimes as a compromise to accomplish another purpose. Remember from above that professor Paul Craig Roberts at George Mason University did the work on the first tax cut bill of the Reagan era. In addition to getting legislation passed to reduce taxes on the wealthy, Reagan went after the Internal Revenue Service by reducing staff numbers so that the agency had a reduced ability to find those taxpayers that were not paying what tax laws required. George W. Bush and Trump have continued in his footsteps by attacking and reducing the staff and capabilities of the IRS.

In the same vein, is the disparagement of government workers. Remember from President Reagan: government is the problem—not the solution. Reagan said, "the most feared words when you are in trouble are, 'I'm from the government and I'm here to help you.' " (I guess the chief administrator of the government was not part of the government.)

Discussing the failure of the Minerals Management Service (MMS) of the US Department of the Interior to adequately monitor oil drilling rigs in the Gulf of Mexico before the Deepwater Horizon oil-spill disaster, Obama writes: "That MMS wasn't fully equipped to do its job, in large part because for the past thirty years a big chunk of American voters had bought into the Republican idea that government was the problem and that business always know better, and had elected leaders who made it their mission to gut environmental regulations, starve agency budgets, denigrate civil servants, and allow industrial polluters do whatever the hell they wanted to do." *Obama*, p. 570.

How the Wealthy Conspired to Make the US an Oligopoly

This all came together after David Koch ran as the vice-presidential candidate for the Libertarian Party in 1980. The party's platform, if enacted, would have changed the federal government to something like it was in 1900. The party proclaimed that the only valid function of the government was to protect individual and property rights. For inspiration, it relied on much of the position of the Freedom School founded and ran by Robert LeFevre.

Thus, the Libertarian position was that kids should not be forced to go to school, it was called, "compulsory education." Essentially all agencies and programs of the federal government enacted from the 1930s to the 1970s should be abolished—the Federal Election Commission, all government health-care programs, including Medicaid and Medicare, Social Security, the SEC, the EPA, the FBI, the CIA, the FDA, the Occupational Health and Safety Administration, and laws including seat belt laws, of all campaign-finance laws, as well as, the abolition of public schools, and all forms of welfare for the poor. No wonder the Party had trouble getting traction.

Libertarians argued that tax evaders should not be prosecuted—so much for "law and order." They called for doing away with laws that kept people from being employed—meaning minimum wage and child labor laws. In the view of the Kochs and other members of the Libertarian Party, government should only do one thing: protect individual and property rights. *The above from Mayer* pp. 70 – 72, and, and *Buck*.

In April 2021, *Jane Mayer* reported that Lee Atwater got Reagan to start his campaign in Philadelphia, MS, the site of the 1964 murder of the three civil rights workers. Atwater also developed the story of Willie Horton for the George H. W. Bush campaign.

The disastrous performance of the Libertarian Party in the 1980 election confirmed for the Koch brothers that engaging in the political process did not accomplish their long-term goal. Instead of winning over the population to their philosophy the usual way by campaigning and governing, their sole strategy was to control society from outside the government. In keeping with the Koch brother's practices, they adopted a long-term view. If something didn't work—analyze the reason and then change tactics. To do this, they would assemble tons of money. And most important, work to make sure that the money you spend accomplishes the intended purpose.

The Donor Network

Led by Charles Koch, a few wealthy families decided to form a donor network of like-minded persons.

Two months before Lewis Powell was nominated by Nixon to the Supreme Court, he was commissioned to write a special memorandum for the business league. The five-thousand-word memo titled "Attack on American Free Enterprise System," was a call to the business community to get organized and fight for its very survival. It laid out a blueprint for a conservative takeover of the American political system. The plan showed how conservatives' business interests could reclaim American politics by a devastating surprise attack on the bloated bureaucracy. He wanted to create a popular public opinion network to counter what was called the elite press. This one would be privately funded to push the pro-business—and political agenda.

The Kochs found an ally in Lewis Powell. His memo got the attention and support of corporate giants that were willing and able to put big money into the cause. Among the first was Joseph Coors, the Colorado beer magnate. Like his parents, he was far to the right of most politicians and was a supporter of the John Birch Society. Coors thought all the government programs of the 1930s up to 1960s including organized labor and the civil rights movement, as well as the youth counterculture were ruining the country.

As a regent at the University of Colorado, Coors, had tried to bar left-wing speakers, faculty, and students on campus. His attempt to require faculty to take a pro-American loyalty oath was defeated by the other regents. Paul Weyrich who worked for Colorado senator Gordon Allot alerted Allot to the possibility of tapping into Coors money. Coors readily agreed and lobbied powerful Congresspersons for several years. The Coors family immediately enlisted. By the time Joseph Coors connected with Paul Weyrich, he already believed that the Right needed new and more militant national institutions of the kind Weyrich was pushing.

Another supporter was Richard Mellon Scaife, as noted above, an heir to the Mellon fortune. Richard Mellon Scaife, got his inheritance just as intellectuals on the right were debating the idea of building a movement to counter the liberals. Lewis Powell, the future Supreme Court justice, as noted above, was an early leading voice of the radical conservatives and was a member of Scaife's League to Save Carthage. Before being appointed to the Court, he was a prominent corporate lawyer from Richmond Virginia.

Keep in mind the names mentioned above— Robert LeFevre, Lewis Powell, Joseph Coors, Paul Weyrich, Richard Mellon Scaife, and the DeVos family. They all hated taxes, were afraid of universal voting, and had no interest in the common good for the nation.

Kochs' goal: to govern outside the government. This gives them all the power but none of the responsibilities of governing. Charles Koch, as noted below, swept in hundreds of national and state legislators to do his bidding.

Of course, rich patrons on both the left and right have long wielded disproportionate power in American politics. George Soros, a billionaire investor who underwrites liberal organizations and candidates, is often singled out for criticism by conservatives. But the Kochs in particular set a new standard. As Charles Lewis, the founder of the Center for Public Integrity, a non-partisan watchdog group put it, "The Kochs are on a whole different level. There's no one else who has spent this much money. The sheer dimension of it is what sets them apart. They have a pattern of lawbreaking, political manipulation, and obfuscation. I've been in Washington since Watergate and I've never seen anything like it. They are the Standard Oil of our time." *Mayer*, Page 7, 8.

> The issue here is not one of morality. On the moral level, George Soros and other Democratic big spenders are on the same moral level as the big spenders on the Right. What is different is that George Soros mostly acts alone. Those on the right led by the Koch brothers have an organization with many millionaires to funnel hundreds of millions into selected goals. And the Kochs in particular, in addition to their law-breaking and skirting the law, and as noted above, have used the federal tax laws to avoid millions in taxes. This enables them to spend lavishly on issues of their choice.
>
> Just spending money on elections doesn't necessarily get results. Ask Michael Bloomberg about his Year 2020 spending, first to get the Democratic nomination, then to win the Florida election for Biden.

The Kochs knew where they wanted to take the US. Their mantra has always been spending for <u>effectiveness</u>. They, along with scores of other millionaires and wealthy individuals, had practically unlimited money to put into their goal. The next step was to create a unified organization, that would take them from idea generation all the way to implementing the ideas through legislation, court challenges and to street demonstrations, disrupting candidates and elected officials, etc.

They created a linked system of 1) academic programs, 2) think tanks, 3) non-profit foundations,4) big donors and secret meetings, 5)) issue advocacy organizations, 6) federal and state elected officials, 7) the loud speakers of radio, TV, and 8) Tea Party groups all to make their money way more effective in accomplishing their objective.

> If the term "think tank" were not used so frequently in this discussion, I would put it in quotes each time. I would like to believe that a think tank is an organization that seeks to understand and interpret political, economic, and social issues. Instead, most of the organizations discussed here are not much more than mouthpieces for the super-rich who want to direct our society in ways that benefit them.

Among the other capabilities of the Kochs was organization and planning. They developed an incredible strategic plan that enabled them to push for their policies and all kinds of areas. And in control was Charles Koch who decided where money was spent—that is, for pro-large business and small, weak government. Funds were channeled in three directions. They made political contributions to party committees and candidates, such as Robert Dole.

Their business made contributions through its political action committee and exerted influence by lobbying. And they founded numerous nonprofit groups, which they filled with tax-deductible contributions from their foundations. This was coordinated with other wealthy activists who made political contributions, and engaged in lobbying. This strategy of control meant that their spending was way more effect than more random contributions. *Mayer*, pp. 176, 177, 178.

The group recognized that to make permanent changes, the next generation had to be brought on board. George Pearson, a former member of the John Birch Society in Wichita, who served as Charles Koch's political lieutenant during these years, advised that to attract young people to the movement they must be taught the conservative position in schools and colleges. Gifts to universities should have strings attached, requiring they be used to push the Libertarian ideological position. They must not follow the usual tradition of gifts made without strings attached. Their gifts, he argued, should be made on condition that the donor can influence academic staff hiring and other decisions and at the same time, hiding their aim of promoting radical conservatism.

Pearson taught that, "it would be necessary to use ambiguous and misleading names, obscure the true agenda, and conceal the means of control. This is the method that Charles Koch would soon practice in his charitable giving and later in his political actions." *Mayer*, pp. 68, 69.

To support building their own youth movement, the libertarian historian Leonard Liggio, a part of the Koch-funded Institute for Humane Studies from 1974 to 1998, urged using the successful model of the Nazis. In a paper titled *"National Socialist Political Strategy: Social Change in a Modern Industrial Society with an Authoritarian Tradition,"* Liggio described the Nazi's successful creation of a youth movement as **key to their capture of the state**. Like the Nazis, he suggested, libertarians should organize university students to create group identity. *Mayer*, p. 68.

Take Over of the Republican Party

Recall that David Koch ran as vice president of in 1980. With the failure of David Koch and the Libertarian Party to attract enough interest to compete with the Republican and Democratic Parties, the Kochs then went after the Republican Party to make it theirs.

The Party was already primed for this takeover. As covered above, William Buckley and Barry Goldwater set the Republican Party on a path of small government, anti-taxes, and racism. Richard Nixon followed up by his "Southern strategy" to bring the Southern Democrats into the Republican Party. Reagan made sure the white southerners stayed Republican by following Buckley/Goldwater and by lambasting welfare cheats—implying most of them were—and by his War on Drugs which targeted mainly Black Americans. For a fuller discussion of Reagan's War on Drugs, see, *Alexander*, The New Jim Crow, pp. 97 - 114.

Campaigning for the 1980 election, Ronald Reagan talked about "the big tent" for all Republicans. It wasn't long before many long time Party supporters and office holders learned that the tent didn't include them. Either change your philosophy and voting positions or you will find the Party supporting a more conservative candidate for your office. US Senator Arlen Specter, apparently was too liberal for the Party. He stood by his principles, but this cost him his Senate seat. His parting shot was to refer to those who undermined him as "cannibals" who seek "the end of governing as we know it." *MacLean*, pp. xxvii, xxix.

George H. W. Bush initially campaigned against Reagan's anti-tax philosophy, but then changed his tune after becoming vice president. He thus departed from his father, former senator Prescott Bush, who supported many of the programs of the Eisenhower administration. [Bush also, as did most politicians, accepted the findings of climate scientists and his administration participated in the first international summit of climate scientists. *Mayer*, p. 250]

In 2012, Senator Orrin Hatch of Utah, exploded after being targeted by a primary challenger: "These people are not conservatives. They are not Republicans. They're radical libertarians. ... I despise these people." But by 2018 Hatch was calling on fellow party members to obey the president. *MacLean*, pp. xxvii, xxix, xxx.

Mitt Romney, after years of supporting actions to reduce greenhouse gas emissions, changed his tune and in October 2012, declared that spending trillions and trillions of dollars to try to reduce carbon dioxide emissions is not the right course for us. Soon afterward, Romney proposed to cut all income tax rates by one-fifth. ... The Tax Policy Center said the proposal would add five trillion dollars to the federal deficit over the next decade. *Mayer*, p. 387.

Take Over Academia

Many rich people give significant amounts of money to colleges and universities. No doubt they are hopeful that the recipients use the money in a way that the donor wishes. But the almost universal expectation is to get their name on a plaque or maybe a building named after them. The Koch organization makes huge donors to colleges and universities—but with strings attached. Their money is to go to uses that they specify and they keep track to make sure that is happening. In their usual strategy, they want control.

Koch's most important control of an institution is George Mason University in Virginia in a suburb of Washington DC. *Mayer* cites *The Washington Post*, as the source for reporting that Koch family foundations donated around thirty million dollars to the school, with the Mercatus Center receiving the bulk of it. The beginning of the Mercatus operation took place at Rutgers University by Richard Fink but transferred to George Mason. Fink is a chief political adviser to Charles Koch. The Fink operation was based on Austrian economics—a system that considered "free" markets the basis of national wealth.

The Post said the Mercatus Center was a "staunchly anti-regulatory center funded largely by Koch Industries Inc." The Center was entirely funded by outside donations, largely from the Kochs, but it was physically located in the midst of the public university's campus, and used this to claim that the University was the source of developing knowledge of market-based economics.

With the Koch organization providing major funding and directing of the Mercatus Center, could the University claim that the Center fulfilled the expectations of universities to be for the purpose of advancing scientific knowledge, or was this just one way for the Kochs to lobby for its position? Clayton Coppin, a history professor at George Mason considered this question and concluded that the Mercatus Center was "a lobbying group disguised as a disinterested academic program." Moreover, as Coppin pointed out, the Kochs could take tax deductions for charitable contributions but were actually a lobbying operation for them. Free market economists and Nobel prize winners, Vernon Smith and Tyler Cowen found a friendly home at the Center.

But this is not all of the embedding itself into George Mason U. Another Koch organization, the Institute for Humane Studies moved from California to the campus of George Mason University was set up in the same building as the Mercatus Center. This Institute was established by F. A. "Baldy" Harper. Harper was a firm believer in "free markets." His idea of free markets was that taxes were theft, welfare was immoral, labor unions were slavery, and freedom required opposition to court-ordered racial integration. The stated mission of IHS was to groom libertarian intellectuals by doling out scholarships, sponsoring seminars, and placing students in internships at like-minded organizations. *Mayer*, pp. 182, 183. Recall that George Mason had already become a center of free-market research and scholarship.

Now we again bring up James Buchanan, the founder of "pubic choice" theory and Nobel prize-winner. Charles Koch became enamored with Buchanan in the 1970s and worked with him to develop his ideas. Buchanan's philosophy was that elected officials and government workers were nothing more than people that were looking out for themselves— there is no such thing as a public servant.

No surprise, this was popular with those that thought the only proper role of government was to protect private property. Koch thought Buchanan's ideas could transform America into the truly capitalist society that Koch wanted. Both men agreed that this transformation had to be done without going through the political process because it would take a long time for the public to accept these ideas. Therefore, the process of transformation had to be done by stealth—put things in place before most of society realized what was happening. *McLean* p. xxii.

When Buchanan moved from the University of Virginia to George Mason University, Koch's money went with him. Recall that Buchanan moved to the George Mason University economics department after being invited to leave the University of Virginia.

George Mason's economics department, is responsible as much as any place to put the US on the path of today's emphasis on lower taxes and restricting federal programs. The lower taxes were mainly by reducing income tax rates on high income taxpayers—restricting government programs were directed to social programs, consumer safety, and industrial safety. The economist, Paul Craig Roberts, an adjunct professor at GMU, was the intellect behind the Reagan tax cuts. A testament to its clout; Mercatus recommended 14 of the 23 federal rules targeted on the incoming Bush Administration's regulatory "hit list." *Mayer*, pp. 182, 183, 184, and *Schulman* p. 262.

GMU is where the idea of supply side economics was made part of the Reagan administration. Supply side economics supposes that the economy is helped the most by encouraging businesses and industries to produce more. Little attention is given to whether consumers are able or willing to buy what is produced. The countervailing theory is that if consumers and businesses have the money, they will buy the items of their choosing from what is available. The latter is the basis for stimulus spending starting in the 1930s and has been used—where politicians allow—on each time there is serious downturn in the economy, such as the 2008 financial disaster.

At West Virginia University, the Charles Koch Foundation's donation of $965,000 to create the Center for Free Enterprise again came with some strings attached. The foundation required the school to give it a say over the professors it funded, in violation of traditional standards of academic independence. A strategy here was to target a small organization, and in this case a poor state, so it could dominate its programs. Moreover, coal mining was the dominant industry in the state—Kochs, as noted earlier—has a large stack in fossil fuel industries.

At Florida State University, Charles was not a passive donor. He provided $1.5 million to hire economics professors but on condition that Charles could veto candidates for the jobs. *Schulman*, p. 265.

Supporters of the Koch organization claimed that the donations were made to diversify the ideas on college campuses. But critics pointed out that much of the work coming from this support lacks the scientific vigor that is a hallmark of university research. One of the funded projects was a book edited by Russell Sobel called "Unleashing Capitalism: Why Prosperity Stops at the West Virginia Border and How to Fix It, arguing that mine safety and clean water regulations only hurt workers." *Mayer*, pp. 189, 190.

The Koch organization spread millions of dollars to colleges and universities. It was always evaluating its efforts to determine how effective they were—by measuring results. To do this on campuses, they increased the size of student seminars to get a better sample. Then, a test was given at the beginning of the week and again one at the end to find out if their political beliefs had changed during the week. Another activity was to scrutinize scholarship applications to see how many times the "right names" … were mentioned—regardless of what was said about them!" *Schulman*, Page 250, 251.

Getting the study results that Koch wanted was only the first step. The next was to get these academic papers out into the public in a form that the general public would read and understand.

For this, Charles Koch hired Abel Winn, a former student at the Mercatus Center. Winn was made a director of a joint project Koch Industries and Wichita State University, to test how well the MBM matched reality and look for ways to an academic center that would "test the veracity of Market Based Manangement's claims and pioneer new discoveries about markets and human behavior." The new partnership was called the MBM Center at WSU. Wichita State administration provided several classrooms to house the center. *Leonard,* Page 369.

Think Tanks

Another strategy focused on grooming the <u>intellectual class</u> through education, research funding, and other efforts—who would, in turn, shape public opinion and influence lawmakers. The "intellectual war" George Pearson said, would not be won overnight. "It took years to bring this country around to believing that government could solve problems better than the market, and it will take years to get rid of that destructive notion. **Belief that government participation is necessary or helpful and that governments are beneficial needs to be challenged.**"

The Cato Institute opened in early 1977, with Ed Crane as its leader, Murray Rothbard its top scholar, and Charles Koch provide much of the funding. Charles decided to establish the Cato Institute under the laws of Kansas whose laws allowed nonprofits to issue stock shares. By knowing how to get what they wanted, this allowed Crane, Charles Koch and Rothbard to appoint the think tank's board members and control Cato's mission. *Schulman,* p.103.

"Who is against liberty? Or prosperity, which we are told, comes as a bonus with it?" wrote social critic Ernest Van Den Haag in Cato's magazine cover story. "But how to get it, and keep, both? The libertarian answer is beguilingly simple: **the government is the problem, not the solution.** Do away with it, and we will all be free and prosperous. Society has been wrong for the last few thousand years in making laws and demanding obedience to them. *Schulman,* p.107. Is this where Reagan got his idea?

A disaffected Libertarian, Samuel Konkin III, coined the term "Kochtopus" to describe the many tentacle operations funded by Charles, whom he accused of trying to "buy the major Libertarian institutions—not the Party—and run the movement as other plutocrats run all other political parties in capitalist societies." *Schulman*, p.108.

In addition to The Cato Institute, we have The Heritage Foundation, and the Mercatus Center itself, among dozens of others all with the same message. Favorite topics were, arguing for the privatization of Social Security, accusing public employee unions of causing state budget crisis, attempting to debunk climate science, and making the case for slashing the welfare system and Medicaid. Sound familiar?

Bringing Big Donors Together

When we hear "oligarchy" we think of Russia and perhaps other nations that we try to distance ourselves from. Definitely, most of us never thought that there was a real possibility that the US would become and oligarchy. But some analysts say it is already happening. Jeffrey Winters, a professor at Northwestern University who studies oligarchies says it is already here where the wealthy are bending our politics to serve them and not the general public. As the authors cited here have noted, these oligarchs don't rule directly, but rather force office holders to vote for the agenda of the oligarchs. This force is applied by withdrawing campaign support, excluding them from seminars and conferences, and running candidates against wayward office holders. Columbia University professor Joseph Stiglitz, a Nobel Prize-winning economist, put it, "Wealth begets power, which begets wealth." *Mayer*, pp, 14, 15.

> And above all, where we are and where we are going has been and is being done in stealth, without large bodies of the population knowing what is going on. It has taken extra effort by journalists and others to find out that well-funded power groups push a

lot of legislation and attempt to hide their activities
from the public.

Wealthy opponents of government have donated to politicians and lobbying groups for decades. Each have their own agenda. The Koch organization, again emphasizing effectiveness, organized several of these big donors into a group so that it could agree on common goals—primarily to take over and change American politics. Donors includes individuals and families mentioned above, and adds more. These were: the Kochs; Richard Mellon Scaife; the Coors brewing family of Colorado; the DeVos family of Michigan, founders of the Amway marketing empire; Harry and Lynde Bradley who had gotten rich from defense contracts; and John M. Olin, a chemical and munitions company titan. *Mayer*, pp. 6, 7, 13, 14.

The next step was to bring others into the group—they didn't need to be ultra-wealthy, only to have the same political goals as the Koch organization. To coordinate, seminars were set up. Getting an invitation meant that you had arrived. Participants could rub shoulders with the movers and shakers of conservative politics, including Supreme Court Justices Antonin Scalia, and Clarence Thomas, congressmen, senators, governors, and celebrities. (I know, Supreme Court Justices aren't supposed to be called politicians—judge for yourself.)The Kochs set up periodic seminars with this group and other like-minded wealthy. The participants at the Koch seminars reflected the broader growth in conservative causes. *Mayer*, pp. 13, 14.

Not to miss an opportunity, the seminars added on major fund-raising from the group. This topped any previous money raised and spent on campaigning and lobbying. *The Washington Post's* Dan Balz observed, "When W. Clement Stone, an insurance magnate and philanthropist gave two million dollars (eleven million in today's dollars) to Richard M. Nixon's 1972 campaign, it caused public outrage." In contrast, for the 2016 election, funds accumulated by the Kochs and their small circle of friends was projected to be $889 million. *Mayer*, pp. 11 - 14

All preparations and arrangements for conferences were done by the Koch organization. Smartphones, computers, recording devices were banned. White noise makers were planted all around the periphery to prevent outsiders from listening in. If anyone was found to have disclosed what went on at the conference that was the end of their participation. *Mayer*, pp. 12, 13.

To make sure the public was kept in the dark about these gatherings, there was the utmost in secrecy about them. One might think it was a gathering of Churchill and Roosevelt held in the middle of a war zone. The agenda and participants were kept secret, participants were not to talk to the media, nor keep any notes or records of what happened. Secrecy about the conferences was everything. "There is anonymity that we can protect," Kevin Gentry, vice president for special project at Koch Industries and vice president of the Charles G. Koch Charitable Foundation, told participants, according to a recording that later leaked out. *Mayer*, pp. 12, 13, *Fang* p. 11.It is hard to imagine why there was such secrecy. The only answer I can think of is that they were extremely afraid of what the American public would think of their positions.

Billionaires and multi-millionaires dominated these conferences especially during the Obama administration. Of the eighteen billionaires attending, their combined fortunes were more than $214 billion in 2015. "In fact, more billionaires participated anonymously in the Koch planning sessions during the first term of the Obama presidency than there were billionaires in 1982, when *Fortune* began listing the four hundred richest Americans." *Mayer*, pp. 13, 14.

A related organization was started by Paul Weyrich. His operation was periodic lunches with right-wing groups and became known as the Weyrich lunches. Their viewpoint was close to the Koch organization and had some of the same participants. Sponsors of the lunch include the 60 Plus Association, designed to attract senior citizens, Let Freedom Ring, a group funded partially by John Templeton, Jr. a billionaire who pushed the agenda for Christian evangelicals, the American Society for the Defense of Tradition, Family and Property, an extremist Catholic organization, Judicial Watch, the Right to Work Committee, Family Research Council, James Dobson's political organization, etc. *Fang*, pp. 52, 53, 54.

Even though I question whether elected officials should be closely associated with the Weyrich luncheons, Republican elected leaders became regular attendees. Congressman—and later vice president—Mike Pence have also gravitated more and more to the lunch. During the first two years of the Obama administration, Pence committed to attend every meeting, or send John Boehner or Eric Cantor to report on what was going on in the Republican caucus as well as upcoming legislation. This had the potential of informing on Republican officeholders that were not adhering to the agenda of luncheon organizers. Some Republican lawmakers at the Lunch have been attacked and had to explain any votes the leaders thought violated right-wing values. A 2004 *National Review* article about the general atmosphere of the lunch described it as inquisitional. *Fang*, pp. 52, 53, 54.

> I think it is legitimate to question whether elected officials (and as reported below, Supreme Court Justices) should attend such sessions.

When Obama was elected president, this apparently threw many in the right-wing power structure and wealthy individuals and families into a massive defense position. Who knows how much was race-related, but remember the Republican Party has largely eliminated members with tolerant racial views beginning with Buckley/Goldwater in the 1960s?

As soon as it was confirmed that Obama had won, another related group assembled, this one emphasizing more political conservatives rather than just multi-millionaires. L Brent Bozwell III, with family connections to the Goldwater campaign, organized a meeting. Twenty conservative leaders plus several others joined to discuss where the right-wing movement should go from here. Some of the leaders were, Grover Norquist, Richard Viguerie, Greg Mueller, head of the right-wing PRA firm Creative Response Concepts, Tony Perkins of the Family Research Council, Leonard Leo, an executive member of the Federalist Society, the Leadership Institute's Morton Blackwell, pollster (later advisor to President Trump) Kelllyane Conway, and conservative publisher Al Regnery. *Fang*, pp.44, 45

Fang used as a source the *Washington Times*, to report that most of the attendees were glad that they didn't have to explain the views of George W. Bush and John McCain. (Remember, McCain had introduced legislation to control campaign financing and was known to be concerned about global warming. Bush's description of himself as a compassionate conservation didn't sit well with many on the right.) The goal was not to control the Republican Party, but to bend it to the group's will.

The primary focus of the participants was on the 2010 midterm elections and 2012 presidential election. The most important work for them was to defeat Obama, according to R. Emmet Tyrell, editor of the *American Spectator*, who attended the meeting. *New York Times* columnist, David Brooks was attacked for endorsing Obama, and calls were made to evict centrists from the GOP. The plea was for big increases in contributions and for purifying the message in the steps of Sarah Palin. The goal was clear, "the conservative movement is going to retake America," predicted Bozell to the *Washington Times* after the meeting. *Fang*, pp.44, 45

Steve LaTourette, a longtime Republican moderate congressman from Ohio who was a close friend of Boehner's explained, "in the past, it was rare that someone would run against an incumbent in their own party. But the money that these outside groups have is what gives these people courage to run against an incumbent." He described the outside donors as "a bunch of rich people who you can count on maybe two hands who have an inordinate impact." *Mayer*, pp. 211, 212.

This manuscript was written before President Obama's book came out. He reports what he belatedly learned about the Koch operation, which tracks closely what is presented here. "They didn't want compromise and consensus. They wanted war." *Obama*, see especially, pp. 250, 251.

Newspaper Columnists, Magazine Writers, Elected Officials, The Tea Party and Related Groups

Writers looking for material to use for a newspaper column or magazine article could find ready sources in the conservative think tanks. As a reader of political magazines and articles over the years, I now recognize where the material came from. Important topics have been, opposing the Affordable Care Act, denial of global warming, and opposing campaign financing reform. **The reader of such material, unless informed by the knowledge provided by the books used for this Topic, would be unaware that the end purpose of all this source material was to replace our democracy with an oligarchy.**

The next link in Kochs' takeover of the nation was to give all-out support to the Tea Party. The Kochs did not create the Tea Party movement, but saw it as the vehicle to complete their total control of public policy. This followed the long line of groups—noted in previous Parts of this book—of the powerful convincing those on the lower end of our social and economic system that their interests and those of the most powerful were the same, so they must organize against those "others" who are trying to destroy "the American system."

In Topic I, of this book, we see how the English and Dutch elites treated other ethnic groups, in particular, the Ulster Irish with disgust and used them to push to the western frontiers to occupy land and do battle with the residents—the Indigenous people, thus making it safer for the landowning class to move into the territory. This was also the time when the elite worked to create in the minds of those outside this circle, such as the Ulster Irish, that their interests were the same as the elites and that they should join the elites against the African captives.

In Topic III, especially in the South, the powerful repeated the propaganda to convince the white populations who had little power that their interests were the same as the powerful and that therefore they must join with the powerful to destroy any power that the descendants of Africans might have. This spawned the KKK and similar organizations that are with us today.

Today's version is the Tea Party. Koch and others claim their interests are in line with the Tea Party. This vehicle is used for Topic IV (the one here) and for the issue covered in Topic V. As in earlier versions, the powerful has convinced most of the Tea Party crowd that they should support issues that actually are harmful to them—opposing health care systems that would be of tremendous benefit to them and opposing efforts to control global warming.

Of course, not all wealthy people are money grubbing. But without government protection, the wealthy can: 1) market dangerous products, 2) build dangerous equipment, 3) require people to work in unsafe conditions, 4) hoodwink people with some money to invest in products that mostly benefit the financial brokers and leave the investor worse off than before he or she invested, 5) sell faulty insurance products—life, health, casualty, property, that make money for the insurers, but provide limited protection for the buyers, 6) operate industries that cause air pollution and global warming, 8) destroy the environment in the process of extracting some natural resource, and 9) destroy wildlife.

But you may say, organizations such as labor unions provide some of these services and protections. True, but labor unions exist only if the government allows them—remember Scott Walker of Wisconsin.

Former Congressman Dick Armey, had the original idea of a grass roots organization to push right wing causes. He had thought of doing this for the tobacco industry in 1992 to fight regulation of that industry. Imagine being on the side of known killers. For a while he was chairman of Koch's Citizens for a Sound Economy (CSE). CSE got its start by pushing for a flat income tax. CSE later broke into a new group chaired by David Koch, called Americans for Prosperity, and another merged with a group called Empower America to form FreedomWorks, which Armey led.

When the Tea Party caught the public's attention in 2009, the Koch brothers grabbed onto the Tea Party's opposition to big government. Kochs turned the Tea Party activists into supporting big business, rather than opposing it, as they had been doing. From this, Eric Odum formed what he called the Nationwide Tea Party Coalition with other activists from FreedomWorks and Americans for Prosperity.

> I suspect readers may get bored with all the organization names. There is no need to remember them all. The purpose for naming them is to show the vast network, but also it is often the case that new organizations are formed just to make it hard to follow them all. A new one with a patriotic name or neutral-sounding name may attract adherents who are not aware of the underlying goals.

The Koch brothers controlled and funded groups supporting the Tea Party such as the Institute for Humane Studies, the Reason Foundation, the Bill of Rights Foundation, the Cato Institute, Americans for Prosperity, and the Institute for Justice. Along with think tanks, media allies, etc. the Tea Party was ready made for them to take over, which they proceeded to do. *Mayer*, Page 206. *Fang*, p. 111.

The Tea Partiers held a rally soon after Obama was inaugurated but a more powerful one was held on April 15, 2009—they called it national tax day. This time there were rallies across the country with a total of around 300,000 participants. In case there was any doubt who was sponsoring these rallies, speakers, talking points, press releases, transportation, and other logistical support were provided by The Heritage Foundation, the Cato Institute, and Americans for Prosperity. Lee Fang in his web site *ThinkProgress*, found that Americans for Prosperity was suddenly planning protests "coast to coast" and FreedomWorks seemed to have taken over. They sail in pass out material, take some pictures and they're off.

Thomas Frank, author of *What's the Matter with Kansas?*, observed that **"it's a major accomplishment for sponsors like the Kochs that they've turned corporate self-interest into a movement among people on the streets."** *Mayer*, pp. 221, 222.

A major link in the controlled operation is the likes of Glenn Beck. He was the most prominent voice of the American Tea Party movement. Beck's show is credited with creating the 2009 Tea Party movement. So now we have the chain from Dick Armey to the Koch brothers to media celebrities Glenn Beck and Sean Hannity.

In January 2009, several House Republicans got together to defeat Obama's program. At a retreat, these congressmen chose as the model to emulate was the Taliban. Texas congressman, Pete Sessions, showed how this group could wage "asymmetric warfare." He presented the case that they were not here to govern, but to become the majority. This group became the Tea Party caucus in Congress. *Mayer*, pp. 211, 212.

On Tea Party rally day April 15, 2009, at least 35 Republican members of Congress spoke at rallies in their home districts. The idea was to bring the crowds to a frenzy. Republican Senator Vitter of Louisiana introduced legislation formally honoring April 15 as "National Tea Party Day." Also, Republican governors, Rick Perry of Texas and Mark Sanford of South Carolina, addressed Tea Parties and declared they would block stimulus aid to their state designed to get the nation out of the 2008 recession (both later backtracked and accepted the money). Mark Kirk, a leader of the Republican Main Street Partnership, suggested that the Democratic governor of Illinois ought to be assassinated over proposed tax increases. *Fang*, pp. 40, 41.

> The stimulus bill before Congress was a time-tested approach used extensively in the 1930s to get the nation's economy going again after plunging into the Great Depression. What was enacted in 2009 was, by many accounts, only about a third as much as was needed. As a result, the recovery after the 2008 recession took much longer than it would have if it had been more adequately funded.

Some of the organizers of Tea Parties may have thought they would be a force to deal with the inequality of income and job opportunities they were experiencing. They most likely had in mind that they would be a protest group to oppose the breaks that the super-rich were enjoying, such as the massive tax reductions going to the super rich since the days of the Reagan Administration and continuing on to the twenty-first century. Any Tea Partiers who expected support from the Koch organization and allies to deal with income inequality have been gravely let down.

But the Koch machine tapped into another strong issue—gun rights. So Kochs lent their support for keeping gun rights totally off the congressional agenda.

The Obama Administration was taken almost totally by surprise by the vigor of the Tea Partiers. As was John Boehner, who had recently been elected as Speaker of the House of Representatives, and a few years later resigned, singing Zip-a-dee-do-da as he rid himself of the albatross of the Tea Party.

What soon became obvious was that the big money interests were dictating the issues pushed at Tea Party rallies. Not only because major speakers at these rallies were Koch allies, but often some of the Tea Party members were given scripts and talking points that they had little idea what they were talking about. Lee Fang interviewed Jenny Beth Martin, one of the most visible leaders of the Tea Party movement. Fang asked her about the Republican pledge to defund the Consumer Protection Agency, one of the hallmarks of Obama's financial regulatory reform laws. She said she had no idea. Then later she said she would have someone from a conservative think tank, such as the American Enterprise Institute, "come and talk about Wall Street reform, so that she could make a decision." *Fang,* p. 9. So much for taking power by the lower and middle class.

Eric Odom, once connected to the Sam Adams Alliance, was responsible for creating Tea Party groups then using his connections to create web sites to grow and be on message across the country. All of Odom's sites are centrally-planned and operated. Some Tea Party groups he created, like the Patriot Caucus, were aimed at a national audience, others were very localized. But they all came from the top. This is this reverse of the popular understanding that Tea Party groups come "from the people." David Axelrod, Obama's senior adviser, said, "What they don't say is that this is a grassroots citizens' movement brought to you by a bunch of oil billionaires." *Fang,* pp. 165, 166.

Every major Tea Party organization was connected to Odom's communication web. Smart Girl Politics, with the help of Odom, created a web site for Tea Party women. Ginna Thomas, wife of Supreme Court Justice Clarence Thomas, used her Liberty Central group to help Tea Party organizations in Florida build web sites. Other organizations aided or even created were, Libertus Global Partners created Regular Folks United. And, sold its list of addressees to corporate and political interests.

Grassroots Action, Inc., which had led anti-immigration protests for years re-named itself ResistNet and became a Tea Party organization. Republican Party sources operatives and consultants control what goes out. They send out material to very local situations asking Tea Party groups to support or oppose issues making it sound like it was created locally. *Fang*, pp. 165, 166. *Fang* cites other similar examples.

Other organizations saw the power of the Tea Party and joined in. Gun Owners of America mobilized Tea Parties by claiming that Obama was going to confiscate everyone's gun. Neo-Nazi websites like Stormfront immediately seized upon the Tea Parties as recruiting tools. Pro-life activists attended Tea Parties en masse to protest Obama's pro-life beliefs. Local Republican volunteer groups, the State Policy Network of state-based conservative think tanks, and of course various strands of the libertarian movement, found a big tent in the Tea Party movement. *Fang*, p. 39.

These are prime examples of how the wealthy use the middle- and low- income people to do their bidding. The Consumer Protection Agency is an example of an agency designed to protect most people who are attracted to the Tea Party. Yet, the anti-government push leads them to oppose the agency. As a larger issue, the wealthy have to a large extent convinced the middle- and lower-income people that government in general is bad—is against their interests. Actually, government is the source that can, if it is working properly, protect middle- and lower-income people from the wealthy.

After the money groups had inserted themselves into the Tea Party, the Tea Party started requesting money for themselves. The Tea Party Patriots presented a wish list to the Council for National Policy.* They wanted $110,000 for campaigning, $250,000 for GPS-enabled smartphone walk lists, and in keeping with the way big money people operate, $125,000 for "collateral material," meaning whatever we want it for.

*CNP and allies met once a week with White House officials under President Trump. *Washington Post*, January 18, 2021.

For efforts after the election, they wanted $110,000 for fighting legislation in Congress, $175,000 to entertain newly elected Tea Party politicians, $500,000 for "Younger Generation Outreach" at least $500,000 for a renewed advertising budget, $200,000 for help organizing tax day Tea Parties in 2011, in addition to other requests. *Fang*, p.11.

You may be surprised that some of your supposed friends got on the band wagon and received support from Koch-funded organizations. The health insurance company Aetna apparently accidentally revealed that it poured some $7 million into undisclosed nonprofits, like the American Action Network to help elect Tea Party Republicans promising to repeal health-care reform. To help this along, the front group, American Majority held nearly 400 training sessions on how to abuse platforms like Twitter to spread their cause. *Fang*, p. 146, 171.

All of this activity created the impression among many that the Tea Party had attracted a significant portion of the population. However, the *New York Times* estimated that at most, it had the support of 18 percent of the population. And the researcher Devin Burghart estimated that the core group was about 330,000. So, this size is not unusual. But the use of the internet, a ready source of unlimited money, and popularization by newspaper and radio supporters pushed it to center stage. *Mayer*, Page 241.

In April, 2009, a Koch company spokesperson, denied that the Kochs had direct links to the Tea Party, saying that Americans for Prosperity is "an independent organization and Koch companies do not in any way direct their activities." Later, she issued a statement: "No funding has been provided by Koch companies, the Koch foundations, or Charles Koch or David Koch specifically to support the tea parties." David Koch said, "I've never been to a Tea Party event. No one representing the Tea Party has ever even approached me."

Here is a different story. Peggy Venable, who was head of the Texas chapter of Americans for Prosperity was proud of her involvement in the Tea Party. At a Koch-sponsored event called Defending the American Dream. She said, "I was a member of the Tea Party before it was cool."

She later described how Americans for Prosperity helped "educate" the activists. They give the supporters "next-step training," so that they can be more effective. They gave activists lists of politicians to target in their demonstrations. Venable spoke without checking with Koch operatives and said, "they're certainly our people. David's chairman of our board. I've met with them and am certainly appreciative of what they do. We love what the Tea Partiers do because that's how we're going to take America back." *Mayer* pp. 222, 223.

Take Control of State Governments

As this century has gone forward, *MacLean* shows us a growing trend where the radical right has more frequently gone farther than just pushing conservative causes. The push is to diminish the power of government to protect those with less political power. The right has found, if they didn't already know, that many State governments are rather weak. This means that money spent to influence policy at this level has a potential for great rewards. Most State legislatures meet for a limited time each session and this is only a part-time responsibility for the legislators. Unlike federal legislators, most in the state have other ways of earning their living. Because of this, they are vulnerable to groups who provide research, write proposals, etc. to help the legislators get through their restricted schedules and resources.

Therefore, State legislators have been fertile ground for the Koch organization to essentially take over State governments. This has happened in surprising places. For decades, Wisconsin has been a reliable liberal area. Without most of the country being aware of what was happening, Scott Walker was elected governor. Walker wasted no time letting the world know what his political positions were. *MacLean*, p. xvii.

In 2011, Walker attacked public employee unions. He claimed that the unions had illegally bound the State to pay the employees what was agreed to in their contract with their employer, the State of Wisconsin.

Only the state legislature, he argued, could authorize state expenditures. His solution was to do whatever it took to destroy the union. He had no interest in compromising or re-negotiating what was in the contract, even though the unions had already agreed to re-negotiate the agreement. His attacks on the union were more about establishing his political credentials than to solve a State budget issue. This led to great political turmoil. *MacLean*, p. xviii.

New Jersey Governor Chris Christie joined in attacking teachers. The teachers and many others were bewildered by these attacks apparently coming out of nowhere. *MacLean*, p. xviii.

In this environment, several states rushed to cut funding for public education and support charter schools as well as subsidies for private education. Another attack on education was state universities and colleges that have long been associated with economic development and the source of pride for many states. These included Wisconsin, North Carolina, Louisiana, Mississippi, and Iowa. Chancellors who dared to resist their agenda were fired. *MacLean*, p. xviii.

The biggest threat to democracy has been the work to suppress voting. With the passage of the Voting Rights Act of 1965 which prohibited the practices in the South to disenfranchise Black voters, the objective has been the same, but the tactics more subtle and varied. Requiring voter ID, making it harder to register to vote, scrubbing registered voter rolls to remove targeted groups, opposing mail in voting, closing voter polling sites in Black areas, and more. These have been targeted at a few voting groups including black and brown citizens, and younger voters. These groups have the common characteristic of overwhelmingly voting Democratic. Not since Reconstruction was defeated has there been so much work to disenfranchise voters.

> I have maintained that requiring voter ID is not a crazy idea. This could be done if phased in over a few years. When registering to vote, the State Boards

of Elections could issue a voter ID. And those that are already registered could be required to, say over a two-year period, arrange to get a voter ID card from the Election Board.

After this multi-state drive to weaker unions, public schools and access to voting became more obvious, journalists and professionals began getting information and analyzing what was found. William Cronon, a University of Wisconsin historian and at the time, the incoming president of the American Historical Association, looked into the Wisconsin governor's attack on employee unions. He reported that it had originated from outside the state and was a part of a well-planned and well–coordinated national campaign." He suggested that others find out more about the American Legislative Exchange Council (ALEC).

ALEC had been trying to stay out of the public awareness, but at the same time had produced hundreds of "model bills" provided mostly to Republican legislators. Around 20 percent of these had been enacted. In addition to laws to weaken labor unions, those to change tax laws, eliminate environmental protections, move public lands to private ownership, and do battle against undocumented immigrants. *Wikipedia,* August 2020.

Even though it is entirely legitimate for any member of the public to be searching into a topic of importance to them, Cronon was the target of attacks for looking into how the politics of Wisconsin changed so fast. He wrote a blog, What's was going on? "Who's Really Behind Recent Republican Legislation in Wisconsin and Elsewhere, (Hint: It Didn't Start Here) Scholar as Citizen (blog) March 15, 2011. *Wikipedia,* August 2020.

The Wisconsin Republican Party among other things demanded that they have access to his private e-mails on the topic of the Wisconsin election, arguing that as a professor, his private e-mails should be made public. David Walsh, GOP Files FOIA Request for UW Madison

Professor William Cronon's E-mails," History News Network, March 25, 2011. *Wikipedia*, August 2020.

In back-and-forth exchanges, Cronon stated that he was not strongly partisan in his views, but the attacks on him did more to confirm for him that indeed there was an outside campaign to take over Wisconsin politics. His critics claimed he was a liberal all along and was just cloaking his political position in academic wraps. *Wikipedia*, August 2020.

Thomas A. Roe of South Carolina founded the State Policy Network in 1992, a national coalition of conservative state-based think tanks. By 2012, the network had sixty-four separate think tanks, including at least one in every state. In North Carolina, both of the think tanks founded by the Pope fortune (see below) were members. The organization's president, Tracie Sharp, described each as "fiercely independent." But they could only choose from the SPN menu. "Pick what you need," she said, and customize it for what works best for you." Roe has been reported to have told a fellow at the Heritage Foundation, "You capture the Soviet Union—I'm going to capture the states." *Mayer*, pp. 424, 425, 428.

In 2011, the SPN's budget was $83 million. Coordinating with the think tanks were over a hundred "associates" members that included conservative nonprofit groups like Americans for Prosperity, the Cato Institute, the Heritage Foundation, and Grover Norquist's Americans for Tax Reform, which the Koch also helped to fund. *Mayer*, pp. 424, 428.

Perhaps independently, Ed Gillespie, a Republican Party official, came up with a plan after Obama's election. This was to go to the state level and work there to gain Republican control. His idea was to create REDMAP, Redistricting Majority Project. To implement his idea, he got control of the Republican State Leadership Committee (RSLC) because he needed funding for his project. He got funding from tobacco companies, Altria and Reynolds, Walmart, the pharmaceutical industries, and other private donors including the Kochs.

His target state was North Carolina. Local politicians joined in to provide insights into state politics. One such notable person was Art

Pope. Pope had many connections with the Koch organization, one of which was to serve on the board of Americans for Prosperity. In spite of never holding public office nor serving in some capacity for a political party, he had worked for years to move North Carolina politics sharply to the right. His entry in the process was his money.

Pope went out to find candidates with his views and supported them in elections—and also used negative advertising against the opponents. Pope was well-acquainted with the Kochs and spent a summer program with the Cato Institute, attended the Koch donor conferences, and served on the Board of Americans for Prosperity, and previous years had contributed heavily to shift North Carolina politics to the right. The first focus of this effort was to find candidates for election or re-election and target selected ones with negative and false advertising. *Mayer*, pp. 300 – 307, 321, 322.

Between Pope's activities and Gillespie's REDMAP data and activities, their favored candidates took over the North Carolina legislature. Then they went about gerrymandering the state's congressional districts so that Republicans won even more congressional seats. *Mayer*, pp. 410, 411.

Similar efforts in other states enabled Republicans to hold on to the majority in the US House. Kochs used what they learned in North Carolina to control other state governments. *Mayer*, pp. 410, 411.

A primary part of the operation was the time-tested method of gerrymandering to get the districts redrawn so that likely liberal voters were concentrated in as few districts as possible, thus they would likely have fewer districts where their candidates could win. In North Carolina, with the use of modern data techniques they could get voting preferences of populations down to the smallest geographic locations. Then they could draw the congressional districts to suit their objective.

This was run by a Tom Hofeller who was paid $166,000 by a group called the State Government Leadership Foundation. The Hofeller group used extreme measures to make sure their work was done in secret. To get the maximum benefit for its money, it went through the Republican State Leadership Committee which in turn was created by the group that Gillespie used to run REDMAP. This was actually an offshoot of the group that Gillespie had used to run REDMAP, but unlike the parent group, the offshoot was a 501 (c) (4) "social welfare" organization that could conceal the identities of its donors. *Mayer*, pp. 411, 412. With some exceptions, a 501(c)(4) organization is not required to disclose their donors publicly. According to OpenSecrets.com, spending by organizations that do not disclose their donors increased from less than $5.2 million in 2006 to well over $300 million during the 2012 election season, but has declined since then.

Presumably, the Republican State Leadership Committee is not to be confused with any aspect of the Republican Party.

> Gerrymandering is not confined to those on the Right. In Maryland, a heavily Democratic state, gerrymandering was used to draw contorted congressional districts after the 2010 census to cause the defeat of Republican candidates. Leaders in this process were US Congressman Steny Hoyer, and then governor, Martin O'Malley.

Gerrymandering was invented early in our history, even before it was named. The first use was by Patrick Henry to defeat James Madison who was at the time a candidate for a congressional seat. It has always been with us. But after *Citizens United*, it has been the method of the unelected rich. *Citizens United* makes it easy to hide who is funding what.

This money supported the large expense of going down to the precinct level to identify voting history so that districts can be drawn with great precision. There is sometimes no pretense that a district is contiguous. Streets and highways are all that connects parts of some districts. "The Kochs were instrumental in getting the GOP to take over state legislatures," observed David Axelrod. "The GOP is top-down, but the Kochs had a different plan, which was to organize the grass roots. It's smart. There's no equivalent on the Democratic side." *Mayer* pp. 411, 412.

Within a few months, the North Carolina legislature had overhauled the state's tax code and budget from top to bottom. On almost every issue, the proposals came directly from two think tanks, the John Locke Foundation and the Civitas Institute, which were founded by Pope and largely funded by the Pope family's $150 million John William Pope Foundation. Pope funded more than 97 percent of Civitas' budget—some $8 million since its founding in 2005. Critics said this was as Pope's way of pushing the state's politics ever farther to the right. Pope's defense—I don't own Civitas. He was, however, on its board of directors and rejected the description. The Pope family also had supplied about 80 percent of the John Locke Foundation's funding. Most of the rest came from tobacco companies and two Koch family foundations. *Mayer*, p. 416.

Pope's actions in North Carolina were somewhat of a model for doing the same in other states. The network of the super-rich was operating in almost every state by 2012, when Obama was re-elected.

On top of all this, an umbrella group the American Legislative Exchange Council (ALEC)—started by Paul Weyrich—was especially active at the state level. Richard Mellon Scaife provided most of the startup funding. It is a venue for thousands of businesses and trade groups to meet in closed-door sessions with elected officials to draft legislation and then present it as their own. So far, ALEC has averaged producing about a thousand new bills a year, some two hundred of which became state law. Users are cautioned not to mention that ALEC was the origin of the proposals. The State Policy Network's think tanks, some twenty-nine of which were members of ALEC provided legislative research. *Mayer*, pp. 424, 428.

Before ALEC, little attention was given to state legislatures. But Paul Weyrich saw an opportunity. As noted, state legislators were often overworked and underpaid. So, at relatively little cost, ALEC could greatly influence state lawmaking. He was right. *Leonard*, p. 273.

Well-known companies like Proctor and Gamble and Coors Brewing joined ALEC. But over it all was Koch Industries. They supported ALEC financially, served on the board, and contributed freely to friendly lawmakers' campaign. In the early years, a few thousand dollars could influence the outcome of a campaign. *Leonard*, pp. 274, 275.

In spite of what ALEC does, it has gotten designated as a tax-exempt 501 (c)(3) "educational" organization. But it brags to its funders that there is nowhere else that you can get a return this high. As one member-only newsletter boasted, ALEC made a good investment for companies. "Nowhere can you get a return this high," it said. The former Wisconsin state legislator (and later governor) Tommy Thompson admitted, "Myself, I always loved going to these ALEC meetings because I always found new ideas then I'd take them back to Wisconsin, disguise them a little bit, and declare that 'It's mine.'" *Mayer*, pp. 424, 425, 426.

ALEC, The State Policy Network, (now with its own "investigative news" service) and the Franklin Center were able to create the buzz for a new conservative era by making it look like there was a wave coming from the bottom when in reality it was mostly from the top down—only the positions of ALEC/SPN were allowed. Much of the funding was from giant, multinational corporations, including Koch Industries, the Reynolds American and Altria tobacco companies, Microsoft, Comcast, AT&T, Verizon, GlaxoSmithKline, and Kraft Foods as well as a few mega rich individuals. *Mayer*, p. 427.

In 2012, a political unknown, Mark Meadows (later Trump's chief of staff), was nominated as the Republican candidate for the US House from a rural district in North Carolina. The state's gerrymandering after the 2010 census left the incumbent, Heath Schuler, former NFL quarterback and conservative Democrat, in a no-win situation, so Schuler decided not to run seeing it as a waste of time. So, Meadows won. *Mayer*, p. 427, 428.

Soon after arriving in Washington, Meadows became one of the leaders to do away with the Affordable Care Act. His most drastic proposal was to shut down the government if ACA wasn't ended. He was able to get more than seventy-nine Republican congressmen to sign on to this plan, forcing John Boehner, who was opposed, to accede to their demands. *Mayer*, pp. 428, 429.

This didn't succeed so in 2013, a group led by Edwin Meese III proposed an idea that Meadows eventually championed, which was to hold up congressional funds for the health-care program. *Mayer*, p. 431.

> What we see in Topic IV is the intention—to a large extent already achieved—to recreate this oligopoly and become oligarchs of the United States by a few hundred people. They do everything in their power to take away any power of the federal government. They worm their way into state legislatures to sway legislation in their favor. They put great effort into disenfranchising voters. They are opposed to any federal law or action that gives power to any group besides themselves. They spread fear and deception throughout society. They cast doubt on valid scientific findings that don't agree with their selfish interests. They get involved with controversial causes—even if they will not personally benefit from any outcome, just to cause arguments and dissention. To the extent they can achieve their goals, they become today's and tomorrow's American oligarchs.

Contrary to predictions, the *Citizens United* decision hadn't triggered a tidal wave of corporate political spending. Instead, it had empowered a few extraordinarily rich individuals with extreme and often self-serving agendas. The nonpartisan Sunlight Foundation concluded in a post-election analysis, that the superrich had become the country's political gatekeepers. "One ten-thousandth of America's population, or "1% of 1% percent," was "shaping the limits of acceptable discourse, one conversation at a time. *Mayer*, p. 408.

Why Opposing Climate Change Science is a Major Issue

The quick explanation is that Charles Koch made it so.

My understanding of being conservative is that if a major threat appears, you take action to protect against the threat. If the threat doesn't happen, then you can still know that your preparation was the right thing to do. For example, if a hurricane is forecasted for your location, you board up, or maybe evacuate. If the hurricane doesn't hit your area, you still know you did the right thing. But in the case of the threat of global warming—it is the conservatives that look at the warnings from world-renowned scientists and the conservatives that say the research is uncertain and therefore, we shouldn't prepare for global warming.

We now have around 40 years of analysis and research on global warming. James Hansen, director of NASA's Goddard Institute for Space Studies and climate modeler, and associates published their first studies in 1981. In 1985, based on meteorological studies, they concluded that the earth's mean temperature had risen 0.5 to 0.7 degrees Celsius over the past century. In 1988, Hansen testified before a Senate Committee that the earth was warming, and mankind was causing it. His testimony got the attention of the public when the *New York Times* placed his dramatic finding on its front page. *Mayer*, pp. 250, 251 and Wikipedia September 2020.

As early as 1988, the Intergovernmental Panel on Climate Change (IPCC) started issuing warnings that the easily measured carbon dioxide concentration in the atmosphere was increasing. This results in more heat being trapped which could lead to global warming.

The Panel did not issue serious warnings at first, only stating that more studies were needed. This is the usual performance of serious science—that it only concludes what is possible from the studies so far.

As more research was done by the participants of the Panel, it started issuing reports that more clearly showed that atmospheric carbon dioxide concentration was increasing. The increase in carbon dioxide concentration was due largely to the industrial revolution that began in the early 1800s. It reported that because of the increasing levels of carbon dioxide in the atmosphere, global temperatures would rise. At that time the impacts were largely unknown, but there could be more severe storms and areas of the world may become drier. As a consequence of this concentration, global temperatures would rise. *Leonard*, pp. 400, 401. In 2020, what do you think of their warning?

Congress slowly came to the consideration that attention should be given to global warming. After Nancy Pelosi became Speaker of the House, Henry Waxman, California (of tobacco legislation fame) and Edward Markey of Massachusetts submitted a cap-and-trade bill to control carbon dioxide pollution from fossil burning electric generating plants by adopting a cap-and-trade system.

Cap-and-trade as an approach to air pollution originally had a lot of support from both Republicans and Democrats. It was largely a market-based system that penalized large organizations for heavy pollution and rewarded organizations that cut back on air pollution. This was how our air was cleansed of sulfur dioxide from coal-burning electric power plants—an initiative of the George H. W. Bush administration. The system reduced the output of sulfur dioxide and at lower cost than any alternative conceived at the time.

In addition, George H. W. Bush, like most political leaders of both parties at the time, supported responding to whatever the scientific community was reporting on global warming. He vowed to protect the environment, promising to fight "the Greenhouse Effect with the White House Effect." He sent secretary of state, James Baker, to the first international summit of climate scientists, the Intergovernmental Panel on Climate Change. Bush didn't get much opposition from others in the Republican Party. *Mayer*, pp. 250, 251.

The Koch brothers would have none of it. **Their opposition to addressing global warming had nothing to do with the cost of producing energy or energy prices.** In fact, many of the various plans from Democrats to tackle global warming would have lowered energy prices for the vast majority of Americans, according to the congressional Budget Office. Denying the threat of global warming permitted the Koch brothers to make vast amounts of money from their pollution-based empire. But the Koch brothers weren't interested in an honest debate. They wanted to kill attempts to regulate their pollution, and were willing to say or do anything to provide middle- and lower-income voters to turn against Obama. *Fang*, pp. 110, 111, *MacLean* p. 216, *Mayer* pp. 439, 440.

Lobbying and Political Spending

As the scientific consensus grew in support of global warming, the industry's efforts to fight it also grew. The presidential candidacy of the environmental activist Al Gore in 2000 posed an obvious threat to the fossil fuel industry. This brought the Koch organization into action. It wanted to defeat any candidate that might consider climate change as real and therefore spent over $800,000 to support George W. Bush and other Republicans. The Koch organization increased its political spending from about one million dollars in 2004 to $20 million in 2008. This is how concerned the Kochs were that one of their main financial interests may be affected by legislation. *Mayer*, p. 258.

Again, secrecy and deception were the tools of choice. The Kochs did not publicize their opposition to legislation. When statements were made, they were mildly dismissive of possible negative effects of climate change. David Koch said it might even be a great benefit. "The Earth will be able to support enormously more people because a far greater land areas will be available to produce food." Charles called it "blowing smoke." He claimed that if there was global warming it was beyond our control, so live with it. "Since we can't control Mother Nature, let's figure out how to get along with her changes," he advised. *Mayer* pp. 264, 265.

David Koch has over the years given to main stream causes. One was funding the David H. Koch Hall of Human Origins at the Smithsonian National Museum of Natural History in Washington, DC. It is a great exhibition and I recommend that anyone go see it. It visually displays many of the steps our ancient ancestors traveled to looking like us today—the message being that humans have evolved to live in the existing environment. So far, so good. Then in the part, what's next, he deals with global warming, carrying on the idea that we'll just have to live with it. So, an evolution he suggests might occur is that humans will live in underground cities and develop short, stout bodies or "curved spines" so that "moving around in tight spaces will be no problem." *Mayer* pp. 264, 265. Welcome to the future as envisioned by the Kochs.

In spite of the public image the Kochs presented, a few determined sleuths have traced major funding and massive lobbying for climate change denial back to the Koch brothers. Kert Davies, the director of research at Greenpeace, found that from 2005 to 2008, the Kochs, put almost $25 million into dozens of different organizations fighting climate reform, three times the amount spent by ExxonMobil, even though few of us had ever heard of the Kochs at that time. *Mayer*, pp. 250, 251, *MacLean*, pp. 215 – 217, *Leonard*, p. 450, and Chapters 19 and 20.

Mayer reports hundreds of millions of dollars of Koch and allie's money going to right-wing media and public service organizations. The first peer-reviewed academic study of the Koch's spending added further detail. Robert Brulle, a Drexel University professor of sociology an environmental science, discovered that between 2003 and 2010 **over half a billion dollars** was spent on what is described as a massive "campaign to manipulate and mislead the public about the threat posed by climate change." The money went to think tanks, advocacy groups, trade associations, other foundations, and academic and legal programs. This all went to a campaign to undermine climate science and to defeat regulation of carbon emissions. *Mayer*, pp. 250, 251, 252.

Brulle found that around 140 conservative foundations funded the campaign. Readers of this work may see some familiar donor names: foundations affiliated with the Koch and Scaife families, both of whose fortunes derived partly from oil; the Bradley Foundation and several others associated with families participating in the Koch donor summits, including foundations run by the DeVos family, Art Pope; and John Templeton Jr., a doctor and heir to the fortune of his father. Much of this money went through an organization called DonorTrust and could not be traced back to the donor. *Mayer*, pp. 250, 251, 252.

As usual, the Kochs had a multi-pronged approach. These were 1) to raise money for the battle, 2) run a publicity campaign, 3) influence legislators, and 4) get the public buy-in—their favorite group, the Tea Party.

In 2009, Koch began an operation in his lobbying office, where a senior manager directed lobbyists to pay for a third-party economic report that would undermine support for Congress's cap and trade bill or any action to control global warming.

All totaled, Koch financed over thirty-five groups, as well as scores of lobbyists and politicians, all opposed to regulating carbon pollution. As a Koch political deputy later explained his strategy in defeating clean energy legislation to a gathering of conservative bloggers, "if we win the science argument, it's game, set, and match." *Fang*, p. 88.

Here is an example, A program called the Foundation for Research on Economics and the Environment, invited federal judges to a vacation in Montana; hear lectures from climate change skeptics; and provide fellowships for dozens of academics at the Cato Institute and George Mason University. Cato and George Mason used their academic and intellectual status to produce studies showing that the majority of scientific studies are wrong about global temperatures rising. *Fang*, p. 88; also, *Leonard* pp. 450, 459.

They got Mike Pence to be a mouthpiece. He argued that in the midst of the economic downturn, we just can't have a national energy tax increase that the Democrats want to pass. This will raise the cost of living for every American family. At this time there was no public outcry or even much interest in this bill. *Leonard*, pp. 420, 421.

With the Republicans winning the majority in the US House in 2012, they immediately passed legislation to cut the budget for the EPA's Clean Air Act enforcement on carbon emissions. Newly elected Kansas Rep. Mike Pompeo (later Trump's Secretary of State) sponsored this effort. Pompeo was a personal friend of Charles Koch and had worked for an oil company that had Koch Industries funding. *Fang*, pp. 116, 117.

In 2002, Frank Luntz was hired to head the public relations program to fight the regulation of carbon dioxide emissions. Luntz stressed that opponents of carbon regulation "absolutely" **must not admit** that they have a huge financial stake in their opposition. The key was to question the science. "You need to continue to make the lack of scientific certainty a primary issue in the debate" so long as "voters believe there is no consensus about global warming within the scientific community," regulations could be fought off. *Mayer*, p. 256.

From *Leonard*, we learn that the analysis used in the battle against controlling global warming was done by selecting a reliably conservative think tank called the American Council for Capital Formation (ACCF). Koch Industries worked to hide its involvement, so it got the National Association of Manufacturers to "sponsor" the report with the understanding that Koch would pay for it. *Leonard*, pp. 447, 448. The ACCF used a tactic common in many economic/technological studies. This was to make a set of assumptions about the future and then using these assumptions conduct the study using these assumptions. With the right assumptions, you can get the results you want. Note, this is another way of misusing science.

ACCF's predicted that the Waxman-Markey bill of 2010 would destroy 2.4 million jobs between 2012 and 2030 if it was passed. ACCF estimated that electricity prices would jump 50 percent by 2030, and $3.1 trillion in economic activity would be lost. It reached this prediction partly because of its assumption that renewable energy would be more expensive than most other analysts forecasted and therefore, these alternative sources would not come into major use until later. *Leonard*, pp. 447, 448.

The AEA kept up its campaign to publicize ACCF findings. It warned that the cap-and-trade bill was an economic threat to the nation, in the form of job losses higher taxes.

> This is the usual trick of the powerful claiming to be on the same side as the people struggling economically. The ads talk about higher taxes and job losses for the masses. A main thrust of this campaign has been to sow doubts about man-caused climate warming as well as oppose environmental and safety laws and regulations.

With the publication of ACCF's study, Koch Industries put the results into its network of think tanks, friendly media, etc. The Institute for Energy, a think tank, cofounded by Charles Koch was used to publicize the "findings." After the study was promoted by the IER, it was then publicized by the American Energy Alliance, a subsidiary of the IER. IER could not legally engage in politics, but its subsidiary, could because AEA was organized under the tax code that made it legal for it to be involved in politics. The head of AEA was a former Koch Industries lobbyist named Thomas Pyle. *Leonard*, pp. 447, 448.

The Tea Party Put to Work

Next in the strategy, the Tea Party was called to action. Steve Lonegan and others at Americans for Prosperity (AFP) helped make climate change regulation a central focus of the Tea Party movement. Lonegan sponsored rallies, coached participants on what to say about climate change, collected e-mails from participants and encouraged them to contact congressmen, call in to radio talk-shows, and directed to where they could go for right-wing web addresses, etc. *Leonard*, p. 434.

By late February 2009, the Tea Party movement took off. The small Koch-funded rallies morphed into Tea Party rallies. Koch state-based network of think tanks and front groups quickly became the main drivers of the movement, offering everything from free advertisements to arranging protests. Before long, Americans for Prosperity, the group David Koch served as chairman, became the premier Tea Party organization, hosting the largest rallies, employing the greatest number of organizers, and generating lots of media buzz. It picked up on Tim Phillips warnings about the "clear and present danger" of the Obama administration. AFP launched a "Hot Air" tour warning about the falsehoods of global warming. At the 2009 "Tax Day" Tea Party rallies, the staff of Americans for Prosperity were distributing T-shirts calling the cap-and-trade system the largest excise tax in history." *Mayer* pp. 264, 265, *Schulman*, p. 265, *Fang*, pp. 109, 110.

To stop the EPA from enforcing the Clean Air Act's duty to regulate carbon dioxide emissions, Koch started a new group called Regulatory Reality Tour. The group paid staffers they called "Carbon Cops" who would go to Tea Parties and other events to claim the EPA would hire "Carbon Cops" to regulate churches, refrigerators, and even "the air we breathe." The Regulatory Reality Tour hosted its own Tea Party functions, particularly in states with crucial senators. The citizens, after being fed lies about the EPA, were told to call their legislators and demand legislation to gut the Clean Air Act.

Over the fourth of July 2009 weekend as congresspersons were home and making public appearances, they found protestors standing along parade routes, waving placards and shouting. At each parade there was a group of four to six people in the parade screaming and yelling, "No cap and trade! No cap and tax! It stretches the imagination that the general public, on their own, would ever have heard of cap-and-trade, much less how, if implemented, it would affect their livelihood.

Most of the congresspersons were caught off guard. They expected the usual parades of people clapping and waving and in general having a good time getting out into the community. Why on earth were people so up-in-arms about cap-and-trade? And, in one case, protestors went to a town hall meeting calling Republican Mike Castle of Delaware a traitor for supporting cap-and-trade. It was obvious this was a coordinated campaign from the top down. *Leonard*, pp. 424, 425.

If you think this was all that Koch Industries did to oppose carbon dioxide legislation, read on. It is chilling.

Attack on Professionals

All the publicity, lobbying, and media blasts against legislation to control carbon dioxide emissions was not enough for the Koch organization and allies. The next step was harassment, deception, and professional and personal threats, directed at individuals who favored control of these emissions. Tom Perriello, a Virginia congressman who supported cap-and-trade began getting messages from constituents charging him hurting the poor. Two such letters were from the NAACP and the American Association of University Women. These letters were on official-looking stationary. After investigation, it was found that both letters were fakes, and that the sender was Bonner and Associates, a Washington-based public relations firm. *Mayer* p. 266.

Next, is how the opponents of controlling carbon dioxide emissions sought to destroy a professional's career and threaten the safety of his family. This is the case of Michael Mann a tenured professor of meteorology and environmental sciences at Penn State. Mann had to be convinced about what was being reported about global warming. He and colleagues did a study published in 1999 which showed the earth's temperature for the past thousand years in the northern Hemisphere. The temperature was steady for nine hundred years, then began a sharp rise in the twentieth century. The shape of the graph was so distinct that it became the hockey stick graph. *Mayer*, pp. 243, 244, 245.

Mann considered his role was to report on scientific findings—leaving to others the development of laws and policies to deal with global warming. Mann was not particularly interested in politics. In 2008, he was glad that both presidential candidates had a concern for global warming. By now, Mann was fully in agreement with most researchers in this field that burning fossils fuels was trapping heat in the atmosphere and causing climate change that could lead to disasters. For example, the America Association for the Advancement of Science, the world's largest and most prestigious scientific society, warned that "we face risks of abrupt, unpredictable and potentially irreversible changes" with potential "massively disruptive consequences." *Mayer*, pp. 243, 244, 245.

Beyond the scientific world, policymakers were taking action. The Pentagon, evaluating how world developments affected the threats to national security concluded, "the danger from climate change is real, urgent, and severe." An official US National Security Strategy report declared that the situation was a growing national security threat, arguing, "The change wrought by a warming planet will lead to new conflicts over refugees and resources; new suffering from drought and famine; catastrophic natural disasters; and the degradation of land across the globe." The report left no doubt that if nothing were done, "climate change and pandemic disease" would directly threaten the health and safety of the American people *Mayer*, pp. 243, 244, 245.

By early 2009 the Koch network was attacking Mann from every source—talk shows, web sites, etc. Glenn Beck of Fox News, talked about a vast conspiracy to steal from the middle class and give to the wealthy. A prime way of doing this was to convince the public that scientists were lying about what they had found about global warming. The conspiracy, according to Beck, was between Islam, the United Nations, and the Communist Party that was working to hoodwink listeners. *Leonard*, p. 439.

Mayer identifies other organizations and individuals that attacked Mann from various sides. Someone posing as a former CIA officer offered a reward to anyone around Mann who could dig up dirt of him. An organization claiming the status of think tank, tried to get Mann's National Science Foundation grants revoked. The Commonwealth Foundation for Public Policy Alternative tried to get Mann fired and lobbied to get the legislature to withhold Penn State's funding until the university took "appropriate action" against Mann. The university agreed to investigate Mann. Two law firms tried to sue him. These were all paid for by the Koch network under the guise of charitable contributions. Mann's private e-mails were stolen and then their contents falsely reported. Others including US Senator Inhofe of Oklahoma and Ken Cuccinelli Attorney General of Virginia joined in to discredit Mann. *Mayer* pp. 270-275.

Still, this was not enough. Death threats began appearing in Mann's inbox. "I tried to shield my family as much as I could," he says. Then one day he opened a letter and a white powder spilled out. The FBI found the substance to be harmless.

After two years, and after all the investigations demanded were completed, he was found not to have done anything wrong. What worries me Mann said, "is that this circus-like atmosphere may have scared off many young scientists. It actually has a chilling effect. It prevents scientists from participating in the public discourse, because they fear they, or their department head will be threatened." *Mayer* pp. 270-275.

In the State of Kansas, before the Kochs got involved, there was bipartisan support for wind energy mainly because it created jobs for building and maintaining wind farms. Koch hated renewable energy. The state was considering approval—and later approved--construction of a new coal-fired plant, and the mandates to buy renewable energy were included in the approval. Wind power was getting cheaper by the year.

Tom Moxley a rancher and life-long Republican from the town of Council Grove was elected to the state legislature in 2006. Around 2011, he watched Koch Industries take charge of energy legislation. From his membership on the House Energy and Environmental Committee, Moxley saw how the Koch's worked. In 2013, one after another "experts" or heavy hitters" as Moxley called them, came to the legislature to teach the legislators about renewable energy. They testified about the deeply damaging economic effects of wind power and government mandates. The "scholars" came from think tanks like the Cato Institute and also, Koch-funded groups, including AFP, the Heartland Institute, and the Beacon Hill Institute. Moxley wondered why these people came to Kansas. You never see people like this at most legislative hearings. The Kansas Chamber of Commerce also testified. *Leonard,* pp. 478, 479, 480.

These hearings greatly influenced Moxley. He learned a lot about what scientific research had found about carbon dioxide emissions and the dangers this posed. At the hearing, Moxley was impressed by the presentation of one of the opponents of renewable energy. The guy showed legislators a chart on the Earth's climate that <u>conveniently omitted the last hundred years</u>. "I'm open to good science but those guys were just throwing dust in the air and not making a case," Moxley recalled. *Leonard,* pp. 478, 479, 480.

In the next election Koch's team pulled all stops with negative messages about the candidates Kochs opposed by using postcard mailings, advertisements, and door-knocking campaigns. This got rid of all the traditional Republicans and were replaced by Koch supporters. *Leonard,* pp. 478, 479, 480.

"They're a bunch of numbskulls. All they're going to do is take orders from the Chamber and Koch and so on," Moxley said. "They're not thoughtful. They're not people that read the newspaper or have a history background. They just do what Koch wants." Moxley left the legislature in 2016. *Leonard,* pp. 478, 479, 480. **Is this the way we want to govern?**

> No matter whether politically you want to go back to 1900 when the federal government was a fraction of what it is now, or whether you are politically, for example, hoping to have Medicare for all, do you want our political decisions made the honest way by candidates and their political parties by going out and making speeches, organizing rallies, making phone calls, etc., or do you want our political decisions made by outside groups who secretly spend whatever it takes to get candidates of their choice elected and then do their bidding after being elected? Who threaten the lives and livelihoods of those that have other preferences? I assume nearly everyone wants campaigns and elected officials acting on their best judgement and preferences rather than their decisions being dictated by outside secret groups and money.

And finally, as was done for other issues, the Koch brothers through the American Legislative Exchange Council (ALEC) was active at the state level. ALEC adopted a model bill for the states saying that the role of human activity in causing climate change was uncertain, that man-made climate change could be "deleterious, neutral or possibly beneficial," and that the cost of regulating greenhouse gas emissions could cause "great economic dislocation."

In 2015 Common Cause and the League of Conservation Voters accused ALEC of denying climate change. ALEC responded by threatening legal action, denying that ALEC supports climate change denial, and saying it has more recently welcomed debate on the subject and supported renewable energy and carbon tax policies to curb global warming. *Wikipedia*, November 2020.

And Now

The Republican Party is now a creature of the radical Right. In the Trump administration, in addition to Mike Pence, Mike Pompeo, and Mark Meadows, Congress is dominated by those that got elected by the support of the Kochs and other billionaires. Mike Pompeo and Mark Meadows came directly from Koch Industries or a subsidiary. In addition, the Koch machine dominates many state governments who will toe the line. Most will not deviate much from the source of their support. I suspect that Trump was not the first choice of the network and no doubt they had tremors with the disorganization of Trump, as opposed to their tight control on messaging and policies. But there is no doubt that this machine will have a major influence on our society for years to come. *Mayer*, p. xxii.

Note from the list below, the persons that joined the Koch conservative movement and cooperating conservative movements along the way.

G. Warren Nutter, Richard Fink, Grover Norquist, Paul Weyrich, Richard Mellon Scaife, The DeVos family, Joseph Coors, Robert LeFevre, Clarence Thomas, Ginna Thomas, wife of Clarence Thomas, Eric Cantor, L Brent Bozwell III, Richard Viguerie, Greg Mueller, Tony Perkins, Leonard Leo, Morton Blackwell, Kelllyane Conway, Al Regnery, R. Emmet Tyrell, Dick Armey, Pete Sessions, Rick Perry, Mark Sanford, Mark Kirk, Eric Odom, Peggy Venable, Scott Walker, Chris Christie, David Walsh, Ed Gillespie, Art Pope, Tom Hofeller, Thomas A. Roe, Tracie Sharp, Mark Meadows, Edwin Meese III, Frank Luntz, Thomas Pyle, Steve Lonegan, Mike Pence, Mike Pompeo, and Tim Phillips.

Organizations Supporting the Koch Network

American Action Network; American Enterprise Institute; American Society for the Defense of Tradition, Family and Property; Americans for Limited Government; Americans for Prosperity; Bill of Rights Foundation; Buckeye Institute for Public Policy; Cato Institute; Center for Free Enterprise; Century Strategies; Charles Koch Charitable Foundation; Christian Coalition; Citizens for a Sound Economy (CSE); Competitive Enterprise Institute; Conservative Action Project; Council for National Policy; DonorTrust; Earhart Foundation; Empower America; FreedomWorks; Family Research Council; Flint Hills Resources; Foundation for Research on Economics and the Environment; Grassroots Action; Gun Owners of America; Heritage Foundation; Hot Air Tour; Independence Women's Forum; Institute for Humane Studies; Institute for Justice Foundation; James Madison Program in American Ideals and Institutions; John M. Olin Fellowship in Military History; Koch Foundation; Koch Industries; Law and Economics; Let Freedom Ring; Libertas Global Partners; Liberty Central, founded by Ginni Thomas, wife of Justice Clarence Thomas; Liberty Fund; Ludwig von Mises Institute; Media Research Center; Mellon & Sons; Mont Pelerin Society; Olin Foundation; Pacific Research Foundation; Philanthropy Roundtable; Phillips and Reed; Reason Foundation; Regular Folks United; Regulatory Reality Tour; ResistNet; Right to Work Committee; Sam Adams Alliance; Scaife Family; 60 Plus Association; Smith Richardson Foundation; State Policy Network; Stormfront; Taxpayer Bill of Rights (TABOR); Tea Party; Tea Party Patriots; and Weaver Terrace Group.

References for Topic IV

Buck, Rinker, How Those Libertarians Pay the Bills, New York Magazine, November 3, 1980

Fang, Lee, The Machine: a Field Guide to the Resurgent Right, The New Press,38 Green Street, New York, 10014,ISBN 978-1-59588-639-1, 2013.

Fang worked his way into several conferences and meetings, interviewed Koch supporters to obtain first-hand accounts of speeches and events.

Leonard, Christopher, Kochland, The Secret History of Koch Industries and Corporate Power in America, Simon and Schuster, 1230 Avenue of the Americas, New York 10020, ISBN 978-1-4767-7538-8, 2019.

Leonard's book took years of finding how the Kochs have managed to transform the American system against democracy. Multiple sources were used.

MacLean, Nancy, Democracy in Chains, The Deep History of the Radical Right's Stealth Plan for America, Penguin Books, 375 Hudson Street, New York, 10014, ISBN 978110980972, 2017. MacLean's main contribution is her discovery, analysis, and reporting on files and archives belonging to James M. Buchanan that had been abandoned on the George Mason University campus.

Mayer, Jane, Dark Money: The Hidden History of the Billionaires Behind the Rise of the Radical Right, Anchor House, a division of Penguin Random House LLC, New York, Doubleday, ISBN 978-0-385-53560-1, 2016. Mayer was one of the first investigators to pierce into the secretive world of the Kochs and their allies. In addition to her own findings, she used multiple sources.

Schulman, Daniel, Sons of Wichita: How the Koch Brothers Became Americas Most Powerful and Private Dynasty, Hachette Book Group, Grand Central Publishing, 1290 Avenue of the Americas, New York 10104, ISBN 978-1-4555-1872, 2014.

Schulman as an investigative journalist found multiple sources and evidence of the origins of the philosophy of the Koch brothers and how they went forward to create the current danger to our democracy.

Zinn, Howard, A People's History of the United States, HarperCollins Publishers, 10 Est 53rd Street, New York 10022, ISBN 978-0-06-196558-6, 2003.

For Further Reading

Anderson, Kurt, Evil Geniuses: The Unmaking of America: A Recent History, copyrighted in 2020. I have not read this book, but its author says it is about the takeover of our nation by the ultra-rich starting around the 1970s.

Machiavelli, Niccolò di Bernardo dei, The Prince (Il Principe), 1513.

Berman, Ari, Give Us the Ballot: The Modern Struggle for Voting Rights in America

Mayer, Jane, "Covert Operations: the Billionaire Brothers Who Are Waging a War Against Obama," The New Yorker, August 30, 2010;

See also,); Kenneth P. Vogel, Big Money: 2.5 Billion Dollars, One Suspicious vehicle, and a Pimp—On the Trail of the Ultra Rich Hijacking American Politics (New York; Public Affairs, 2014: William Cronon, "Who's Really Behind Recent Republican Legislation in Wisconsin and Elsewhere, (Hint: It Didn't Start Here) Scholar as Citizen (blog) March 15, 2011. The Wisconsin Republican Party became so nervous that it demanded his e-mails: David Walsh, GOP Files FOIA Request for UW Madison Professor William Cronon's E-mails," History News Network, March 25, 2011, http://historynewsnetwork.org/article/137911.

Niven, John, John C. Calhoun and the Price of Union, a Biography, Louisiana State University Press, ISBN 0-8071-1858-3, 1988.

Obama, Barack, A Promised Land, Crown, Random House, Penguin Random House, LLC, New York, ISBN 978-1-5247-6316-9, 2020.

Roesch, James Rutledge, An *abridged version of a chapter which will appear in the forthcoming, From Founding Fathers to Fire-Eaters: The Constitutional Doctrine of States' Rights in the Old South,* Aug 25, 2015

Stevens, Stuart, It Was All a Lie, copyrighted in 2020. Stevens, a former
Republican writes that racism became the central core of the
Republican Party starting decades ago. Everything else has just
masked this core. I have not read this book.

Topic V

The Federalist Society

In addition to serving as US Attorney General under President Reagan, Ed Meese, along with several dozen other prominent lawyers in and out of government, set about to capture the US judicial system to favor right wing philosophy. There was a ready vehicle for this—The Federalist Society.

Beginnings at Yale and University of Chicago

Following the New Deal of the 1930s and 1940s, and civil rights movement and the Great Society of the1950s, 1960s and 1970s, many conservative politicians and others were looking for ways to regain status they had for decades before the 1930s. This was particularly felt among lawyers, both practicing and in law schools. The view was that the three to four decades of liberal politics and justice had crowded out the conservative approach. Thus, in 1980 law students at Yale, in particular Steven Calabresi, and Lee Liberman, and David McIntosh at the University of Chicago began searching for ways to regain a conservative basis.

The three students went on to form the first chapter of the Federalist Society at Yale. The organization soon established chapters at many colleges and universities. Other chapters have been formed that are not directly associated with any college campus. Edwin Meese soon recognized the potential of the Federalist Society. He took on Calabresi as an advisor during the Reagan and George H. W. Bush administrations. *Avery and Mclaughlin*, p. 1, and *Fletcher*, p. A 21.

Founders of the Society, all in law school, looked to getting judges in decisive positions. Thus, judges in sympathy with the Society would in effect change laws by their judicial decisions. As we shall see below, they have very much succeeded.

The goal was and is to preserve the old order. They were able to tap into the resentment that the South's power structure had against *Brown v. Board of Education*. In addition, upset by rulings on crime of the Warren Court, they took up the mantle of "law and order" popularized by the Nixon administration. And *Roe v. Wade* created anger at the Supreme Court among large segments of Republicans and conservatives in general.

The election of Ronald Reagan created a massive boost to the Society just as it was rapidly gaining members. Large segments of the population favored a judiciary that would reverse these initiatives which in turn created the demand and opportunity to put a new generation of Federalist Society lawyers in the federal judiciary and train them for future nominations to the Supreme Court

Since the early years of the Federalist Society in the 1980s, its members have believed that the easiest way to change the law is to change the judges. They have been phenomenally successful in doing so. "'I think the Federalist Society and some other conservative organizations have played a really important role in changing the terms of legal and, ultimately, political debate in the United States,' said Peter J. Rubin, a Georgetown University law professor and founder of the American Constitution Society, which aims to do for liberals and centrists what the Federalist Society has done for conservatives and libertarians." *Fletcher, p. A 21.*

During the administrations of Reagan, and those of the two Bushes, Federalist Society members have had prominent positions in the White House and Justice Department. Society members in private practice essentially have a veto over selecting candidates for federal judges. And with these judges in the majority, decisions have moved to way more conservative positions. *Avery and Mclaughlin*, pp. 20, 21.

Size of Federalist Society and Early Strength

It is obvious that the positions of the Federalist Society have a strong following in our society. There is of course, nothing wrong with building strong organizations and institutions that the people want. Where the Society has gone astray in our society is that they have worked and succeeded in <u>suppressing</u> other beliefs and points of view. They have done this in several ways, a primary method was and is to get only Society members and others holding similar philosophies to dominate the federal courts, including the Supreme Court. Especially since the George W. Bush administration, Republicans in the US Senate refuse to approve judicial nominees with other philosophies and political leanings and approve only those in agreement with the Federalist Society.

The idea of the Society founders was to bring lawyers to campuses who represented conservative positions. This succeeded almost without bounds and now nearly all the 200 or so law schools have chapters. Frequent speakers at these events and at other Society gatherings include Frank Easterbrook, Richard Epstein, Edwin Meese, Steven Calabresi, Thomas Merrill, Lino A. Graglia, A. Raymond Randolph, John McGinnis, Leonard S. Leo, Theodore Olson, Lillian BeVier, Charles J. Cooper, John C. Yoo, and William H. Pryor.

Politicians who are strong supporters include Ted Cruz, Mike Lee, and Mike Pence. Many federal judges and justices have no qualms about participating in its conventions. A number of Supreme Court Justices, including Samuel Alito, regularly attend and sometimes speak at Society conventions.

According to the Federalist Society, there are over 45,000 lawyers and law student members of which around 13,000 pay dues. Five Supreme Court justices—Clarence Thomas, John Roberts, Samuel Alito, Brett Kavanaugh, and Amy Coney Barrett—are current or former members. The late Antonin Scalia was an early and long-time member. With this army of lawyers, great changes have been made in how our justice system operates. It has also greatly influenced our political system. The Society works to stay out of the news, but at their conventions it celebrates its accomplishments and those persons that have been notable in supporting the positions of the Society.

Meetings and intellectual debates held in many locations help to clarify and solidify positions of the Society. These then flow through the Society's networks so that many unifying positions are developed. The networks also serve to inform decision-makers—politicians and others as to topics and positions of the Society. *Avery and Mclaughlin*, p. 18.

Connection to Republican and Conservative Racism

The philosophy of the Federal Society has its roots in the development of the modern Republican Party. Recall from Topic IV, that Barry Goldwater, as a politician, and *National Review* editor William F. Buckley Jr., provided political and intellectual grounding for the Republican Party we have today. The goal of these men and others was to protect the way of life that well-to-do men and their families had enjoyed for long periods of our history. At this time, Black people, women and others were beginning to get rights formerly prohibited by custom, law, and court rulings. As recounted in Topic IV, both Goldwater and Buckley seized on the opposition to civil rights as a way of protecting the power of white men.

Topic V follows very much Topic IV in which the Federalist Society is in lock step with the Koch brothers' network. The Society has received substantial financial backing from foundations supporting a large menu of conservative causes. The Society supported investigating the personal life of former president Bill Clinton. Note the names and organizations that support both the Koch brothers and the Federalist Society, include the John M. Olin and Charles G. Koch foundations and Richard Mellon Scaife. *Fletcher p. A 21.*

In recent decades, the approach to protecting the powerful in our society as noted before, was opposition to civil rights court rulings and legislation in the 1950s and 1960s. This handle of racism was Nixon's "southern strategy" and "law and order," Reagan's saying that welfare queens drive up with their Cadillacs to collect their food stamps, and his administration's War on Drugs, George Bush, Sr. using "Willy Horton" as a scare tactic to work his way to the presidency, and currently, Trump in his innumerable instances of support of racism—the most recent, trying to frighten white suburbanites by warning that "those people will be moving into your neighborhood."

Goals of the Federalist Society

The political right, of course, does not say openly that they are opposed to racial equality and healing. Rather, their stated goals, are: limited government, protection of individual rights, and added on to the list, the concept of "originalism." The first belief listed in the Federalist Society's statement of principles, that the "state exists to preserve freedom." Frank S. Meyer, argued that "the state" has only three limited functions "national defense," the preservation of the domestic order, and the administration of justice between individuals. Each of these goals have as their <u>results the protection of the powerful.</u>

Limited Government

Limited government in general means that those with power are left alone to do as they wish; the less powerful without money and influence, are dependent on government to protect and extend their rights. For Federalist Society and allies, the goal of limited government often means 1) not having to protect worker rights and safety by among other things, weakening and destroying unions, 2) opposing consumer safety by not requiring safe consumer products, and 3) working against laws and regulations that prevent financial institutions from defrauding consumers or coming to the government for bailouts, 4) opposing actions that slow down climate change, and 5) opposing laws designed to provide equal opportunity to oppressed groups.

Protection of Individual Rights

Protection of individual rights sounds appealing—who is opposed to an individual having rights? But the way this is interpreted by the Society and like-minded people is using government to protect ways of life that conservatives favor including; prohibition of same-sex relationships, opposition to abortion, protecting "Christian values" such as opposition to recognition and celebration of other religions. Spreading fears that "those people" are trying to cancel Christmas is an example.

Originalism

Originalism according to Society members' statements means that only the original meaning that the founders intended for the Constitution is acceptable for deciding cases today. Not surprisingly, the Constitution doesn't provide much guidance for a large portion of the cases now coming before the courts. So, proponents of originalism spend a lot of effort trying to discern and then interpret what the founders intended.

The society's promotion of originalism as the only legitimate method of constitutional interpretation was given a solid beginning in the Reagan Justice Department under the stewardship of Meese. Meese had described originalism as the notion that "judges should issue rulings based on the original understanding of the authors and ratifiers* of the Constitution and the Bill of Rights, rather than on outcomes that reflect the judges own bias or policy preferences." Meese became interested in the subject while serving in Reagan's California administration and made it a national priority while serving as attorney general. *Avery and Mclaughlin,* pp. 8, 9. *Good luck on agreeing what the original understanding of the ratifiers was, see Topic II.

One of the means of success of the Society is a much-used strategy of saying something is true over and over until it becomes accepted as the truth. Lawrence Tribe of Harvard University, said that Meese was "successful in making it look like he and his disciples were carrying out the intentions of the great founders, where the liberals were making it up as the went along. It was … very misleading with a powerful public relations effect." *Avery and Mclaughlin,* p. 8.

Recall from above that Meese did not hesitate to use his salary, not only to run the Justice Department, but to transform the nation's judiciary in his image. This was especially true in his launch of the concept that only the original meaning of the Constitution was legitimate. He launched his originalism campaign in a speech to the American Bar Association in July 1985. He later spoke at the Society's lawyer's division in Washington, DC. It was a heady moment for some of the student attendees (one likely reason is that the concept seems so simple until it must be applied to real situations). Meese also started having lectures within the Justice Department and related it to current issues such as civil rights and criminal justice.

It takes no great imagination to understand why Meese would choose these issues. We have come a long way since the late 1700s in terms of a journey of extending civil and human rights and dignity for individuals and groups. Originalism seeks to reverse these gains.

A few months later, Supreme Court Justice William Brennen Jr.in a speech called attempts to figure out the intent of the Constitution writers, "arrogance cloaked in humility." Brennan said, it was "arrogant to pretend from our vantage that we can gauge accurately the intent of the framers on application of principle to specific, contemporary questions." *Avery and Mclaughlin*, p. 8.

A reminder—there were only incomplete notes kept on the deliberations leading to the proposed Constitution, so there has to be a lot of guessing as to what the intent was when words and phrases were chosen. As readers of these pages know by now, the Federalist Papers are not a guide for the intent of the Constitution—the Papers were written to <u>advocate</u> for ratifying the Constitution because of fears that ratification would fail. Advocating for a certain position is not the same as providing an unbiased analysis. The incentive for writing the Federalist Papers, mostly be Hamilton and Madison—proponents of the proposed Constitution, was that the proposed Constitution was in serious jeopardy of not being ratified especially by New York.

My Perspective

One of the reasons I started this effort was because of writings by members of the Federalist Society. The Society urges—with considerable public success—that it possesses the knowledge to provide the true meaning of the Federalist Papers and has worked to establish the Federalist Papers as *the* interpretation of the US Constitution. The Society seems to insist that the Federalist Papers have some legal standing—that is, if a court issues a ruling that is in conflict with what is found in the Papers, then the court has erred.

I have been troubled by several of Federalist Society positions, so decided to do a deep study of the Papers to find if there are other possible interpretations. I focused on just a few issues, but added more as I did my studies. In many instances, I reach quite different interpretations of the Federalist Papers than does the Federalist Society. Let's have a look into the Federalist Society.

"The Federalist Society has become kind of mythologized," said Nadine Strossen, president of the American Civil Liberties Union, who often speaks at the group's events. "For those who don't really know what they do, the ACLU can be shorthand for the liberal agenda and the Federalist Society can be shorthand for the conservative legal agenda." *Fletcher, p. A 21.*

The naming and icon chosen for the group is itself propaganda. The original identification of "federalists" was a group that was energized by Alexander Hamilton and James Madison. As discussed in Topic II, these men saw the weakness of the Articles of Confederation and believed that the United States organized as a Confederation could not survive. They therefore, set about working to create a stronger federal or national government. This led eventually to the calling of the Constitutional Convention and ultimately to the ratification by states and adopted as the foundation of our government and our society.

Later, as the government was launched under the Constitution, Madison broke from his former allies because he disagreed with positions taken by Washington and Hamilton to create a strong federal government. In these early battles, Washington, Hamilton, and John Adams were now called federalists and Adams ran for president as a Federalist. Madison now took positions along with Thomas Jefferson that rights were being taken from states. Recall that some of their positions went so far as to argue that if the federal government took actions that states could not agree with, then states had the right, under the Constitution, to not abide by the federal actions—the term <u>nullification</u> was used to describe this position.

Thus, a more descriptive name for the Federalist Society would be "The States' Rights Society" and its icon would not be James Madison, but someone such as James Rutledge or John C. Calhoun, both of whom were from South Carolina and strong advocates for states' rights. Calhoun directly advocated for nullification*, although he was usually talked out of it. *From Roesch.* *Nullification became a term used to argue that states had the right to disregard federal laws and regulations that they did not think were legal.

Even the word federalism or "our system of federalism" has been co-opted by those favoring stronger states' rights. It is often used to mean that the federal government must allow states' rights to take priority.

The Federalist Society as a body, takes every opportunity to emphasize the States' rights position in the Constitution. Look again at Amendment 10: "The powers not delegated to the United States by the constitution nor prohibited by it to the States, are reserved to the States respectively or to the people."

Compare this to *Federalist Paper Number 45* language. "The powers delegated by the proposed constitution to the federal government are few and defined. Those which remain with the State governments are numerous and indefinite." The Constitution does not say United States powers are "few."

But remember my favorite passage recorded in Topic I: "…We have heard of the impious doctrine of the Old World, that the people were made for kings, not kings for the people. Is the same doctrine not to be revived in the New [World] in a different shape—**that the solid happiness of the people is to be sacrificed to the laws of political institutions** of a different form? …It is too early for politicians to presume on our forgetting that **the public good, the real welfare of the great body of people, is the supreme object to be pursued, and that no form of government whatever has any other value than as it may be fitted for the attainment of this object.** Were the plan of the convention adverse to the public happiness, my voice would be, Reject the plan. Were the Union itself inconsistent with the public happiness, it would be Abolish the Union. **In like manner, as far as the sovereignty of the States cannot be reconciled to the happiness of the people, the voice of every good citizen must be, Let the former be sacrificed to the latter.** How far the sacrifice is necessary has been shown. How far the unsacrificed residue will be endangered, is the question before us."

The Federalist Society argues that the Constitution is unchangeable, that its value is good for all time. But based on the above, would Madison today say that some major changes should be made in our governments so that we can pursue that supreme objective—the real welfare of the great body of people? Would he still argue that, the powers delegated by the proposed constitution to the federal government are (should be) few and defined and those which remain with the State governments are (should be) numerous and indefinite?

I have found in doing this study, that the Society is selectively interpreting the Federalist Papers and using these interpretations to bolster arguments for limited government, protecting actions of ultra-rich people, etc. The fault lies, not in their objective, but in their restricted conceptions of who "the people" are (or were). Their concept of "the people" was white, property-owning men.

The Society, it seems, insists that these papers show that States should have default powers, that is, if the Constitution does not give a power to the national government, then it cannot expand its powers. This is in contrast to what *Madison* wrote in *Federalist Paper Number 41*, where he treats the basis for granting of named powers to the federal government. He writes of the trade-offs that must be made in any of the arrangements. "This method of handling the subject cannot impose on the good sense of people of America. It may display the subtlety of the writer; it may open a boundless field for rhetoric and declamation; it may inflame the passions of the unthinking, and may confirm the prejudices of the misthinking; **but cool and candid people will at once reflect; that the purest of human blessings must have a portion of alloy in them; that the choice must always be made, if not the lesser evil, at least of the GREATER, NOT THE PERFECT, good; and that in every political institution, a power to advance the public happiness involves a discretion which may be misapplied and abused.**"

The Federalist Society Captures the Federal Judiciary and Other Victories

"The Federalist Society ... says that it "is founded on the principles that the State exists to preserve freedom, that the separation of governmental powers is central to our Constitution, and that it is **emphatically the province and duty of the judiciary** to say what the law is, not what it should be." *The Federalist Society*

> You may want to get out a tablet and note how many instances where this <u>emphatic province</u> is disregarded by Federalist Society members in the following pages.

With the founding of the Federalist Society and implementation of its goals, it has moved the judiciary further to the right than the traditional orientation of judges appointed by Republican presidents. Studies of judges on the Circuit Court of Appeals and federal district court judges show what is largely believed, that Republican-appointed judges take more conservative positions and Democratic-appointed judges take more liberal positions. But the studies also show the ever-increasing influence of the Federalist Society on the Republican Party. One of the studies shows that the judicial decisions of appointees of Reagan, George H. W. Bush, and George W. Bush were more conservative than the appointees of Presidents Eisenhower, Nixon, and Ford. Scherer and Miller state that their results show a statistically significant and large impact by members of the Society on judicial decisions of the US Court of Appeals. Professors Sunstein, Scherer, and Miller, et. al. in *Avery and Mclaughlin*, p. 44, 45, 46.

The Federalist Society "has played a significant role in moving the national debate to the right on the Second Amendment, campaign finance regulation, State sovereignty, and the Commerce Clause. It plays a central role in networking and mentoring young conservative lawyers. *Hollis-Brusky*, p. 213.

Elliot Minchberg, former legal director of People for the American Way, stated that he had "never seen courts of appeal nominations as politicized as they were during the George W. Bush administration." The Senate had rejected a number of the president's nominations during the first term, but in his second term, he challenged the Senate and nominated them again. *Avery and Mclaughlin, p. 34*

Not only did Republican administrations appoint only candidates with ties to the Society, the younger lawyers were far more extreme. In writing speeches for Meese, they advocated abolishing parts of the federal government that had been in place for many decades that had been built to make the system more effective in carrying out the legislation that had been passed by Congress and signed into law by presidents. One such instance was questioning the constitutionality of independent federal agencies. [The Constitution does not provide for these agencies, nor does it prohibit them. And as we know from Topic II, the Constitution also does not provide for a cabinet.]

Taking a page from the "nullification" arguments of the early 1800s, these lawyers also suggested that the president did not need to obey Supreme Court decisions if he disagreed with the decision. [One can reasonably ask if the advisors to Trump had access to these writings.]

As noted earlier, Attorney General Edwin Meese was the energy behind the move to totally dominate the federal judiciary with persons known to hold the views of the Society. A strategy totally under Meese's control was to prepare young conservative lawyers and leaders in the Society by hiring them into key positions in the Justice Department. Prominent members receiving nominations to appellate judgeships in the Reagan and Bush administrations were two of the Society's original faculty advisers—Robert Bork and Antonin Scalia—to the U.S. Court of Appeals for the District of Columbia Circuit and later the Supreme Court. Bush nominated Clarence Thomas to both courts.

The administration of George H. W. Bush took the practice a step farther by giving the responsibility for finding and promoting lawyers in sympathy with the Society to Lee Liberman Otis on the White House staff, a founder of the Society.

If lawyers want to succeed to judicial appointments in Republican administrations, it is not good enough that they be conservative. They must be approved by the Society. The most notable case was when George W. Bush nominated White House staff member, Harriet Miers, to the Supreme Court. Bush made the mistake of not first getting the okay from the power structure in the Federalist Society. Right away after her nomination, Society members began attacking her credentials, among which that she was not a member of the Federalist Society. As is well-known, Bush withdrew her nomination and then nominated Samuel Alito.

On the other side, the Society has gone after nominees. President Clinton nominated Lani Guinier to head the Civil Rights Division in the Justice Department. Clint Bolick was prominent in defeating the nomination. Members have been active in opposing the appointments of prominent liberals. *Avery and Mclaughlin, pp. 134, 135, 136.*

The Federalist Society passes on the suitability of all federal Judges that are nominated to be approved by Congress when we have a Republican president. Think of that! An unelected organization with their own definition of the Constitution and strong conservative views gets to choose our federal judges. The Federalist Society puts a lot of effort into keeping from the public the fact that they have this power to get judges into the federal courts.

Before the Federalist Society had much clout, the American Bar Association reviewed candidates for federal judges, especially Supreme Court nominees and issued an opinion to Congress, which was made public. One may argue against the ABA, which is also an unelected body, passing on the suitability of judges. But at least the process was well publicized. With the Federalist Society acting as a filter, the public is largely unaware of its involvement—rather perhaps thinking nominees are chosen for their judicial accomplishments, instead of their conservative political views. <u>It would be much better if all candidates were evaluated by a number of political and professional organizations and all these evaluations widely publicized</u>.

We now see the results of this long-term strategy implemented by Edwin Meese decades ago. Not only the federal judiciary as a whole is dominated by judges approved by the Society, the majority of Supreme Court Justices as noted above are or have been members—Roberts, Alito, Gorsuch, Kavanaugh, and Barrett. The late, Antonin Scalia, also a member, helped found the society as a faculty advisor at the University of Chicago Law School. Most if not all of these justices were chosen from a pool of Society members that had gotten appointments to lower courts. For example, as David Kirkpatrick noted in the *New York Times*, the appointment of Alito to the Supreme Court was "the culmination of a disciplined campaign begun by the Reagan administration to seed the lower federal judiciary with like-minded jurists who could reorient the federal courts "toward the philosophy of originalism" *Avery and Mclaughlin*, pp. 21, 22.

The strategy is self-perpetuating. As Society members are appointed to judgeships, they hire young lawyers who are also members of the Society as clerks, thus putting these lawyers on a path to future appointments to the bench. Edward Lazarus, a former Supreme Court clerk, called membership in the society during the eighties "a prerequisite for law students seeking clerkships with many Reagan judicial appointees as well as for employment to the upper ranks of the Justice Department and the White House." *Avery and Mclaughlin*, p. 23.

The Society much prefers to avoid publicity about their activities and strength. It is not uncommon for public officials and candidates for public office to downplay or even deny any connection to the Society. The most well-known case of denial, was when George W, Bush nominated John G. Roberts for the Supreme Court. it was widely reported that Roberts was a member of the Society. The administration vigorously denied this until it was shown that Roberts was once listed as serving on the steering committee of the group's Washington chapter. The administration insisted that Roberts has no recollection of ever being a full-fledged member of the Society. *Fletcher. p. A 21.*

Federalist Society members were at their peak in the George W. Bush administration. Vice president Dick Cheney was proud to point out close ties between the Society and the administration and the many members that were in the administration. He told the Society that we're especially proud to have two of your founders at the Department of Energy—the general council, Lee Liberman Otis, and Secretary Spence Abraham.

In 2001, three cabinet members were either Federalist Society members or active participants: Energy Secretary Spencer Abraham as noted, Interior Secretary Gale A. Norton, and Attorney General John D. Ashcroft. Society leader, Ted Olson was the solicitor general. Five of the eleven lawyers in the White House Counsel's Office were members. Because of the power of Federalist Society members, from the gutting of the civil rights division of the Justice Department, where 60 percent of the professional staff was driven out and not a single discrimination case was filed, to breaking Article Three of the Geneva Convention against torture, (which White House counsel Alberto Gonzales termed 'quaint' in a memo to the president). *Avery and Mclaughlin*, p. 11.

Next battle in the war, the Society worked to get friends appointed—the most important was getting Clarence Thomas on the Supreme Court. Among other acts, in a case analyzed below, Thomas criticized the Seattle school board for getting involved in making decisions on the basis of race. He mocked (1) the school board's definition of "cultural racism" and (2) the fact that the school district sent a delegation of students to a conference on the topic of white privilege.

> This gets right to a major question. Should civil and human rights be put to a popular vote? The starkest example in our history is slavery. Put to a popular vote, it would have been supported by the voters in

most of the south and a good share of the rest of the US. But this didn't make this evil right.

Mitch McConnell has been either Senate Majority Leader or Minority Leader since 2006. He has worked tirelessly, and using a variety of techniques to block liberal causes and enhance those of the conservatives. He came to prominence in fighting against campaign finance reform by opposing Republican Senator McCain and Democrat Russ Feingold. These two saw the evils of unlimited campaign spending. McConnell took the position of the Federalist Society to oppose any legislative restrictions on campaign financing.

In recent years he has taken on an unrelenting fight to turn the entire federal judiciary into a system that is aligned with those of the Society. His approach is not hidden—it is in front of everyone to see. When he has the power, he refuses to approve of candidates nominated by Democratic presidents and rushes through the approval of those nominated by Republican presidents. His most famous is blocking Obama's candidate for the Supreme Court, Merrick Garland.

He voted against Obama's Supreme Court nominee, Sonia Sotomayor but called her "a fine person with an impressive story and a distinguished background." Then said that he did not believe she would withhold her personal or political views while serving as a justice. His has no shame in saying or doing what he can to get his way. At Elena Kagan's confirmation, McConnell announced his opposition to saying she was not forthcoming enough about her "views on basic principles of American constitutional law."

When McConnell became majority leader in 2014, he put up a near blockade on judicial appointments, creating many vacancies. Then when Trump became president, Senate Republicans broke a record for largest number of appeals court judiciary and circuit court judges confirmations during a president's first two years. When Trump became president, his three nominees for the Court, Neil Gorsuch, Brett Kavanaugh, and Amy Coney Barrett were rushed through quickly. McConnell stated that he considers the judiciary to be the item of Trump's first two years with the longest-lasting impact on the country.

The Society has a periodical called *ABA Watch* which goes into great lengths to take issue with the ABA on their judicial ratings. Just the existence of *ABA Watch*, shows how politicized is the process of getting judicial nominees. I presume most of the population would like to have judges that make decisions for the welfare of the nation and who have judicial accomplishments, rather than based on their political preferences.

Lott writes, "While Democratic Court of Appeals nominees who were clerks on the Supreme Court had an average rating of slightly below "well qualified," similar Republican nominees were rated on average as only "qualified/well qualified." Likewise, of nominees who attended Top 10 law schools and served on their law reviews, Democrats had an average rating as "well qualified/qualified," but Republican nominees were only "qualified/well qualified." Overall, Republican nominees had lower ratings than the nominees of either President Carter or President Clinton."

"Moreover, the A.B.A. rating system was a poor guide to how judges will do once they are on the bench. [This is good! It is at least an indication that they review the cases with an open mind. Their decisions may be more likely to depend on the facts of the case—not because of a political viewpoint.] According to The Almanac of the Federal Judiciary's lawyer survey, judges who had "good" judicial temperament got lower A.B.A. ratings than judges whom lawyers rated as only 'fair.'" *Lott*

The takeover of the federal judicial system advanced greatly under the two Bush presidents. Every single federal judge appointed by George H. W. Bush or George W. Bush, was either a member or approved by members Society. The Justice Department hired all or mostly all young lawyers aligned with the Federalist Society. The same was true for other federal agencies. During the administrations of the two Bushes, multiples of cases were brought to federal courts by Society members. Favorite cases were government regulations, affirmative action, weakening workers' access to courts, same for consumers and environmentalists, opposing LGBTQ rights, for tax support for private schools, and opposing abortion, and finally giving more power to the president. *Avery and Mclaughlin*, pp. 2, 3.

After achieving the mostly Democratic-supported civil rights legislation, the actual implementation of its goals was only partly achieved. As soon as Republican administrations were elected, there was a concerted effort to undo the organizations and programs designed to carry out the legislation. the liberal legal network achieved only qualified success. *Avery and Mclaughlin*, p. 7.

Federalist Society Supports Reinterpretation of the Second Amendment*

Through most of the history under our Constitution, the Second Amendment was not interpreted as an individual right—rather, it was to provide a militia for the common defense. In a 1939 ruling *United States v. Miller*, the Court ruled that the Second Amendment was not a right for an individual to bear arms. Justice James Clark McReynolds wrote that "in the absence of any evidence tending to show that possession or use of a 'shotgun having a barrel of less than eighteen inches in length' at this time has some reasonable relationship to the preservation or efficiency of a well-regulated militia, we cannot say that the Second Amendment guarantees the right to keep and bear such an instrument." Most political scientists agreed with this interpretation. *Hollis-Brusky* pp. 31, 32. *See also, *Wikipedia Heller*, September 2020 and *Nash*, pp. 117 – 120.

But in 1997, Supreme Court Justice Thomas said that there were more and more opinions that the Second Amendment was an individual right. Thomas hoped that the Court got a case where they could rule on this new viewpoint. Thomas's viewpoint signaled to members of the

Federalist Society that the Supreme Court might get them a ruling to their liking. *Hollis-Brusky* pp. 33, 34. So much for calling balls and strikes.

This opportunity came in 2008 when *District of Columbia v. Heller, 2008* was brought to the Supreme Court. Heller brought the case to challenge the District of Columbia law which restricted how hand guns could be used and secured by the owner. A favorable ruling that struck down the law could validate Justice Thomas's position—that an individual had the right to bear arms. So, in 2008, members of the Federalist Society network filed a case that got to the Supreme Court. Justice Thomas was glad the case came to the Court so it could reconsider the restrictions on an individual right to have guns which, in his opinion, was what the Second Amendment said. *Hollis-Brusky* pp. 33, 34.

In *Heller*, the Court ruled for the first time, five to four, that the DC firearms control regulations violated the Second Amendment, which protected individual right to bear arms. The opinion was written by Antonin Scalia—John Roberts, Anthony Kennedy, Clarence Thomas, and Samuel Alito voted in the majority.

Three of the lawyers leading the case (Clark M Neily III, Robert Levy, and Alan Gura) had ties to the Federalist Society and twenty-one members of the Federalist Society network signed on to eight different *amicus curiae* briefs submitted on behalf of Heller. *Hollis-Brusky* p. 45.

To get to the position that the Amendment protects an individual right, the Federalist Society and others favoring this interpretation are claiming that this was the original intent of the Amendment and that providing for a militia to protect the nation was an add-on to the primary purpose. Put another way, Society network members argue that the Originalist reading of the Second Amendment commands us to read it **backward**. *Hollis-Brusky* pp. 36, 37.

> The wording now is, "a well-regulated militia, being necessary to the security of a free State, the right of the people to keep and bear arms, shall not be infringed."

The society would have us read it, "the people's right to bear arms, shall not be infringed, a well-regulated militia, being necessary to the security of a free state.

In my reading of the State constitutions from around the time of the Revolution and during the Articles of Confederation period, some states provided for some individuals to have guns. So, the wording in the US Constitution didn't come out of nowhere. The larger question that I pose in *Nash* is whether the Constitution should be interpreted today <u>to **require** the population to be in danger from gun violence</u>. *Nash*, p. 50.

Waldman has a detailed review of how Justice Scalia made the argument for the majority's opinion. Scalia went right to the argument that "the right to bear arms," is the controlling wording, according to Scalia, because that was how people wrote in the 1700s. The opinion, which he wrote for the majority, parses every word in the Second Amendment and giving each word a meaning, not always the meaning that the word has when written in sentences. *Waldman*, pp. 121 – 126.

"According to adjunct Professor of Law at Duquesne University School of Law Anthony Picadio, who said he's not anti-gun but rather "anti-bad-judging," Justice Scalia's reasoning in *Heller* is the product of an erroneous reading of colonial history and the drafting history of the Second Amendment. He argued that the Southern slave states would never have ratified the Second Amendment if it had been understood as creating an individual right to own firearms, because of their fear of arming free blacks. After a lengthy historical and legal analysis Anthony Picadio concluded: "If the Second Amendment had been understood to have the meaning given to it by Justice Scalia, it would not have been ratified by Virginia and the other slave states." *Wikipedia*, January 2021.

So, after all these centuries, the Court has found the "lost meaning" of the Second Amendment. But as a Judge Sprecher stated, the meanings are never "lost." What happens is that advocates of a position work and work through various methods over a long period of time to create in the minds of a critical mass of lawyers and intellects that the wording should be re-interpreted.

In *Heller*, Justice Scalia was able to draw on Society members and their decades of writings, speeches, and conferences to put together the individual rights justification. Society members and allies saw the Heller decision as a starting point to advance other favored positions and to protect those cases already won.

George Will, who delivered an address at a Society convention in 2000, remarked in 2008 in a *Washington Post* editorial "of conservatives' few victories this year, the most cherished came when the Supreme Court, in *Heller*, held for the first time that the Second Amendment protects an individual right to bear arms." Society network actors celebrated these victories (or at least protecting them from being narrowed or eroded in the lower courts) as just beginning making our society over in the image of the Society. *Hollis-Brusky* pp. 57, 58.

A mere two years later, in 2010, in an opinion written by another Federalist Society member—Justice Samuel Alito—the Supreme Court declared that the states could not legislate in opposition to the finding of the Supreme Court on this issue. So much for conservatives giving deference to States.

Opening the Money Floodgates—Citizens United

The road to getting the Supreme Court to adopt *Citizens United* is a prime example of how the Federalist Society and other conservative groups accomplish their goals—they take the long view, as has been shown in initiatives already discussed. For campaign finance especially, conservatives providing money to the cause, knew that this was a war of ideas—it takes a long slog to get important members of society to buy in to the ideas. Not surprisingly, one of the money bags in this long view was David and Charles Koch, who are staunch supporters—and funders—of the Federalist Society.

For most issues, liberals don't keep at it for the long run. Conservatives have learned to take the long view, learning from mistakes in strategy and then changing their strategies. *Avery and Mclaughlin*, p. 17. [This is a warning and lesson to liberals—if we want political changes, we have to take the long view—do the leg work, pester politicians, put money into it, and talk to friends and family. Rev. Martin Luther King understood this and tried to educate followers.]

As is well known, the Supreme Court held in *Citizens United v. Federal Elections Commission*, that First Amendment protections included corporations. The ruling means money has rights. Among lead advocates through the courts was Society member James Bopp and Theodore Olson presented the case before the Supreme Court. *Avery and Mclaughlin*, p. 12.

Common Cause tried to make the case that Justices Scalia and Thomas should have declined to participate in the case because they had associated with corporate leaders whose political aims were advanced by the ruling. This went nowhere.

The objective to get unlimited campaign financing was started by the newly formed Free Speech and Election Law Practice Group of the Federalist Society. Its first primary activity was to defeat the Bipartisan Campaign Reform Act (BCRA), often referred to as the McCain–Feingold Act. Senator Mitch McConnell got into his leadership position in the Senate by leading the fight against BCRA, calling McCain-Feingold as "an unprecedented power grab." He argued that all Americans should be horrified by professional reformers forcing a bureaucratic takeover of the American political process. [Notice McConnell's choice of words to get an emotional, rather than a rational response.] *Hollis-Brusky* p. 65.

McConnell is saying that the power structure that has been in place and restricts most of society from having a say in the democratic process should continue; that freedom and liberty for the powerful should be protected. Remember the statement from the Federalist Society that, "the state exists to preserve individual freedom." Nothing is said about a responsibility to create and preserve participatory democracy, where each individual has a means to be heard.

Others have warned that limiting campaign financing will enable a liberal takeover of our nation. One such argument, "pluralistic roots of the First Amendment should make us suspicious that any attempt to restrict expenditures for political speech is actually an attempt to entrench a legislative majority." [Up is down and down is up.] *Hollis-Brusky* pp. 68, 69.

Here is how The Free Speech and Election Law Practice Group worked; publication of newsletters, commenting on previous Supreme Court decisions, hosting panels of "experts" at every Society's National Lawyers Convention, and Election Law Series" as a "Special Project" publication, all to keep the issue before the Society. At the 2003 Convention, Daniel Ortiz, Trevor Potter, Kenneth Starr, David Thompson, and Fifth Circuit Judge Jerry Smith all pushed the topic of "Campaign Finance Reform in the Supreme Court. Now you can see the prime movers all in one place. *Hollis-Brusky* p. 67.

Jumping ahead to the 2010 decision, here are the players in that action. In addition to Theodore Olson, who took over the lead from James Bopp, there were other Society network members pushing for *Citizens United*, including Edwin Meese, Bradley Smith, Charles Cooper, David Thompson, Floyd Abrams, Joe Gura, John Eastman, Laurence Gold, Steven Law, Steven Shapiro, Reid Cox, and Allison Hayward. Of the four Federalist Society affiliated Supreme Court Justices in the majority in *Citizens United*, two wrote separate opinions in the case— Roberts and Scalia.

The first modern ruling on campaign financing by a modern Court was issued in 2003. The decision was by vote of five to four that the federal government had a compelling interest and it was constitutionally permissible to regulate "the corrosive and distorting effects of immense aggregations of wealth that are accumulated with the help of the corporate form." *Hollis-Brusky* p. 76.

The majority opinion was written by Sandra Day O'Connor and John Paul Stevens. They relied on the 1990 Court ruling in *Austin v. Michigan.* This held that: 1. Section 54(1) does not violate the First Amendment. (a) Although § 54(1)'s requirements burden the Chamber's exercise of political expression, see FEC v. Massachusetts Citizens for Life, Inc., they are justified by a compelling state interest: preventing corruption or the appearance of corruption in the political arena by reducing the threat that huge corporate treasuries, which are amassed with the aid of favorable state laws and have little or no correlation to the public's support for the corporation's political ideas, will be used to influence unfairly election outcomes." *Hollis-Brusky* p. 76, and Wikipedia November 2020.

Needless to say, this angered the Federalist Society members and allies. They did not like the use of *Austin v. Michigan* which narrowed the freedom for corporations to finance political campaigns. The original Court proponent of unlimited campaign spending, Clarence Thomas wrote that "because *Austin's* definition of 'corruption' is incompatible with the First Amendment, I would overturn *Austin* and hold that the potential for corporations and unions to influence voters … is not a form of corruption justifying any state regulation or suppression." *Hollis-Brusky* p. 76.

Roberts's dissenting opinion strongly argued that the majority relied too heavily on prior opinions. He said that if prior opinions were in error, then it was the duty of the Court to issue contrary opinions. Relying on prior opinions was not an end in itself—it only provides a savings of effort if a prior opinion can be cited. Roberts continued, "fidelity to any particular precedent does more to damage this constitutional ideal than to advance it, we must be more willing to depart from that precedent." *Hollis-Brusky* pp. 85, 86.

Roberts, of course, is right. The Court rightfully departed from settled law in many cases, most famously in *Brown v. Board of Education* in abandoning *Dred Scott v. Sandford*, and *Plessy v. Ferguson,* rulings that legally instituted racism. The issue is, should you depart from precedent so that you can take away human rights—forgetting that the public good, the real welfare of the great body of people is the supreme object to be pursued, as Madison taught us.

In the first set of arguments before the Court, Theodore Olson had presented *Citizens United* to the Court in a **narrow** way ... the main issue was whether the McCain-Feingold law applied to a commentary, presented on video on demand, by a nonprofit corporation." At this time, *Citizens United* was not asking the Supreme Court to overrule the relevant portions of McCain-Feingold, in *McConnell v. Federal Election Commission* because—the organization did not think that necessary. **However, a discussion was held outside the public's knowledge where it was decided that the argument would be withdrawn and presented later.**

After this out-of-sight discussion, Roberts announced that a new round of arguments would be heard and invited Olson and his assistants to file new briefs to the next Court session to address whether *Austin* and *McConnell* should be overturned. *Hollis-Brusky* pp. 81 - 83.

Instead of waiting for the first Monday in October (when the Supreme Court's new term traditionally begins), the second round of oral argument in *Citizens United* was scheduled for September 9, 2009.

Proponents of unrestricted financing argued that the Constitution does not distinguish between individual speech and corporate speech. [This is obviously true; the Constitution does not specify lots of things.]

In the final opinion released on January 10, 2010, Justice Kennedy wrote for the majority, holding that by barring corporations and unions from using general treasury funds to make independent expenditures that advocate the election or defeat of a candidate, the federal government violated the First Amendment by wrongly suppressing political speech by corporations.

This was the culmination of the long march of Scalia, Thomas, and Kennedy. This decision effectively overruled the precedent established in both *Austin* and *McConnell*. *Hollis-Brusky* p. 83.

The January 2010 decision in *Citizens United* which removed any restrictions on campaign financing totally changed our society. A vast number of liberal politicians, including Nancy Pelosi, Charles Schumer, and promised to introduce legislation to overturn *Citizens United*. It was obvious to large segments of society that the Court had overreached. Rather than waiting for cases to come before the Court—just as it did in the Second Amendment ruling, it brought up the case on its own initiative. Again, so much for just calling balls and strikes. *Hollis-Brusky* pp. 61, 62.

Jerrold Nadler, chair of The House of Representatives Committee on the Constitution, Civil Rights and Civil Liberties said that, "One of the things that strikes me, … is the extent to which an extraordinarily activist Court reached out to issue this decision. The justices answered a question they weren't asked in order to overturn a century of precedent which they had reaffirmed only recently." *Hollis-Brusky* pp. 61, 62.

Justice John Paul Stevens in his dissenting opinion, argued that "the Court addressed a question not raised by the litigants when it found BCRA §203 to be facially unconstitutional, and that the majority "changed the case to give themselves an opportunity to change the law". He argued that the majority had expanded the scope beyond the questions presented by the appellant and that therefore a sufficient record for judging the case did not exist." *Wikipedia* September 2020.

> Again, I repeat Madison's words in Federalist Paper No. 45: We have heard of the impious doctrine in the Old World that the people were made for kings, not kings for the people. Is the same doctrine to be revived in the New in another shape—that solid happiness of the people is to be sacrificed to the views of political institution of a different form? It is too

early for politicians to presume on our forgetting **that the public good, the real welfare of the great body of people**, is the supreme object to be pursued, and that no form of government whatever has any other value than as it may be fitted for the attainment of this objective. Were the plan of the convention adverse to the public happiness, my voice would be, reject the plan. Were the Union itself inconsistent with the public happiness, it would be, abolish the union. In like manner, as far as the sovereignty of the States cannot be reconciled to the happiness of the people, the voice of every good citizen must be, let the former be sacrificed to the latter.

Property Rights and the "Takings" Clause

Avery and Mclaughlin has a chapter devoted to property rights. This gets into complicated arguments when the cases have come to the Supreme Court. The Constitution has very little guidance, so the justices have crafted their positions as each case is presented. I could not see a lot of consistency from case to case. [You are invited to read them and form your opinion.] The one constant is that the conservative judges have defended property rights of individuals—and corporations. But the way they have arrived at their opinion is quite variable. Sometimes they have relied on precedent, other times finding a new interpretation of some previous case, or going back to common law or medieval law. *Avery and Mclaughlin*, p. 44.

It takes a deep plunge into the issue to understand the legal battles that have taken place and it is beyond the purposes of this treatise, but here is some introduction. In 1922, the Supreme Court heard a case, *Pennsylvania Coal v. Mahon*, where the issue was whether the government must compensate property owners whose property lost value because of a government action. Justice Oliver Wendell Holmes pointed out that government simply could not function if it had to compensate every person whose property lost value.

Experts going back to the Constitution say that, yes, James Madison, the author of the takings clause in the Constitution, was concerned about the issues of the day but a clear statement about property rights was not one of them. One has to do a little searching in the Constitution to even find the "taking." It is in Amendment V. titled, "Rights in criminal cases." The last phrase of this amendment reads, "<u>nor shall private property be taken for public use, without just compensation</u>."

Richard Epstein was an early promoter of the idea that any action the government takes that effects the value of one's property, such as rent controls, minimum wage laws, zoning laws, the owner should be compensated. This position went way past anything that can be found in the Constitution. He went back to the Magna Carta and English common law as interpreted by John Locke. John Locke is considered by many as the intellectual source for our Constitution.

Arguments about property rights gets into deep philosophical discussions and assertions. Douglas A. Kendall takes on Epstein for misinterpreting Locke. One argument from Locke is that each individual owns his own labor; no one owned the external things of the world until the first possessor acquired them." *Avery and Mclaughlin*, p. 52, 53. [This passage goes on to criticisms of Epstein's work by both the left and right in politics, including Robert Borke, which is beyond the purpose of this work.]

> This idea of "first possessor" is deeply disturbing to me. Who is the "first possessor?" The migrants from Africa who moved into Europe, Asia, and Australia some 40 to 50 thousand years ago? The migrants who moved onto land at the end of the last ice age? When they fought off another migrating group, were they the first possessor? Or, in Europe, was it the Roman

invaders of Gaul? I'm sure they had papers. The kings, despots, and the church, all of whom claimed the land was given to them by "divine rights"? European invaders of the Americas who claimed via the Doctrine of Discovery, that the residents, the Indigenous people, had no rights? I say we should be very careful when we say this is mine—not legally, but **morally**.

The Indigenous people of the North America did not have the concept of ownership of land. Rather the concept was/is that the land is part of the environment and is to be treasured for the gifts it provides for their use and livelihood. *See, Dunbar-Ortiz*. I assume that a similar concept was held by "landless" people of Europe. For example British Enclosure Acts, enabled the powerful to <u>enclose</u> <u>open fields</u> and <u>common land</u> in England and Wales, creating **legal** property rights to land previously used by local residents. Between 1604 and 1914, over 5,200 individual enclosure acts were passed, affecting 6.8 million acres (2,800,000 ha; 28,000 km^2). Wikipedia, October 2020. I wonder how many people were therefore thrown into poverty and became dependent on others for their livelihood. Note that <u>legal</u> rights were established—not <u>moral</u> rights.

A hard insistence on property rights makes itself known by such acts as attacking someone for throwing a candy wrapper on your property, or the neighborhood kids accidently throwing a ball onto your property and you yell at them or worse maybe call the police. It also shows when a person acts as though a public resource such as a highway is his alone to use and everyone else has to get out of the way.

Some people are so protective of their belongings that they spend a lot of emotional energy fearing anything that may damage them. A hairline scratch on their car, a minor imperfection on clothes coming back from the cleaners, worrying if a house cleaner may steal a spoon, etc., etc.

Lost is the tendency to be generous when neighbors near and far suffers and we insist that everything I have is mine. A little reflection lets us realize that we have not gotten anything at all by our own efforts without the dedication of generations including our parents, neighbors, teachers, scientists, philosophers, soldiers, governments, etc. And then there is the gift of our environment that we did nothing to create. Realizing this dependence and interdependence leads to gratitude and generosity.

One more thing. Think about all the people present and past generations—farm workers, factory workers, hotel cleaning staff, various groups of non-citizens, nannies, house maids, chauffeurs, some teachers and other professionals and other people who were/are not paid a living wage. This enables the rest of us to have money for our use and enjoyment that **morally** belongs to them.

Those that insist on one hundred percent keeping what they consider theirs are the most unhappy among us.

A case decided by the Supreme Court in 2005, *Kelo v. City of New London*, lit a fire under the conservatives. This was a finding that Kelo's property could be condemned so that a private developer could "make a better use of the property." This has been referred to many times as showing that the liberals on the Court were re-writing the Constitution. *Avery and Mclaughlin*, pp. 60, 61. (I happen to agree. One private party should not be able to get a court to condemn another's private property. Who would agree to have their property subject to such a policy?)

An organization, Foundation for Research on Economics and the Environment (FREE) has seized on the public outcry from *Kelo* and has been in the forefront in opposing taking of private property for environmental and other land use regulations.

Supporters of FREE reads like lists of anti-government individuals and organizations found in Topic IV. Koch family, Claude E. Lambe Charitable Foundation, the John M. Olin Foundation, and the Sarah Scaife Foundation. For example, between 1988 and 2008, the Charles R. Lambe Charitable Foundation donated more than one million dollars to FREE.

During that time period, the Charles R. Lambe Charitable Foundation also contributed to the Cato Institute, $9.5 million, the Federalist Society, $1 million, the Heritage Foundation, $3.4 million, and the Institute for Justice, $1 million. FREE's board of directors includes influential conservatives such as John Kannon, vice president and senior counselor at the Heritage Foundation, and Judge Edith Brown Clement, now on the Fifth Circuit Court of Appeals. Jonathan Adler of Case Western Reserve University School of Law is on the Executive Committee of the Society's Environmental Law of Property Rights Practice Group. Ed Meese was formerly a director. The strategy of the Koch brothers to use funds wisely is evident here. The money goes to where it can be most effective. *Avery and Mclaughlin*, pp. 64 – 66.

Further emphasizing the importance of property, President Reagan greatly increased the power of the Office of Management and Budget to oversee regulations in the areas of health, safety, and the environment. OMB was given a final say over whether each regulation would be approved. On its face, this may sound like good management to make sure the regulations were not overly burdensome and that they did not duplicate or contradict other existing regulations. But OMB's control was narrower. <u>Its review simply was to assure that costs to industry were eliminated</u>. Interests representing the environment and consumers and workers were concerned that the agency was overstepping its legislative authority and did not provide for a process of public review of its decisions.

Under Reagan, an office within OMB called the Office of Information and Regulatory Affairs, (OIRA) under Jay Plager, and Executive Order 12, 630, (authored by Roger Marzulla from Mountain States Legal Fund,) reviews of proposed regulations were greatly expanded. The expressed purpose of such initiatives was to assure that the federal government would not be subjected to increased litigation. The requirement was that "a proposed regulation that restricted the use of private property must be proportionate to the problem that the regulation sought to address." Justice Scalia had proposed this language in a dissenting opinion of the Court. *Avery and Mclaughlin*, pp. 64 – 66.

George H. W. Bush used OIRA and Executive Order 12, 630, to create an anti-regulatory environment. The purpose of OIRA was to look into whether a proposes regulation was likely to result in litigation. A risk assessment was to be performed as the analysis of potential litigation. These were for the purpose of determining whether the restricted use of private property was proportionate to the problem that the regulation sought to address.

George H. W. Bush appointed vice president, Dan Quayle as chair of OIRA. His strong support for business assured that their position was always going to be looked upon favorably. Not only was this point of view on regulation given priority, but Quayle was conducting business behind closed doors—the very opposite of how federal rule-making is legally done. (I was rather heavily involved in federal rulemaking for a good share of my career as a federal employee.) That Quayle operated in secret is evidenced by his refusal to respond to Freedom of Information

Act requests or to testify before committees overseeing the agencies whose rules the council reviewed. *Avery and Mclaughlin*, pp. 67, 68.

That the OIRA had a lot of power is shown by heavy hitters who served on the council, including Richard Thornburgh, attorney general from 1988 to 1991 and later joined the Federalist Society's Criminal Law and Procedure Practice Group, William Barr, who for years has argued that the president should have more power and Congress less. OIRA was even at that time said to be the best example of this presidential power. Barr is active in Federalist Society affairs.

Under Quayle, David McIntosh, was in charge of actual implementation. Among his goals was removing about half the country' wetlands from regulation and therefore these could be developed. Later as a congressman, McIntosh continued pushing the issue emphasizing that the Constitution prohibited the government from taking private land without just compensation. *Avery and Mclaughlin*, pp. 68, 69.

Race and Gender Discrimination

Racism has been part of the Republican strength since the takeover by Goldwater and William F. Buckley Jr. The Federalist Society took up this mantle as one of the methods of preserving the centuries-old power structure. Following *Brown v. Topeka Board of Education*, the Society, mostly in sympathy with the Republican Party, set about dismantling it.

Even though there were some earlier cases, the Reagan administration provided a launching pad for the conservative campaign against affirmative action, school desegregation and similar initiatives. Many Federalist Society members were part of this. Ed Meese, who was very proud of his accomplishments, was the leader. Others with significant influence were Carolyn Kuhl and Michael McConnell, who would be appointed as Court of Appeals judges by George W. Bush; Charles J. Cooper, director of the Office of Legal Counsel; T. Kennedy Cribb, Jr., Meese's counselor and later a member of the Board of Directors of the

Society; Michal Carvin, who became senior advisor to the Civil Rights Practice Group and a cofounder of the Center for Individual Rights; Linda Chavez, staff director to the US Commission on Civil Rights in Reagan's first term and later the founder and chair of the Center for Equal Opportunity, Roger Clegg, later the president and general counsel of the Center for Opportunity; and Gerald A. Reynolds, then president of the Center for New Black Leadership. William Bradford Reynolds, an ally of the Society, and as head of the Civil Rights Division of the Justice Department led this effort. *Avery and Mclaughlin, p. 121.*

Reynolds's actions as head of the Civil Rights Division were so controversial that his nomination to the position of associate attorney general was rejected by the Senate Judiciary Committee, despite the fact that it was led by Republicans. Critics claimed that he "had refused to enforce civil rights laws and ignored court rulings with which he disagreed." Republican senator Arlen Specter "accused Reynolds of giving misleading testimony, 'disregarding the established law,' and 'elevating his own legal judgements over the judgements of the courts.

Clarence Thomas was chairman of the Equal Employment Opportunity Commission (EEOC) from 1982 to 1990. The direction of the EEOC under Reagan was set by the 1980 EEOC transition team that included committed conservatives Jay Parker, the chair; Thomas; Hugh Joseph Beard, Jr., later counsel to the Center for Equal Opportunity, Andrew W. Lester former membership director of the Civil Rights Practice Group; and William Keyes.

Chairman Thomas waged "a counterattack on the received wisdom of the civil rights community." Thomas turned the EEOC away from the sweeping enforcement activities that had been focused on goals, timetables, and the use of tests and other hiring requirements disadvantageous to minorities. Instead, he focused on individual claims of discrimination. Thomas argued, "Law enforcement, not social engineering was the proper mission of the agency."

Bolick who worked for Thomas at the EEOC "learned to spin the debate" by avoiding terms like "affirmative action" "goals" or "timetables" and using terms like, "quotas" and "racial preferences." *Avery and Mclaughlin, p. 122.*

Thus, they got active in court cases and litigation where the purpose was to extend rights to other groups. A primary case was *Parents Involved in Community Schools v. Seattle School District No. 1.* Two voluntary school integration plans had been struck down, one in Seattle and one in Jefferson County Kentucky. The ruling was that the plans violated the equal protection clause of the Fourteenth Amendment. They ruled that it was unconstitutional to take race into account in assigned students to particular schools.

It cannot be emphasized too much that this was a great victory for a well-organized and funded operation. It affirmed a favorite of the Federalist Society—to do away with government decision-making based on race. The Society was in the lead on this issue, Harry. F. Korrell, spoke for the position of the Society; he was a member of the Society's Puget Sound Lawyers chapter and a member of its Labor and Employment Practice Group's national executive board. Paul Clement, solicitor general of the US and other Society members filed amicus briefs for a variety of conservative groups. *Avery and Mclaughlin, pp. 99, 100.*

Affirmative action was fought primarily by the now the time-worn argument about the harm coming from promoting unqualified students. One of Ed Meese's favorites, Clint Bolick, who is one of the Society's, most influential members on the topic of affirmative action had written against affirmative action since his student days at the King Hall School of Law at U. C. Davis in California.

He called it irresponsible and a cruel hoax to send law school graduates into the world that can't communicate properly or competently represent clients. It is better to screen students before they are admitted and accept only those that are qualified. We should avoid the frenzy of trying to get more minority students regardless of qualifications. Law school is too late to acquire these basic skills and King Hall is not the place to conduct remedial education no matter whether their disadvantage was caused earlier. Bolick was criticizing a "frenzy" to admit Black students to an institution named for Dr. Martin Luther King. *Avery and Mclaughlin, p. 101.*

Perhaps Bolick did not have some of the knowledge or concepts that have been developed regarding equal opportunity. (It's also possible that he was just looking for a justification to prohibit racial and ethnic minorities from being admitted to King Hall.) The concept is that if some of the students that are admitted are not as well educated as others due to living with racism their whole lives, a solution is to create equal access—not equal opportunity.

Visualize some people standing on the ground and looking over a fence that you can't see through. Some are tall and some are short. The tall people can easily see over the fence. The short group can't see over at all. Equal opportunity means they are all standing on the same ground so each group has equal opportunity. [This is what Bolick advocated.]

Equal access means that for the short people, you provide a stool for them to stand on. For the tall people no stool is provided, they are tall enough to see over the fence. With the short people on stools, all of the people have equal access to seeing what is on the other side of the fence.

In case the message is lost with the analogy, it means that for the short people, you provide some help at King Hall—correct the deficiencies some students had coming into the law program. By the time of graduation, the decision then could be to graduate only those that are "clearly qualified."

Think for a moment that it is in the national interest to enable all residents to perform at their highest capabilities. If we do not do this, then we have whole segments of our population performing below their capabilities. If they were given the opportunity to contribute their talents, the nation would have a higher income, clients would be better represented, and fewer people would be in the income category where they must depend on others.

Reinterpreting the Fourteenth Amendment

Again, Chief Justice of the Supreme Court, John Roberts has **reinterpreted the Constitution. This time it was** the Fourteenth Amendment. Contrary to overwhelming evidence, he says that the Amendment should apply only to individual acts of discrimination—not a population of Americans. He stated, "There is no ambiguity in that statement." **Can you imagine?** The Fourteenth Amendment was enacted at the end of the Civil War. Throughout its wording it refers to those that were involved with the insurrection and their not having the right to serve in public office, nor will debts incurred in the insurrection be paid off by the US or any state. If the Amendment was not about ending enslavement of a category of people (those of African descent held in chattel slavery), it would never been enacted.

Roberts argued that the court's decision in *Parents Involved*, was "faithful to the heritage of *Brown*." This was immediately challenged by those that had worked so hard to get to the *Brown* ruling. Jack Greenberg called it "preposterous." William T. Coleman Jr. said it was "dirty pool," and Carter, a senior judge of the US District Court in New York, said it stood their argument on its head." Rather than watering down *Brown*,

Carter said it should be interpreted as the legal team had intended—that *Brown* requires integration. If this interpretation had been kept, the nation would not be still in the situation where so many Black students are attending low quality schools with mostly minority students. *Brown* was meant to improve the educational opportunities of Black students. That this largely has not happened is due to the powers of Justice Roberts and those in power that agree with him. *Avery and Mclaughlin, pp. 102, 103.*

The Federalist Society has adopted a Court designation from 1944, called strict scrutiny. Where this came from is beyond this inquiry. But the idea is that legislation must not only serve a "compelling interest" but it must be "narrowly tailored" to fit the purpose. This is a convenient concept to use when the Court wants to reject an argument and once this standard is adopted, the Court rarely upholds legislation as constitutional.

The Court has done this in all racial classification cases in 1989 and 1995 to require set asides for racial minorities in construction. Roberts argued that strict scrutiny is justified in all cases where there are racial classifications, in part because it is just too difficult to determine if the loss of opportunity was an individual thing or because of racial discrimination. He therefore wants to take the determination out of the hands of lower courts, or even administrative deliberations.

The minority in the Court, Breyer, Stevens, Souter, and Ginsberg, disagreed and argued that given the purposes of the Fourteenth Amendment "to bring into American society as full members those whom the Nation had previously held in slavery," the framers of the amendment "would have understood the legal and practical difference between the use of race-conscious criteria in defense of that purpose, namely to keep the races apart, and the use of race-conscious criteria to further that purpose, namely to bring the races together."

Even though a majority of the Supreme Court has been using strict scrutiny, many federal court judges and constitutional law specialists continue to argue that racial classifications for the purposes of affirmative action should be reviewed more in the nature of the original intent of the litigants in *Brown*. Justice Stevens has concluded, "There is no moral or constitutional equivalence between a policy that is designed to perpetual a caste system and one that seeks to eradicate racial subordination."

Justice Ginsburg concluded that "consistency," with respect to the standard of review, regardless of the purpose for which racial classifications are employed, would only be fitting "when our Nation is free of the vestiges of rank discrimination long reinforced by law." She emphasized, however, that "the effects of centuries of law-sanctioned inequality remain painfully evident in our communities and schools." She understood the relevance of social discrimination in employment, access to health care, and residential housing to diminished educational opportunities. *Avery and Mclaughlin, p. 104, 105.*

To say that two centuries of struggle for freedom from oppression is not about racism is to trivialize the lives and deaths of those who suffered under the system. To pretend that a white person denied access to an institution is the same as a Black person denied access, is to pretend that history never happened and that the present doesn't exist.

Racism is not merely a system that distinguishes one race from another, but more importantly it allocates power to the white race and denies power to minority races. *Avery and Mclaughlin, pp. 106, 107.*

> This is the appropriate place to put a quote I heard recently in a discussion group. "Is it White Supremacy? If it benefits whites and holds back Blacks, it is White Supremacy." The larger issue here is that White Supremacy is not confined to the KKK and other hate groups. It is the system we live in today, where the major institutions— government, large business, (including laws that give large businesses extraordinary access to government decision-makers), entertainment, the press, are all controlled by the white power structure.

Conservatives argue that when the rational for using racial classifications is previous discrimination, there must be proof of intentional discrimination. Limiting government's role in addressing societal discrimination appeals to conservatives both because of their analysis of race and because in general they prefer small government.

Proponents of this position are Society members, William Bradford Reynolds, Charles J. Cooper, Michael Carvin, and Samuel A. Alito, Jr., who had become a justice of the Supreme Court by the time of the *Parents Involved* decision. Conservatives, especially those associated with the Society lose no opportunity to emphasize that federal courts should not base discrimination systemic social problems, but rather limited to "specific violations." *Avery and Mclaughlin, p. 111.*

In the case of *Wards Cove Packing, Inc. v. Antonio*, a case brought by non-white workers in Alaska, "the Supreme Court held that the act that the cannery workers were predominately nonwhite and the non-cannery workers were predominantly white did not constitute relevant statistical proof of disparate impact. The court reasoned that it was inappropriate to compare the number of nonwhites in one category of employees with the number of non-whites in another category. The appropriate comparison, according to the court, was between the percentage of nonwhites who were cannery workers with the percentage of nonwhites in the labor market for those positions, and between the percentage of nonwhite who were non-cannery workers with the percentage of nonwhites in the labor market for those positions. The court concluded that only in this way could it be determined whether there was discrimination against workers actually qualified and willing to take the more desirable jobs." *Avery and Mclaughlin, pp. 124, 125, 126.*

Do you understand what they said? The Court did every kind of gymnastics to come up with an argument that they liked.

This is clearly an instance where there should have been economists and other social scientists advising the court on the issue of job discrimination. It is quite obvious that they first did an untrained analysis of an area they knew little about and then set out to make a decision—a decision that most likely fit their already preference for how it should be ruled. This is not unlike "scientists" first deciding on what they want as an outcome—then looking for ways to justify their position.

A related question—should there only be lawyers on the Supreme Court?

Federalist Society Changes Strategies—not Goals

Federalist Society members and others were dissatisfied that the courts had not completely eliminate affirmative action. The next step adopted in the mid-1990s was to turn to ballot initiatives. The campaign started in California. In November 1996, the state's voters passed the California Civil Rights Initiative (CCRI). Proposition 209, which barred all use of race and sex preferences in government contracting, employment, and education, including in affirmative action programs. This "direct democracy" measure required big money. The group Yes on Proposition 209 raised $5.2 million and spent $4.4 million to get it passed. Other groups and individuals spent addition hundreds of thousands of dollars.

As I have noted above, putting human and civil rights to a vote is the wrong way to deal with these rights. They should be good for all time—not subject to the whims of politicians or the voting population. Human enslavement, child labor, and dozens maybe hundreds of issues of human dignity were once accepted by the population and protected in law.

Proposition 209 or similar efforts is ongoing in several states with familiar advocates: Society members or supporters, are Clint Bolick, Theodore Olson, Sharon L. Brown, Gary G. Kreep, Ward Connerly, and Kevin Snider. Organizations are: The Civil Rights Practice Group, Independent Women's Forum, Pacific Legal Foundation, Log Cabin Republicans, US Justice Foundation, the Center for Individual Rights, the American Civil Rights Institute (ACRI). Efforts were enacted in other states; Washington in 1998, Michigan in 2006, Nebraska in 2008, and Arizona in 2010.

These successes led to a push to enact federal legislation, the Civil Rights Act of 1997. The House Judiciary Committee tabled the bill and, it was never passed.

Federalist Society Opposes Individual Choice

Next is the Federalist Society and allies using laws and the courts to prohibit individuals from making choices on family planning, choice of marriage partner, equal rights for women, etc. The political and religious right says these are family values.

Even though the religious right went into politics prior to the creation of the Society, the two have found common cause and some of these religious leaders are also active in the Society. Both groups talk of the same principles; religious liberty, individual freedom, and separation of powers. *Avery and Mclaughlin, p. 142.*

> Here is a case of words meaning the opposite of what is expressed. The religious right has for years claimed that the government or someone is trying to cancel Christmas by simply saying, "happy holidays" rather than "merry Christmas." By this claim, they are not <u>for</u> religious freedom, but rather pushing for everyone in this diverse nation be a religious-right Christian. Same with

individual freedom. They oppose allowing a woman to make a decision on whether to have an abortion.

Federalist Society founder Steven Calabresi wrote "How to Reverse Government Imposition of Immorality: A Strategy For Eroding Roe v. Wade." His idea was to use tactics for making other political changes. His idea was to work step by step to take away certain parts of *Roe v. Wade*. When enough of the original rights had been taken away, then to argue that the whole thing should be abolished.

Calabresi argued that a constitutional right of women to have abortion is "deeply" and "profoundly" immoral. By making the legality of abortion "a matter of individual constitutional right," the legal system had "put its highest moral imprimatur on a loathsome procedure that ought to be at least discouraged by the law if not forbidden." *Avery and Mclaughlin, p. 155.*

> But the Constitution says nothing about this and at least a good portion of the population has the goal of increasing individual freedom in this diverse society we live in. "Loathsome procedure" is clearly a value judgement—not an expression of truth. Of course, Calabresi has gone from a legal argument to a moral one. I have concluded in the many years of the debate over *Roe v. Wade* in our society that the right to an abortion is one of those beliefs that cannot be proven nor disproven, which puts it in the same category as "all people are created equal." The issue cannot be settled by constitutional arguments.

From Michael Gerson, opinion writer for *The Washington Post*, October 13, 2020. *Dark trade-offs of a fairy tale* (Gerson was an official in the George W. Bush administration and prominently the face of Bush's "compassionate conservative" agenda.)

Commenting on the Senate hearing to approve Amy Barrett for the Supreme Court.

"[f]inally the King's Federalist Society supporters—the watchmen on the wall of conservative legal ideology—are offered their own version of the temptation. They will get a Supreme Court majority that is committed to judicial restraint and the rule of law—but only if they support a king who despises restraint and cares nothing for the rule of law. Barrett's nomination is being considered; the mad king has lambasted his attorney general for failing (so far) to prosecute political enemies on imaginary charges. This is clearly what the king regards as his October surprise: the disqualification of his political opposition through manipulation of the law.

Of all the king's shills, the Federalists are perhaps the most pitiable. For a Supreme Court nominee who supports their beliefs, they will happily dance around a bonfire of those beliefs. To secure a choice taken from their approved list, they are willing to embrace a leader who constantly tests the limits of the law, refuses to affirm a peaceful transfer of power and talks openly of jailing his rivals.

The king's offer is tainted once again: power for Federalist views, but only if they are revealed as pretense.

In the final, decadent days of the mad king's rule, all these groups within the Republican coalition are being made the same offer: power in exchange for the public disgracing of their ideals. Their response was evident in the garden: the hand-shaking and air-kissing of the maskless, the faithless, and the doomed."

References for Topic V

Avery, Michael, and McLaughlin, Danielle, The Federalist Society, How Conservatives Took Back the Law From Liberals, Vanderbilt University Press, Nashville, Tennessee, 37235, ISBN 978-0-8265-1877-4, 2013.

Batkins, Sam, *ABA Retains Little Objectivity in Nomination Process,* Center for Individual Freedom. August 12, 2004.

Baum, *Lawrence and Devins, Neal, The Law, Lawyers, and the Court, Federalist Court, Jurisprudence,* Slate, January 31, 2017.

Dunbar-Ortiz, Roxanne, *An Indigenous Peoples' History of the United States,* Beacon Press, Boston, ISBN 978-0-8070-5783-4, 2014.

Fletcher, Michael A., *What the Federalist Society Stands For; Group Is Haven for Conservative Thought,* The Washington Post, Washington, D.C. 29 July 29, 2005, p. A.21.

Hollis-Brusky, Amanda, *Ideas with Consequences: The Federalist Society and the Conservative Counterrevolution,* Oxford University Press, ISBN 9780199385539.2006 (2015).

Lott, John R., *Pulling Rank,* The New York Times, Opinion, January 25, 2006.

Nash, Darrel A, *A Perspective on How Our Government Was Built, And Some Needed Changes,* Rose Dog Books, 585 Alpha Drive, Suite 103, Pittsburg PA 15238, ISBN 978-1-4809-7915-4, 2018

Roesch, James Rutledge, *from an abridged version of a chapter which will appear in the forthcoming, From Founding Fathers to Fire-Eaters: The Constitutional Doctrine of States' Rights in the Old South.* Aug 25, 2015.

Sunstein, Cass R., Schrade, David, Ellman, Lisa, M., and Sawicki, Andres, Are Judges Political: An Empirical Analysis of the Federal Judiciary, 2006.

_____, *The Federalist Society ABA Ratings of Judicial Nominees.* ABA Watch, July 1996.

Waldman, Michael, *The Second Amendment, A biography,* Simon and Schuster paperbacks, ISBN 978-1-4767-4745-3 (pbk) 2014.

For Further Reading

Toobin, Jeffrey, *How Chief Justice Roberts Orchestrated the Citizens United Decision,* The New Yorker, May 14, 2012.

Topic VI

Covid-19

When I started this project, I did not in my wildest imagination that I would be writing this Topic.

In conversation with a friend soon after we collectively became aware that the virus was a pandemic, I wondered if the nation would join in a national effort to defeat this, as our parents and grandparents had done for World War II. (Yes, there were some cheaters, but there was a huge outpouring of people at all levels doing what they could to win the war.) For WW II, I bought savings stamps for ten cents every week and pasted them in a book that could be used to buy war bonds when the book was full.

Now, we have the answer. A great body of citizens centered around the medical staff and other workers in the COVID wards have and are working tirelessly for days at a time, often risking their own lives. Researchers are dedicated to finding solutions, both for the immediate response and for developing vaccines. Lots of people are wearing masks when they go out in the public. This is the same dedication millions displayed for WW II.

But to the great misfortune of our nation and for millions of citizens, led by the president, irresponsibility is called a virtue—holding huge gatherings, pooh-poohing face masks, totally disregarding scientific knowledge, promoting quack cures, and on and on. The mantle is—my freedom is number one and I am not responsible for anyone else's safety and well-being. This thinking tears apart any society.

Viktor Frankl, a holocaust survivor, has an answer. He wrote in *"Man's Search for Meaning*, "Freedom, however, is not the last word. Freedom is only part of the story and half of the truth. Freedom is but the negative aspect of the whole phenomenon whose positive aspect is responsibleness. In fact, freedom is in danger of degenerating into mere arbitrariness unless it is lived in terms of responsibleness. That is why I recommend that the Statue of Liberty on the East Coast be supplemented by a Statue of Responsibility on the West Coast." *Frankl*, p. 132.

We are in constant struggle in how to balance liberty and responsibility. In our modern world, with increasing populations, increasing wealth, and increasing economic activity, our actions more and more affect others. Sometimes we affect other individuals, but more often whole populations—locally, nationally, and globally. This pushes us more toward the responsibility end and away from liberty and doing what we please. Destroying or emasculating the EPA will not make the challenge of having clean air, clean water, and lowering carbon dioxide in the air go away. It may increase our individual liberties—maybe lowering our taxes in the short run.

Responsibility extends to other citizens and groups of citizens. At one level of responsibility, we help clean up public places after we have used them, keep our grass mowed and weeds pulled partly because we feel responsible to our neighborhood. But as a nation, this requirement for responsibility goes much farther. We should all be concerned with how our fellow citizens are doing in inner cities and racialized ghettos. What should we know about reservation conditions for our Indigenous Peoples? What should we as a nation be doing about the rapid changes in our economy that leave almost state-wide poverty? How should we react to all the rapid changes in our concepts of sexual orientation and gender identity? **The public good, the real welfare of the great body of people, is the supreme object to be pursued.**

I prefer the concept of citizenship to that of patriotism. Citizenship relates to responsibility to others. Humans living first in tribes and growing to larger organizations for connection took individual responsibility to see that the welfare others in the group was tended to. [There are, of course, many notable exceptions to this—feudalism, Russian communism, etc.] Citizenship in its ideal expression means that you have concerns for not only those close to you, but those that may be left out of access to the benefits of the larger society. *Nash*, pp. 124, 125

The corona virus has put us all to the test of being responsible. So, for our own self-interest we should do what we can and follow guidelines from experts to avoid getting and spreading the virus. The much greater issue is that if we do what we can to avoid passing it on to others, this means we are taking responsibility for the greater good. We should do this even if we aren't concerned about our own welfare.

Here is some of the reasons.

Health care workers from the top doctors, the assistants, the nurses, the technicians, the cleaning crews will all be less burdened if each of us do our part to avoid getting the virus. Some report working 14 hours and day 7 days a week, living apart from their families all for the greater good. Then show gratitude to the manufacturers of ventilators, face masks, and lab clothes and all the other equipment needed by the workers to do their work and avoid getting the virus themselves. Same for the truck drivers, packagers, package handlers and on and on that have this added to their regular work.

Then there are those that don't know what they are talking about, just saying things that make them feel important, those that dispute the experts because, well who knows why? And those that go out and buy the medical equipment for their own use, or maybe so they can sell the items at a higher price, thus depriving the medical workers of the supplies they need to care for any who are affected.

As I wrote in, *How Our Government Was Built*, the US Constitution should be looked on as a covenant—not a contract. A covenant means that we are committed to each other—that we will care about each other. Can't we do better?

References for Topic VI

Frankl, Viktor E., Man's Search for Meaning, Beacon Press, Boston ISBN 0-8070-1427-3, 2006.

Rev. Dr. Martin Luther King, Jr. I have a Dream Speech; we are caught in a web of mutuality.

Nash, Darrel A, A Perspective on How Our Government Was Built, And Some Needed Changes, Rose Dog Books, 585 Alpha Drive, Suite 103, Pittsburg PA 15238, ISBN 978-1-4809-7915-4, 2018

Epilogue

I am angry.

For how a few hundred oligarchs have taken over our country from the dreams and hopes of millions who have worked tirelessly to live the promises and dreams set out by our foremothers and forefathers in creating and building our society.

Instead of the grand visions of the Declaration, the Preamble to the Constitution, Madison's statement for what makes a legitimate government, the Gettysburg Address—especially the beginning and end, the Civil War amendments to the Constitution (Thirteenth, Fourteenth, and Fifteenth), giving women the right to vote (Nineteenth Amendment), labor laws enabling workers to ask for a decent wage and safe working conditions, federal social security and medical insurance programs, the Civil Rights initiatives, protection of our land and water resources, consumer protection for our investments, safety of food, toys, etc., and a judicial system that is just …. We get a massive effort by the oligarchs to re-make the United States into something like Russia is today.

I am angry that instead of enjoying the blessings of liberty and responsibility that millions have worked so hard to achieve:

> That there are some that are filled with greed and hate
> > That a few hundred of these people have a virtual unlimited amount of cash that they are using to impose their future on our democracy

That intelligent and educated people willingly take the money, go to secret and exclusive retreats and then espouse the greed and hate and publish "research" newspaper columns, books, and other sources to make it seem like this greed and hate is legitimate

That vast numbers of persons holding public office and candidates for public office who are so eager to get elected or stay in office that they toe the line of greed and hate

That TV "commentators," mainly some from cable channels spew this greed and hate hours each day

Finally, that some forty percent of US citizens have bought into the message of greed and hate.

What can we as citizens do about this?

One of the big problems we as citizens have is that we too often go on the basis of labels. As examples, the terms "libertarian," "socialist," and "populist" are thrown around and we are supposed to know what these mean. As someone with more than a casual interest in politics, I do not find that there is a common understanding of what any of these words mean. In these cases, they are often adopted by minor political candidates who want to get elected, but have been shut out by either the Republicans or Democrats. But then other politicians fling the words around to put down opponents, hoping listeners will attach some meaning—favorites are accusing an opponent of being a communist or socialist.

So, a big part of protecting ourselves is to do away with, or greatly diminish our reliance on labels to decide if we are for or against something. Look at the proposal on its merits and decide from there if it meets your preference. If an official makes a mistake—let him or her know. If an official does something right—let him or her know. With an open mind, you may surprise yourself how much you agree with someone of a different political party.

Especially in these times of being blasted from all sides on statements and research findings that may or may not be true, we must step back try to find out if the research is to push some political agenda or is the research to advance knowledge. This is a great challenge, I know, but it is very important.

Go to different sources when looking for news. Use differing accounts and opinions to help you think through what is most likely true.

What this means is that we must all spend more time and effort to be citizens. We have to get involved in the public debates and discussions and decide for **ourselves** what is likely true and what most likely will be good policies going forward.

We come to the end of how power is wielded in America. The issue of racism permeates this whole story. Recall that Europe, especially Britain was a horrible place at the time of the European arrivals here— unless, of course, you were one of those that had power. Throwing people out of the Tower of London, putting people on the rack to pull their bodies apart, putting severed heads on fence pikes were common. This practice of inhuman violence was imported here.

This meant that there was a class system already in place, so the upper class without hesitation, set about maintaining a class structure.

The constant from the arrival of the first settlers from primarily Britain, to today's holders of power is this: The powerful falsely tell groups of powerless that their interests are the same as the powerful. Then set about dividing the powerless into groups so that they battle each other, rather than gang up to defeat the powerful.

Thus, without hesitation, the Jamestown settlers enslaved the arriving Africans—a reflection of their experiences in Britain that it was okay for one group to dehumanize another. As time went on, the system of indentured servants arrived—poor and destitute mostly young people were sent to this continent to serve as slaves for around seven years. When the powerful saw that the indentured servants and other powerless European arrivals were allying with the enslaved Africans, the powerful set about turning the oppressed groups against each other and telling the poor whites that they were in danger from the enslaved Africans.

This cycle continued for generations. When the Civil War was ended, there was the possibility that the enslaved descendants of Africans could gain power, the powerful took action and just to emphasize that the African descendants should not have any power set in motion the notion that those of African descent were animals—not really human. With this mentality, there was no need to grant them any civil or human rights. The white people without political clout were then brain-washed into joining this de-humanization of descendants of Africans.

The vestiges of this mentality drive our society today. The most obvious is police officers murdering Black people without any apparent hesitation or regret. But it permeates every part of our society. Efforts to keep Black people from living in white neighborhoods, keep Black students in their own schools, job discrimination of all kinds are all part of daily lives for persons of color. Recall that the Tea Party started as a grass roots organization, dissatisfaction with what they were getting from the government, wanting to protect unlimited rights to carry guns and similar issues. Then the Koch organization took it over, claiming that Tea Party's concerns were the same as those of the rich and powerful. Now the Tea Party does the bidding of the Koch organization and other power groups such as opposing taxes and denying climate change.

Counter to all this has always been a resistance. Enslaved people running away from their captives, oppressed groups secretly helping others, politically, there is the Civil War and the civil rights action and legislation of the 1960s and 1970s. There is some indication that the time we are living in now may be another phase when oppressed people gain some power—note such things as the huge outpouring across racial lines to support Black Lives Matter when protesting police murders of Black people.

end

www.ingramcontent.com/pod-product-compliance
Lightning Source LLC
Chambersburg PA
CBHW032051020426
42335CB00011B/278